Praise for *The Indie Band Survival Guide*

"[Chertkow and Feehan] are the ideal mentors for aspiring indie musicians who want to navigate an ever-changing music industry."

—*Billboard* magazine

"I've seen a lot of books over the years; I've worked on every side of it.... [Chertkow and Feehan] have the most up-to-date reference book for young musicians."

—Matt Pinfield, radio and MTV/VH1 television personality

"Finally! A comprehensive and practical guide for musicians that explains how to navigate today's music world without a label. A must-read!"

—Derek Sivers, founder of CD Baby and HostBaby

"This is just the sort of zero-BS guide to modern artistic survival that should be in every artist's handbag."

—Cory Doctorow

"Dear Parent: I hear your kid's band is starting to sound pretty good! The band is getting regular practices in; they're gigging a bit; they've got a logo and a Facebook page. How can you help them now? ... Take a look at: *The Indie Band Survival Guide: The Complete Manual for the Do-It-Yourself Musician* by Randy Chertkow and Jason Feehan."

—Laura Lamere, *Parenting Creative Kids* blog

"Chertkow and Feehan are plugged-in to the mercurial world that is the music industry. Their straightforward approach to making your own rules in a world without them is exactly what new and experienced artists need.... I'm going to call the publisher to inquire about a quantity discount for studios. Seriously. We should hand these out to every new client who comes in the door."

—Garrett Haines, *TapeOP Magazine*

"The Int ... is an extraordinary opportunity for musicians to make and profit fr ... music. This clearly written and comprehensive book shows exactly ... ess of the law and the promise of the technology, it should be read by anyone who wants to take their talent and share it—for the love of sharing, or for the profit."

—Lawrence Lessig, author of *Code*, professor at Stanford Law School, founder of the Center for the Internet and Society, and CEO of the Creative Commons project

"Jam-packed full of incredible information. *The Indie Band Survival Guide* is a book that all artists, independent or not, need to own."

—Ariel Hyatt, author, publicist, and founder of CyberPR

"[Chertkow and Feehan have] effectively produced a take-along, dog-earable handbook so anyone can follow in these well tread footsteps."

—BoingBoing

"Highly, highly recommended—for not only musicians, but for anyone and everyone living DIY.... It's also an incredibly invaluable resource for techies, writers, bloggers, social/digital media folk, producers, editors, and just about anybody with an interest in Indie/DIY culture."

—Rockthought.com

"[Chertkow and Feehan] have collected a wealth of information and tools to help the indie band in getting recognized and their music distributed to their fans and, more importantly, the rest of the market."   —Cybergrass

"The reason the guide is so good is simple.... It's written by a pair of musicians, Randy Chertkow and Jason Feehan.... I'll be recommending it for years to come."   —*Journal Star* (Lincoln, NE)

"Indispensable ... This lively book offers such essential guidance in these changing times, no band should be without a copy."   —*Publishers Weekly*

the
INDIE BAND
SURVIVAL
GUIDE

ST. MARTIN'S GRIFFIN
NEW YORK

THE INDIE BAND SURVIVAL GUIDE

Randy Chertkow
& Jason Feehan

the complete
manual
for the
do-it-yourself
musician

**SECOND
EDITION**

www.stmartins.com

ISBN 978-1-250-01075-9 (trade paperback)
ISBN 978-1-250-01753-6 (e-book)

Second Edition: September 2012

10 9 8 7 6 5 4 3 2 1

Dedicated to musicians everywhere

TABLE OF CONTENTS

INTRODUCTION

REFERENCE PAGE: IndieGuide.com/Intro
and IndieGuide.com/Book

TO THE SECOND EDITION

WELCOME TO the second edition of *The Indie Band Survival Guide:* remixed and remastered, an even more practical, expansive how-to manual to getting your music heard, distributed, sold, booked, promoted, and seen in today's Internet-powered music industry. In the past, what we cover in this guide would only be possible if you had the backing of a major record label, but you can now do it on your own. We'll tell you how to get started, give you tons of practical ideas you can implement *right now* to build your fan base and get your music in front of people, and, unlike most books on this topic, give you practical, step-by-step "recipes" that lay it all out in plain English so you can put it to use for you and your music.

HOW THE SECOND EDITION IS DIFFERENT

When we wrote the first edition of the guide, we hoped to achieve what one reader of the original online PDF that inspired the print book e-mailed us to say: "I get it. A dog-eared copy in every battered instrument case, eh?" That image stuck with us throughout the writing of that book. It kept us focused on our goal to write a book that indie musicians like ourselves would use in the real world and would refer to often. And, from all the positive reviews, e-mails, and comments we've gotten in the four years since the first edition came out from musicians around the world, it's gratifying to know we hit our goal.

But then, we're not ones to sit still. After all, we're in a band that's written, recorded, and produced twenty albums and released a song every day for an entire year. Sitting still really isn't in our vocabulary.

If the first edition was about *doing,* this second edition is the same, just cranked to 11.

In the first edition we needed to spend a lot of words explaining things like what Twitter was and why that strange site was so important and useful to musicians. Today, it's a given. Everyone knows Twitter.

But because so much since the first edition is now accepted and gone mainstream, we can cut out most of the superfluous explanations and instead outline clear, step-by-step instructions on *what exactly to do*.

We also cut out the little bit we had about major labels. The world has continued to move on, making it better to be a musician today than when we wrote the first edition. Musicians like George Hrab, Gavin Mikhail, and a host of others we wrote about in our previous books have only continued to make their living through music—and they've been joined by other indies in this edition such as The Gregory Brothers, Pomplamoose, Pogo, and more. Jonathan Coulton, in particular, has continued to grow his fan base on his terms. He's funded his album *Artificial Heart* on his own, hired John Flansburgh of They Might Be Giants as the producer, and even put together a backing band. Coulton's broadened the concept of the concert by organizing a weeklong Caribbean trip aboard a cruise ship. And he's continued to create music for video games (Portal 2) and license music to others. He told NPR's *Planet Money* that, as a musician, it makes sense for him to stay indie and just hire the skills and services he needs when he needs them—which is exactly what we talk about in this guide.

So, if you picked up this book to revel in a lament about a music industry long gone by, or the clash between big content versus Silicon Valley, or the debate over whether, if everyone can make music, culture as we know it is over, then we can't help you. Grab any other book on the same shelf if you want theories, debates, or feel-good motivational text. This book focuses on what matters: laying out in clear step-by-step language *exactly* what you need to do to get "out there" and start winning fans.

WHO THIS BOOK IS FOR

Although this book is entitled *The Indie Band Survival Guide,* this book is not just for bands. We use the words "band," "musician," and "artist" interchangeably throughout this book.

This book is for all musicians, from hobbyists to professionals. It's useful for musicians of all ages, from teens starting their first garage band to retirees who have rediscovered their love of music and want to share it with the world. It will be indispensable to you whether or not you have a lot of experience with the Internet. The *Guide* will explain how to use all of the talents that you already have and supplement them with tools and techniques to accomplish what was only possible for major-label musicians in the past. And keep in mind, the guide is intended to show you how to succeed whether you do it yourself or direct other people or services (many of which are free!) to do it for you.

It's also for managers, bookers, labels, promoters, recording engineers, music-video directors, filmmakers, and anyone else who works with music.

And, because this book provides clear and practical techniques on how best to succeed in today's disrupted, Internet-powered music industry, the book is especially useful for music schools, music business schools, and teachers.

But it's not just for those working in the new music industry.

Much of what we share in this book is useful for any creative endeavor—whether you're an indie author, blogger, comedian, podcaster, YouTuber, filmmaker, producer, or director; you don't have to be a musician to get a lot out of this guide, even though our focus is on how each topic relates to music. For instance, when we explain how to create Web sites, we specifically cover the creation of *music* Web sites, even though we share principles of good Web site design that any site should use.

More than anything, at the heart of this book are essential techniques for anyone who wants to get their music into the world.

WHO ARE "WE" ANYWAY?

"We" are lead members of Beatnik Turtle (beatnikturtle.com), an indie band with fifteen years of experience; twenty albums and nearly five hundred songs to our name; years of live shows; music that's been licensed to Disney, Viacom, and others; college-radio play; countless podcast plays; theater shows at venues such as the world-famous Second City; TV theme songs, music videos, Web sites, and a completed Song of the Day project, through which we released one song for each day of 2007 (TheSongOfTheDay.com).

We are also two working professionals—an IT expert and an attorney—and we've brought all the knowledge and experience from our respective fields to bear on this book, just as you will take advantage of your own skills beyond those in music to make your band a success. We're like other musicians who found that they had skills in photography and started to take pictures for bands, or discovered they were good at recording so also set up a studio. Because of this, we've been columnists at *Electronic Musician* magazine, where we wrote the DIY Musician column, as well as feature articles and interviews. We also write for a variety of Web publications, blogs, and journals and teach music business in Chicago at the Music Industry Workshop (miworkshop.com). And, most important, we run the free and open IndieGuide.com, created to help musicians find the resources they need to succeed.

In the end, though, we are musicians in a band. We generated the material in this book by actually solving the problems we discuss here. In fact, this is the book we wish we'd had when we started out years ago. For instance, when we wrote the section about how to submit your music to podcasts, we recorded the steps we'd been using for years, then did another round of submissions to test and refine the process.

So when we say "we," we're talking to you as one musician to another.

OUR ASSUMPTIONS—WHAT YOU NEED TO GET STARTED

We're going to cover *a lot* of topics. Way more than in the first edition. Because of that, we're going to assume three things:

- You've got talent.

- You've got music you want people to hear and content you want to share.

- You're focused on winning fans and motivated to do what it takes.

We're also going to assume you know how to use a computer and know the basics of using the Web. We aren't going to spend a lot of time explaining what hyperlinks are or how to use a Web browser. Many of the opportunities that have opened up for musicians in the last few years are on the Web, so you'll be using it quite a bit to promote your music and get it heard by a worldwide audience. If you're uncomfortable with the Internet, then we recommend some background reading such as *Internet for Dummies*, by John R. Levine, Margaret Levine Young, and Carol Baroudi, for a basic overview, as well as the book *Rule the Web* by Mark Frauenfelder, which can help you get the most out of the Internet.

HOW TO USE THIS BOOK

As we said, this book is about *doing*. We imagine you'll read it like others told us they read the first edition—scribbling notes in the margins, dog-earing pages, capturing ideas on paper or their computer, discussing the strategies and techniques with band members or other musicians, and having it in their bag or guitar case for easy reference.

Although the book is a reference book and therefore can be read in sections rather than cover to cover in sequence, we do recommend you take some time to page through the book so you can get an idea of all the possibilities that are out there for you and your music. That said, you don't have to do everything that the book covers, just be aware that it all exists and decide which tasks you want to take on. More important, just work on each part when you're ready. There's no need to run a marketing campaign if you don't have an album for sale yet.

Each chapter is broken up in the following way:

- **The Strategic Goal.** If you're ever wondering what you should be getting out of a particular chapter, read this brief section.

- **Reference Page.** We set aside a section of IndieGuide.com, and created Web pages with clickable links, information about any reference books we cover; plus extra materials on each chapter to help you with each topic. Just go to IndieGuide.com/Book for links to every reference page chapter.

- **Checklist.** We've created a table that lists what you need for your music as it relates to each core topic covered in the chapter. For example, for publicity campaigns, you need a press kit. We'll provide downloadable checklists at IndieGuide.com/Book to help organize what you need to do.

- **Sections.** Each chapter is broken up into large sections. For instance, the second chapter, "Your Music," contains five sections: Making Your Music, Recording and Mixdown, Mastering, Preparing Your Music for Distribution and Release, and Learning More.

- **Subsections.** Each section is broken down into smaller subsections around a specific topic. Most of the subsections explain "how to do X." Other subsections may be titled "What Every Musician Needs to Know About X" or "The Top X Thing(s) You Should Do." These subsections will explain key concepts or provide context for the topic.

Naturally, as a musician you'll want to improvise on what we suggest in this book and try out new things. Go for it. As we like to say, the techniques and lessons in this book are no substitute for artful practice. When you hit on something that works and it's not in this book, write us at ContactUs@ IndieGuide.com. We want to hear from you, and so does the indie musician community.

USING INDIEGUIDE.COM—YOUR COMPLETE DO-IT-YOURSELF MUSICIAN RESOURCE

You're holding more than just a book—it's a portal to an extensive and free Web site we created called IndieGuide.com, which houses a growing list of musician services, tools, sites, and resources. We created it so the guide could focus on what books are good at: strategy and explanations of what you should do. The links to the latest Web sites, services, and tools—which change quickly in today's music world—are covered at IndieGuide.com, which stays up to date.

To get this information, as well as additional how-tos, exclusive materials, downloadable forms, and a way to connect to other motivated musicians like you, head to IndieGuide.com.

GET TO IT

Now, with introductions out of the way, turn the page and get to it. There are fans waiting for you and this guide will tell you how to get them.

CHAPTER 1   THERE'S NO

REFERENCE PAGE: IndieGuide.com/Intro

BETTER TIME TO BE A MUSICIAN

THE TOOLS and opportunities you have at your fingertips today were nearly unthinkable just ten years ago. You can record music on your computer with technologies and capabilities that used to be only available through costly professional recording studios. You can easily obtain global digital distribution for your music, and with it you can sell millions of copies of your album worldwide with no need for warehouses, shipping, or up-front money tied up in inventory. More opportunities than ever exist to get your music discovered, heard, and seen. And through Web, social, and mobile presences, you can target your audience, connect with listeners, and build a worldwide fan base.

How people create, promote, discover, distribute, sell, and monetize music in today's world has changed. What used to be closed off by "the music industry" is now open for anyone who wants to participate. The traditional players in the music industry were like tollbooth operators, and the price of admission was the rights to your music and a large cut of the income you created. Now you don't have to ask anyone's permission, the cost to you is minimal, and you keep all the rights and money you earn.

We're now in a world where the musicians are in charge. The numerous middlemen who decided which musicians "made it" and which ones didn't have fallen away. Musicians have stopped wasting their time trying to appeal to the mainstream-minded music executives in the hopes of "getting signed" and instead focus on "getting discovered" by the people who really matter: the fans.

For everything a label used to do in the past for their musicians there are now services, sites, tools, and resources available that can let you do it yourself—often for free. You just need to know what to do and how to do it.

And that's the point of this guide.

You're holding the one book written by two indie musicians who, by necessity, navigated and deciphered the confusing worlds of music, business, law, marketing, and technology and wrote it all down so musicians could act on it. This is the guide that we wish that we had when we started our own band over fifteen years ago.

In short, you now have everything you need to do it yourself.

WHY EVERYTHING CHANGED AND HOW IT'S GOOD FOR MUSICIANS

THE FOUR TRENDS THAT HAVE REVOLUTIONIZED THE MUSIC INDUSTRY

There are four trends that have revolutionized and democratized the music industry:

1. **Inexpensive Worldwide Digital Distribution**

2. **Democratization of Media and the Death of Channels**

3. **The Infinite Store Shelf**

4. **Access to Inexpensive Music Production Technology**

1. Inexpensive Worldwide Digital Distribution

In the past, distribution meant manufacturing tens of thousands of CDs, tapes, or records. It meant convincing thousands of stores that it would sell if they'd only stock your product. It meant fleets of trucks to drive the product to the stores in the first place. Most of all, it meant that a great deal of money needed to be invested up front in manufacturing large amounts of the product (creating inventory) and paying middlemen to get the product in front of music fans. Few musicians had the money to fund this themselves.

In today's world, thanks to the Internet, faster computers, and broadband connections, whether you sell one copy or one hundred million, there's no marginal cost, no trucks involved, no money tied up in inventory, and shipping music anywhere worldwide is instantaneous. Even better, these incredible distribution channels are available to any musician, and it costs well under one hundred dollars. In fact, you can even get free digital distribution. You can also sell physical CDs with zero inventory, with all of the production costs being paid for by the customer each time they buy a CD.

This change put music distribution in your hands and made the major labels unnecessary for both distribution and for funding the manufacturing of your product.

2. Democratization of Media and the Death of Channels

The media technology of the past was limited and costly. It meant few channels of distribution, with control concentrated among few players. These players decided what music and shows would be distributed to the masses of viewers and listeners at what time and on what channel. This allowed a handful of companies to control what could be seen and heard, and forced musicians to use music labels to get their music heard, since there were no other options. It was a world of one-way communication—of broadcasting. You were either local, or you were signed.

It also meant that since channels were playing to huge, nearly captive audiences, the gatekeepers focused on music or shows that would appeal to as many people as possible to maximize their audience share. Anything that wouldn't do this got no exposure and was deemed of little value. Generations of people internalized this hits-only economic model and began to assume that there was "a mainstream" that everyone liked. But how much of this was because mainstream entertainment was the *only* entertainment available?

But the means to broadcast media is now in everyone's hands. Want to start your own TV station? Just use Ustream (ustream.tv), Livestream (livestream.com), or just post videos on YouTube (youtube.com). Want to start your own radio station? Use sites like Live365 (live365.com) or create a podcast. Want to have your own newspaper or magazine? Just start a blog or Web site.

This means that the notion of a "channel" is dead. Media is now on-demand, and available for everyone to participate. This change puts media coverage within your reach and has made the major labels unnecessary in getting coverage for your music. People aren't forced to select their music from a small set of options. There are more ways to get your music "out there" and win fans than ever before—and they don't have the same barriers to entry the old media has.

3. The Infinite Store Shelf

When music was only sold in physical record stores, the stores would purchase albums from distributors (which bought albums from labels) to resell to the public. These stores had limited shelf space, so, except for dedicated music stores that featured obscure music, the only music for sale was from major labels. Because of this, the music industry, as well as music stores, only focused on hits. This isn't surprising, since most of the sales for the industry came only from those hits. Why bother with any other music?

But, today, with high-speed Internet connections and digital storage, there is no end of shelf space. There's now room for everything—new artists, unknown bands, obscure music, rare tracks, and more. Everything can stay on the shelf forever since it doesn't take up any physical space. If a customer wants to buy a song, it's always available for purchase no matter how many sales it gets per year.

This change means you are side by side in the same stores as all major-label and established acts and your music can come up in searches and be discovered while customers are shopping.

4. Access to Inexpensive Music Production Technology

A revolution in music production technology occurred because computers and recording gear became powerful, inexpensive, and available to most musicians. Recording, mastering, and music production no longer requires expensive studio time and the financial resources of a label.

"Today's recording technology both equals that of the studios of the past, and at the same time is a fraction of the cost," says Norman Hajjar, the chief creative and customer officer of Guitar Center, the largest musical instrument retailer in the United States. If you have a computer and a microphone, you're ready to record music, especially since software such as GarageBand (apple.com/ilife/garageband), Sonar (cakewalk.com), Reaper (reaper.fm), or free tools like Audacity (audacity.sourceforge.net) can transform your computer into a full-blown recording studio.

As Hajjar points out, this affordable recording technology and gear has "unbottled the creativity that was always there; it was just inaccessible to most people. Musicians today have so many different and exciting ways to not only get access to the creative tools that allow them to express themselves, but also more ways to share their creativity with the world. Ways that were unfathomable in the past. I have zero doubt that we're hearing music today that would not have been created if it weren't for this access to technology."

This change put music production in your hands and has made the major labels unnecessary for funding the recording and mastering process. And since their financing of music production was their justification for keeping the copyright to the master recordings, this means that you can keep all the rights to your music.

YOU NOW HAVE A CHOICE . . .

Back when studio time was expensive and distribution and promotional channels were limited and costly, musicians needed labels to help them record, distribute, promote, and sell their music. But given the four revolutions above, this is no longer the case.

As Jonathan Coulton (jonathancoulton.com), a successful indie musician making a living off his music said on his blog, "The revolution in the music industry (which has already happened by the way) is one of efficiency, and it means that success is now possible on a much smaller scale. Nobody has to sell out Madison Square Garden anymore to make a living. We now have an entirely new set of contexts and they come with a whole new set of tools that give us cheap and easy access to all of them—niche has gone mainstream. It is no longer necessary to organize your business or your art around geography, or storage space, or capital, or what's cool in your town, or any other physical constraint."

In other words, today there's room for every artist.

"Signing with a label today is just a choice," says Jeff Price, former indie label head and founder of TuneCore (tunecore.com), a service that allows anyone to digitally distribute their music. Musicians should evaluate a label deal the same way they would evaluate a contract from any business partner. And it might be appropriate for some musicians. But music fans don't care about whether artists are signed or not; they only care about the music and the musician. And that's the point: a middle man is no longer required. The distinction of whether you're signed or not no longer matters in today's world.

. . . AND YOU'RE NOT ALONE

Every service that a label used to perform for their artists is now available to every musician. Today there are professionals, services, sites, tools, and resources available to meet every need you have to get your music into the world. Best of all, many are inexpensive or even free. The computer and software industries are creating new tools and services almost daily in an effort to reinvent how people discover and purchase music. Plus, many experienced and talented music professionals, such as producers, engineers, graphic artists, publicists, and more are exiting labels to find their niche in the new music industry. Many have started up companies or are hiring themselves out to musicians directly, charging by the hour or per project. For example, when we decided to get the help of a publicist for one of our CD releases, we found one who had worked at Sony BMG promoting major groups for years, had many contacts in the press and media, and was deeply experienced in getting albums noticed and reviewed. And we didn't have to give up the rights to our music to take advantage of that experience.

THE EIGHT WAYS YOU CAN TAKE ADVANTAGE OF THIS
NEW MUSIC INDUSTRY RIGHT NOW

Although the media loves to talk about the impact these four revolutions have had on the old music industry, the fact is, they work in your favor as a musician. You are now free to be who you are, create music the way you want to, and own all the rights.

There's no one you need to impress in the industry to get access to distribution, the media channels, the shelf space, or the recording equipment anymore. The only people you need to impress are your fans.

In fact, now that you're in control, here's a list of what's possible for you and your music right now:

1. You can get worldwide distribution for your music and keep all the profits yourself, rather than a label only paying you a few cents per album sale.

You can get digital and physical distributors to sell your music in stores like iTunes, Amazon, Rhapsody, and more. And you can use a manufacturer to make your CDs, DVDs, or other physical media—including on-demand sites that manufacture CDs or DVDs when they are purchased, requiring you to put up no money up front and making you a profit on every sale. You can also use a fulfillment partner to take orders and ship your products for you. And when you hire your own distributors, manufacturers, and fulfillment partners, you keep all the rights—and all the profits. See chapter 2, "Your Music"; chapter 5, "Your Rights"; and chapter 6, "Your Albums, Merchandise, and Sales" for more information about what you can be doing right now to make all of this happen for your music.

2. You can get your music played on radio stations, webcasts, MP3 blogs, podcasts, Web sites, YouTube, and more so it's discovered by fans around the world.

Radio campaigns are within your reach and digital music services such as Spotify, Pandora, Rdio, Last.fm, and others are available to musicians that submit their music the right way. Also, musicians like Nice Peter, The Gregory Brothers, and Pomplamoose have shown that viral videos can catapult musicians into the spotlight and give them millions of fans. We explain how to run radio and Internet campaigns, make video work for you, and more in chapter 13, "Get Heard," and chapter 14, "Get Seen."

3. You can get journalists, fans, and the media talking about you and your music in articles, Web sites, and videos and on social networks so you get noticed and grow your fan base.

New media is especially friendly to the newest and freshest music out there—something that you can provide for them. And once you get some traction in the new media, you can run your own traditional media campaign, or even hire an independent publicist that has worked in the music industry to leverage their press, media, and Web contacts. We'll show you how in chapter 11, "Your Marketing Strategy," and chapter 12, "Get Publicized."

4. You can get venues demanding you for gigs, pack your shows, and tour no matter where in the world your fans want you to play.

Touring around your immediate area to build your fan base is only part of the story. Today live shows are about getting your music out there on the Web and finding out where your fans live. It's about letting your fans, no matter where in the world they discover you, request that you play in their area, so that you tour places where you're guaranteed an audience. It's also about creating a killer live show that sells out venues and boosts your music and merchandise sales. Finally, it's also about broadcasting your shows live on the Web so your global fans can take part. We'll show you how to do this and more in chapter 7, "Your Gigs."

5. You can get worldwide distribution for your branded merchandise and keep all the profits yourself.

Physical manufacturers and distributors can create and sell your merchandise in stores around the world. Also, with merchandise-on-demand stores, there is no cost to you to upload your images and make branded items available for purchase, making you a profit on every sale. And, of course, your sales improve depending on the strength of your identity, logos, and imagery. We explain everything you need to know in chapter 4, "Your Brand," and chapter 6, "Your Albums, Merchandise, and Sales."

6. You can create a pervasive Web, social, and mobile presence that makes it easy for you to engage and grow your global fan base.

We outline a Web, social, and mobile strategy that makes it simple for you to share pictures, videos, and news in one place and automatically spread them across all of your social presences. Plus, you'll get automated alerts when people are talking about you no matter where on the Web or in the social media they are—perfect for keeping up on radio, press, and media campaigns. Most of all, you'll learn to stay connected and engaged with your fans with as little effort as possible so you can spend more of your time on music. We show you how in chapter 8, "Your Web Strategy"; chapter 9, "Your Web, Social, and Mobile Presences"; and chapter 10, "Your Web Site."

7. You can have complete creative control over your music, the entire recording process, and your business.

When the labels fronted the money for their artists to record, they had a say over the music and whether it ever got released. Today you call the shots. You decide which albums you create, what gets released, how, and when; you also have a choice in recording: you can create an inexpensive home recording setup or hire a local studio. And it's even more important than ever to master your music, a process that's been a mystery to most musicians and yet is one of the best ways to make your music stand out above amateur work. You're also no longer limited to the musicians you know on your block. Session players can record in their own studios and send you the tracks. You can even hire entire orchestras, in other parts of the world, to record your music. We cover all of these topics and more in chapter 2, "Your Music"; chapter 3, "Your Team and Networking Strategy"; and chapter 5, "Your Rights."

8. You can own all the rights to your music and keep all the royalties and profits from music licensing.

Today you have access to licensing options that musicians never had in the past. You can get your music in films, television, radio, commercials, theater, video games, and more. There are seven different registrations you should perform to guarantee all the royalties that you are owed. But that's only half the story. Understanding how to use your legal rights to *promote* your music is critical—especially since you need to get your music on the Web so it can be shared and discovered by fans around the world. We explain everything you need to know in chapter 5, "Your Rights."

GET OUT THERE

Everything that a label used to do for musicians in the past is now within your reach. You have outstanding tools, services, networks, and resources at your fingertips to help you do it yourself. Right now, you have global distribution, unlimited promotional opportunities, and countless new ways to get your music to millions of people all over the world. You don't have to waste time trying to "get signed"; you can focus on building a fan base directly. They're out there. You just need to win them over. The rest of this book has the specific steps you need to make it happen.

Read on to find out how.

LEARNING MORE

Go to IndieGuide.com/Intro for a clickable version of every link, Web site, and service mentioned in this chapter, as well as links to books that cover the changes to the old music industry.

PART ONE
GET PREPARED

CHAPTER 2

THE STRATEGIC GOAL: to create, record, and prepare your music for distribution, promotion, and sales

REFERENCE PAGE: IndieGuide.com/Music

CHECKLIST

What	Description
Recording Studio	Either build a home studio, or find a professional studio to record your music.
Mastering Studio	Either create a home mastering studio, or choose a professional mastering studio to master your music to make the finished product equal to professional recordings.
WAV Files	Make fully mastered, album-ready WAV versions of your music files for videos, podcasts, and licensing purposes. May need different mixes, such as instrumental, vocals up/down, or others as required.
MP3 Files	Create fully mastered, album-ready MP3 files that are high and low quality for sales, promotion, or distribution. These MP3 files should be fully ID3 tagged, and there should be files that are both high- and low-bit-rate quality.
Studio Musicians	Use either local or Internet sources to find musicians to fill in any part or instrument for your recordings.
Samples and Loop Sources	If your music requires it, discover royalty-free samples and loops for your recorded music.

YOUR MUSIC

"Your tools should serve your art, not the other way around."

—SARAH JONES, EDITOR IN CHIEF, *Electronic Musician*

YOUR MUSIC is the foundation of everything you do as a musician. Whether it's marketing, publicity, getting radio play, or music sales, it's all based on the quality of what you create. It's your most important asset for winning fans.

Advances in recording technology have unleashed the creativity of musicians. Professional studio time that used to cost tens or hundreds of thousands of dollars is now inexpensive and within your reach. And if you have your own computer, your studio time is free, allowing you to truly experiment at your own pace.

Of course, the crafts of songwriting, recording, and mastering are broad topics that fill many books, with technology that is evolving rapidly, and new tools and techniques appearing all the time. This guide will focus on recording, mastering, encoding, and tagging issues you'll have to deal with no matter what techniques you're using.

MAKING YOUR MUSIC

WHAT TO CONSIDER BEFORE YOU EVEN HIT
THE RECORD BUTTON

When it comes to increasing sales of your music, the secret is quantity. It takes a lot of time and energy converting a person into a fan. But it takes less time and energy getting someone who is already a fan to purchase additional music from you. This is where having a back catalog of music to sell comes in.

David Hooper (musicmarketing.com), host of the syndicated show *Music Business Radio*, suggests thinking about repurposing your music at the outset. For instance, set out to make one main album and a series of additional albums or EPs (a short album of approximately four songs) with material based on the songs from the main album. That way, while you focus publicity efforts on creating awareness of the main album, you can also build your discography and back catalog with a series of albums, singles, special offers, giveaways, and so on. You could, for example, create an album of

- songs that didn't make the cut (outtakes and b-sides);

- live versions of some of the songs found on your album;

- original demos of the songs you later used to create the album;

- alternate takes and rehearsals of the songs that made your album;

- unplugged versions of many of the songs on your album;

- remixes of the songs on your album; and/or

- a "commentary" album where you tell the story of how you made the album, how you came up with the songs, and so on, much like a director talks over the movie on a DVD.

Although not everyone will be into all these versions, as Hooper notes, "You're not trying to please everybody; you're trying to go after the hardcore fans who will spend money on you."

EIGHT ALTERNATIVE VERSIONS OF SONGS YOU CAN MAKE TO MAXIMIZE SALES AND LICENSING

You can make a variety of different versions of a song on your album. You're not limited to the album version alone. Making different versions of a song allows you to have material for other purposes such as licensing, giveaways, rewards to fans and street teams (people you organize to help promote you and your music), "rarities," and more. For instance, you can take your song and record an

- acoustic/unplugged version;

- live version;

- acapella version;

- instrumental version;

- demo version;

- outtake version; and/or

- "Making of" version.

You can also release the stems from the master recording—the bass track, the drum track, the vocals—so you can get others to make remixes of your work (which we'll talk about later in this chapter).

HOW TO FIND AND COLLABORATE WITH MUSICIANS IN YOUR AREA

When it comes to finding skilled musicians (or any expert for that matter, be it graphic artists, video editors, etc.), the Internet gives you numerous ways to connect, not to mention choices.

1. **Ask for a referral.** By far, the best way to find musicians is from other musicians you already know.

2. **Post an ad at a local store, music school, or studio.** In Chicago, where we live, one of the best places to find musicians is the Old Town School of Folk Music (oldtownschool.org), which has music classes for all types of instruments and styles. But don't forget music stores as well. When we needed a new drummer, we posted an ad at the Drum Pad (thedrumpad .com), one of the largest drum stores in the region, and we connected with the perfect drummer for our group.

3. **Go to where the party is.** You can head to the community sites where the people with the skills you're looking for congregate and hang out with one another. For instance, if you're looking for a bass player, you may hit the TalkBass forum (talkbass.com). If you're looking for drummers, you should check out Drummer Cafe (drummercafe.com/forum/index.php).

4. **Use musician classified sites.** You can post an ad in your area on sites like BandMix (bandmix.com), JamConnect (jamconnect.com), Musicians Wanted (musicianswanted.org), Musolist (musolist.com), or Craigslist (craigslist.org).

5. **Go to contracting sites.** You can head to Web sites where the people with the skills you need post their availability for hire. Sites such as oDesk (odesk.com) and Elance (elance.com) specialize in this. People also post on Craigslist (craigslist.org).

HOW TO FIND AND COLLABORATE WITH MUSICIANS OVER THE WEB

Thanks to the Internet, a musician can record a part for you, or play with you live, anywhere in the world. So you are no longer limited to finding musicians in your area to jam with.

To collaborate with other musicians, try the following:

1. **Virtual jam sessions.** Sites like eJamming (ejamming.com) or programs like Ninjam (cockos.com/ninjam) allow you to jam live with other musicians using your computer and an Internet connection.

2. **Remixing sites.** If you like the idea of remixing, musicians all over the world like to share the source tracks to their songs and see what other musicians can do with them. You can use these sites to both play music and share your own. Try out ccMixter (ccmixter.org), but if you put your music up there, be prepared to put it under a Creative Commons license.

3. **Track-sharing sites.** Mix multitrack recordings with a file-sharing site, and you get the ability to record songs with any musician that wants to take part. On these sites, entire songs are written one track at a time. One might record a bass part. Another might record drums. And before long, there's a song with vocals and even background vocals by entirely different singers—all of this done by musicians who have usually never met each other. Try sites like Kompoz (kompoz.com), and Indaba Music (www.indabamusic.com) if you want to give this a try.

Within each of these areas, there are new sites that pop up all the time, so we will track them for you at IndieGuide.com/Music.

HOW TO FIND SOMEBODY TO RECORD ANY INSTRUMENT FOR YOUR MUSIC

If your local recording studio can't find a session player to fill in on your album, don't give up. With the Internet, you can find people to fill in. This goes beyond just getting a bass player or a drummer for a song. You can hire brass sections, wind ensembles, vocalists, or people who play rare ethnic instruments. The possibilities are endless—for a fee. And the service goes beyond musicians. Note that you can get some very well-known studio musicians to record a track for you at a reasonable rate. You can even hire engineers to mix or master your songs.

To use a service like this, do the following:

1. **Choose a service.** Try eSession (esession.com), Session Players (sessionplayers.com), or DrumsForYou (drumsforyou.com), or go to Indie Guide.com/Music for more links.

2. **Send the musician a rough mixdown.** Give them a rough take, with an explanation of what you're looking for.

3. **Coordinate the recording.** Some services will let you listen in to the session on Skype; others will just let you trade recorded tracks. Adjust the track with the musician if you need it.

4. **Get the WAV.** The musician records a final version and sends you a WAV file with the track.

The good news is that you can use these techniques with any musicians in the world, if they're willing. You could even start a band where none of the band members live in the same city.

EIGHT OTHER WAYS TO COLLABORATE WITH BANDS AND MUSICIANS BEYOND MUSIC

As a musician, you're already a member of one of the most helpful networks you can access. You're reading a book by two of them right now. But we're not the only musicians willing to share what we've learned. When musicians cooperate and share resources, productive things happen:

1. **Booking cartels.** Bands and musicians with a complementary sound can join forces for booking purposes. Being able to offer an entire night of entertainment to venue bookers makes their job easier and can get you more gigs in the long run. We'll talk more about this in chapter 7, "Your Gigs."

2. **Musician exchange programs.** Team up with like-minded musicians in another city online. Each band can book a gig in its respective town and share the same bill. Both bands establish an out-of-town presence.

3. **Substitutes.** Ever had a gig you just couldn't make? It's quite hard to find a substitute unless you know other bands and musicians in the area. Finding an appropriate substitute when you can't meet your commitment can save your relationship with the venue.

4. **Cross-promotion.** Bands and musicians that work together can introduce their music to each other's fans on the Web and onstage, or even by co-writing and playing on each other's albums. We'll talk more about this in chapter 11, "Your Marketing Strategy."

5. **Recommendations and referrals.** If you need to find someone who can help you, other musicians can often refer you to a trusted person or service.

6. **Shared roles at gigs.** Bands can help each other out at shows. For instance, we once ran another band's store while they were playing onstage, and they did the same for us while we performed. We'll talk more about this in chapter 7, "Your Gigs".

7. **Going beyond your arm's reach.** Each band has its own skill and opportunity networks and will often share and share alike. This can be a great resource for referrals of trusted freelancers and other services.

8. **Newbies.** Don't forget that, as you progress, it's a good thing to offer guidance and assistance to other bands and musicians just starting out and add them to your own network. You never know if they'll return the favor someday.

Remember that you don't need to be in the same location to collaborate with other bands and musicians; it can happen online as well. Message boards, blogs, social networking sites, and our own site, IndieGuide.com, can help connect you to other bands and musicians. Often, a solution or an opportunity is just a few clicks away.

AN ADDITIONAL GROUP TO COLLABORATE WITH

Thanks to the Internet, fans have also become empowered and expect to be involved more with the artist. They're no longer limited to watching bands play onstage; they're now a part of that stage. And since you can now create anything—music, videos, artwork—with anyone, you may want to look into collaborating musically with some of your more talented fans. But it could go beyond music. You'll invariably attract fans with talents and skills of their own, which may include skills you don't have within your arm's reach. For instance, fans have shot videos, created mash-ups, recorded tribute songs, created remixes, collaborated on books, recorded podcasts, created T-shirt designs, and more for many indie artists such as Jonathan Coulton, Brad Turcotte of Brad Sucks, George Hrab, and Beatnik Turtle, to name just a few. Fans today want to interact and participate—not just listen. It's a pool of talent that you may want to tap.

RECORDING AND MIXDOWN
DECIDING BETWEEN RECORDING AT HOME OR AT A PROFESSIONAL STUDIO (OR USING BOTH)

Quality sound recording equipment and software have gotten inexpensive enough that a home studio is in almost every band's reach. In fact, by the time you've paid the average professional studio to record just one album, you've probably spent the equivalent of a very capable studio setup for your house, one where you could have recorded as many songs as you'd ever want. And yet, professional studios offer a range of benefits home studios lack. Knowing the advantages each option brings to the table can help you choose.

Note that you can also blend the two. Some bands use recording studios for laying down basic tracks or more complicated work such as recording drums (which is difficult to get right in a home studio environment), and then use their home studios to record overdubs and mix. This gives them the best of both worlds: quality microphones, equipment, and experience for capturing the basic tracks that will shape the sound of the recording, and time back home to experiment and be creative on the overdubs.

Advantages for home recording:

- Once you put together your home studio, you have unlimited time to record, unlike a professional studio, which charges by the hour.

- You have the freedom to work on and release new music whenever you feel a creative spark.

- You have the ability to produce different versions of your songs, including instrumentals, remixes, loops, and samples that can be used for other purposes such as podcasts, promos, and ringtones.

- You have the ability to record live versions of your music, especially if you have a laptop or portable recording solution.

- You're that much closer to producing and editing high-quality videos for yourself and your music. Add a green screen and your home music studio can become a home video studio.

- The act of recording can be part of the musical creative process. The studio and the recording technology can be used as an instrument.

- You can learn new skills and technology that can be marketable.

Advantages for professional recording:

- You can focus purely on the music, and let the professional engineers deal with recording. Plus, if there are any problems, the engineers will handle it, not you.

- Studios usually have multiple rooms acoustically designed for recording—which is especially beneficial when it comes to recording drums and vocals.

- You can get access to a selection of modern and vintage microphones, sound processors, amps, and instruments to tailor your sound. This equipment is usually expensive and not within most musicians' reach.

- Unless you are a proficient engineer, using a professional studio can be faster than doing it yourself. Especially if you don't have a lot of people to help you record.

HOW TO SET UP A HOME STUDIO

When it comes to setting up a home studio, John Lisiecki, a sound engineer for Chicago's Millennium Park who has years of experience recording everything from rock bands to symphony orchestras, advises, "It's the ends that matter. Everything else is a religious question." His advice is to spend your money on the best microphones you can buy and the best monitors so you can hear exactly what you captured. The middle part (mixer, cables, recorder, and so on) can be whatever you'd like it to be, and the particulars are often debated. If you build a studio from scratch, or you want to improve your studio, remember that the ends are what you need to spend money on first.

To get started building your studio, do the following:

1. **Do some research on creating home studios and recording before spending the money.** If you would like a list of links, books, and magazines on these topics, head to IndieGuide.com/Music.

2. **Buy at least one decent microphone.** Having at least one high-quality microphone is essential to getting the best sound. As you grow your studio, you may end up getting new microphones to handle particular instruments and situations. If you'd like a list of recommendations, head to IndieGuide.com/Music.

3. **Get a Digital Audio Workstation (DAW).** As far as free solutions, if you have an Apple computer, GarageBand will work out great. If you have Linux, try the free program Ardour. And for Windows, try out Audacity (audacity.sourceforge.net). Professional DAWs such as Avid Pro Tools (avid .com), Sonar (cakewalk.com), and Ableton Live (ableton.com) can be much more expensive but offer additional features.

4. **Get an analog-to-digital audio-recording interface.** Buying an external interface will allow you to connect an XLR microphone or instruments such as your electric guitar or external keyboards to your DAW via a USB or FireWire connection. There are numerous interfaces available such as the PreSonus Firebox, Avid MBox 2 Mini, Mackie Onyx Blackjack. If you'd like more info on this broad topic, see IndieGuide.com/Music for links, suggestions, and technical details about how to connect your XLR microphone and instruments to your computer.

5. **Buy lots of backup hard drives.** Losing your source tracks can be heartbreaking, and hard drives are cheap. In fact, our own DAW has mirrored hard drives for the main data drive. Even if one fails while we're recording, we have a backup to make sure nothing gets lost.

6. **Buy decent monitor speakers for mixing and mastering.** Monitor speakers are used to listen to mixes and mastering while in the studio. This is where precision comes in. There are a variety of quality monitor speakers available—the higher the quality, the more likely you'll be able to hear nuances in what you've recorded. Don't use headphones to mix or master.

7. **Buy cheap headphones for recording.** You can save money by buying cheap headphones for *recording*. While you would never use headphones for mixing or mastering what you've recorded, when it's all about hearing the backing tracks so you can record your part, a pair of cheap headphones is "good enough" to do the job.

8. **Know your room.** Professional studios have rooms designed for recording. The room affects the sound that's caught in the microphone as you record, not to mention the feedback you get from your monitors. Make sure that the room is either dead (carpeted or otherwise insulated), so you can manipulate your sound in postproduction, or has a sound that you can live with. Also, be conscious of extraneous noise created by fluorescent lights, electronic devices such as cell phones, air conditioning, and snare drums that aren't locked down.

8. **Build it over time.** We recommend building a home studio slowly by just getting the pieces that you need and learning each new one as you go forward. Professional recording equipment can be overwhelming at first, so it's worth your time to learn it one piece at a time. You can replace parts of your studio that you want to upgrade as you go forward. IndieGuide.com/Music has information as well, should you decide to build your own.

HOW TO FIND AND USE A PROFESSIONAL STUDIO

If you go the professional-studio route, know that both the studio and those working there are on the clock. That means time literally equals money. Here's how to find and use a studio most effectively:

1. **Do research.** Referrals from local musicians is the best way to find a good studio. Otherwise, try your favorite search engine, or go to IndieGuide.com/Music for links to recording-studio directories.

2. **Negotiate the contract.** Normally, recording studios will charge a flat rate depending on the amount of music that will need to be mastered. Make

sure that the contract doesn't give the studio any rights to your music and that you own the master recordings.

3. **Make a plan.** Don't spend any time in the studio deciding what to do. Make a list of songs you want to cover, and schedule the musicians ahead of time. Usually, you'll record all of the tracks for a single musician all in a row across all of the songs that they are on.

4. **Rehearse for your session.** The best way to minimize your recording time is to practice and arrange your songs for your session the same way that you'd practice for a live show. Everyone will know their parts and will be able to play them in just a few takes.

5. **Bring extras of everything.** You get charged for the time it takes to go to the store for a battery for your pedal. Take care of logistics ahead of time to save money. Bring extra strings, batteries, cables, tuners, AC plugs, power strips, reeds, tools, and anything else that you might need for your performance.

6. **Prepare your instruments for recording.** Get new drum heads, break in strings, and make sure all of your instruments are ready to go for your session.

7. **Tune your drums.** Or find someone to do it for you.

8. **One tuner to tune them all.** Make sure you use the same tuner for all of the instruments that you record—including the drums. Otherwise, you might need to re-record tracks.

HOW TO FIND AND HIRE A PRODUCER

Producers fill a somewhat misunderstood role in recording. You don't have to get a producer, and many bands don't, but they do bring some advantages to shaping your music.

Although the names sound the same, a music producer is not the same as a film producer. If an album were a film, a music producer would be the director. The producers are usually in the control room during a recording and will help manage the recording session and help realize the full creative potential of the music. The Grammy Award–winning producer Michael Freeman, who has been in the recording business for decades, explained that while a live performance is only played and heard once, a studio album is meant to be heard over and over. Producers can help with pitch, meter, tuning, energy, and feeling during the sessions—a process very different than playing live. Some other examples of what producers do for your band:

- Help decide what kind of sound to aim for, as well suggesting which kind of microphones, equipment, and recording styles to use.

- Arrange the songs' structure to be more effective.

- Come up with ideas for extra parts or different sounds to give a song direction. For example, you might hear, "That's good—but what if you played it this way...." (Freeman's advice on this is to at least try out suggestions that producers make, even if you don't initially like an idea.)

- Supervise mixdown and mastering.

- Help manage the entire process.

Naturally, many bands do all this for themselves, especially when they have their own studios. If you decide to go without a producer, just be prepared to do the same work a producer does if you want the same high-quality result.

You must feel comfortable working with your producers, since you'll be including them in every creative step. They may take your recording in directions that you don't want to go. John Lisiecki says, "The best producers will help you realize your creative vision. Not theirs." If it starts becoming a question of your sound versus their sound, you may want to find other producers.

Freeman's advice is to "find a producer that understands your music. Ask yourself, Does he or she 'get it'?" Freeman said that he spends a month or more working with the band in rehearsals on the songs to prepare for the recording, before even setting foot in the studio. During this preparation, they decide how they are going to play the songs for the recording, and understand the vision for the album, so that they can make the best decisions about instruments, arrangements, and recording.

The following steps can help guide you toward the right choice.

1. **Find a producer.** Use referrals from other musicians, your local recording studio, sites like SessionPlayers (sessionplayers.com), or go to IndieGuide.com/Music for links to producer resources.

2. **Research and then meet with the producer to see if it's a good fit.** Make sure it's someone that fits your musical style and whose work you like. You might also want to check out the person's references. And meet with them first. You'll be working closely with them on your music and you'll want to make sure you're compatible.

3. **Negotiate the contract.** If you hire a producer, make sure that your financial arrangement is both clear and acceptable to you. Most producers nowadays will require an up-front fee as well as a cut of the album sales. Standard industry terms usually gave producers a cut of the royalties ("points" on an album) before the band saw any of its own. Of course, in today's world, you might be able to get one willing to work for a flat fee, and we'd recommend this if possible. Be wary if the producer wants a copyright interest in your songs or sound recordings.

HOW TO FIND PRECLEARED AND ROYALTY-FREE SAMPLES AND LOOPS FOR YOUR RECORDINGS

With the right combination of samples and loops, you can create the illusion of a full band backing you, or just enhance tracks with that little something extra that they need. While these tools have been around for a long time, many new sources will sell them royalty-free, which allows you to legally use this material inside your own music. These sources, found all over the Internet, can add new dimensions to your music.

To find royalty-free samples and loops, do the following:

1. **Check out free sources.** It turns out that there are many free sources of samples and loops. Public-domain recordings are always free, and there is also a great deal of material licensed under Creative Commons (CC) licenses, some of which allow commercial use, while others require you to go back to the creator to get the rights; so please read the license carefully. Check out ccMixter (ccmixter.org) and the Freesound Project (freesound .org). Additionally, the Creative Commons site (creativecommons.org) allows you to search multiple sites for prelicensed material that can be incorporated into your music.

2. **Research loop and sample services.** There's a wide variety of loop and sample sources like Drums on Demand (drumsondemand.com), East West Samples (eastwestsamples.com), and ACIDplanet (acidplanet.com) that

will charge a one-time fee for the use of a sample or loop that you can use in your songs. For more sample and loop resources, see IndieGuide.com/Music.

3. **Make sure that you understand the terms, and verify that they are royalty-free.** Be sure to read the agreements carefully before downloading, buying, or using them. The important point about these tools is that they come with a license that allows you to incorporate the audio into your own songs (sometimes called "derivative works") and that you don't have to pay for each use ("royalty-free"). Don't sample music that you don't own and isn't precleared. To do so is to enter the world of copyright infringement. We'll discuss this more in chapter 5, "Your Rights".

4. **Record a cover version of the sample or audioloop.** One additional thing you can do is record a cover version of the sample or audioloop you wish to use. If you do so, you'll need to obtain permission from and pay a fee to the author/publisher (we discuss this in the "Your Rights" chapter), but the sound recording is yours to sample and use in your song.

MASTERING
WHAT EVERY MUSICIAN NEEDS TO KNOW ABOUT MASTERING—
WHAT IT IS AND WHY YOU NEED IT

Mastering is frequently misunderstood, perhaps because it's much easier to hear its effects than to describe them. The difference between a mastered track and an unmastered one can be dramatic. Mastering is best described as the finishing process for music recording. It occurs after the recording is mixed down, but before it is sent to a CD printing house or uploaded online.

Mastering involves the following:

• **Powerful and Targeted EQ.** The mastering house will apply EQ (boosting or reducing certain sound frequencies) to the entire recording rather than just the individual tracks, which happens during mixdown. They also EQ the songs in relation to each other, so that they share a common sound. A mastering house can bring out qualities in your recording you didn't even know were there.

• **Compression/Limiting.** Mastering houses usually apply some compression (normalize levels) and limiting (prevent clipping) to the whole album, rather than to individual tracks. This, again, helps the entire album develop a consistent amplitude and sound, rather than having some tracks stick out.

• **Volume Normalization.** Well-mastered albums don't have huge volume differences between tracks. During mixdown, each song is mixed at volume levels appropriate for it, but not in comparison to other tracks. Mastering makes the album into a coherent whole and puts all the songs into the same dynamic range.

• **Track Arrangement.** Details such as the ordering of tracks and connections and spacing between the tracks are done during mastering. Mastering houses will often put a final volume drop-off at the end of a track to control how the album flows from one song to another.

• **Sound Smoothing.** Mastering houses usually have a few vintage, vacuum-tube-based systems that can "warm up" a digital recording, which might sound harsh and cold without some analog equipment to smooth it out.

• **Crowd Noise.** Because live albums are often put together in a way that eliminates silences between tracks, crowd noise might be added between tracks during mastering.

Mastering plays a significant role in making a disparate collection of songs you recorded at different times, levels, and with varying instruments into a cohesive whole. You can learn to master your own music, but it's usually a good idea to get mastering specialists to work on the finished product. In fact, many mastering engineers don't do recording or mixdown work so they can focus their ears on mastering alone. Michael Freeman, the producer we mentioned earlier, echoes this point and suggests you never use the same person for mixdown and mastering so you have a different person and a new pair of ears on the music. When your recording sounds professional, you've raised the odds of getting it noticed by audiences, as well as getting it licensed. Mastering is useful whether you record at home or at a professional studio, so although many indie musicians sometimes skip this process, they aren't doing themselves any favors.

If you're not familiar with mastering, many mastering houses will offers to master a track for free, charging you only if you decide to use it. We recommend you try this so you can hear for yourself the surprising things mastering can do.

HOW TO FIND A MASTERING HOUSE

Follow these steps to find a mastering house:

1. **Research the options and select a mastering house.** Find a mastering house in your local area if possible, so that you can be present during the process. To find one, use referrals from other musicians, your local recording studio, or go IndieGuide.com/Music for links to mastering resources. Additionally, there are online mastering houses, including SoundOps (soundops.com) and the Sound Lab (discmakers.com/ soundlab).

2. **Negotiate the contract.** Normally, a mastering house will charge a flat or hourly rate depending on the amount of music that will need to be mastered. Make sure that the contract doesn't give the studio any rights to your music and that you own the master recordings.

HOW TO PREPARE FOR AND USE A MASTERING HOUSE EFFECTIVELY

When you decide to use a mastering house, some musicians don't prepare their music before going in there. In fact, the first time we used one, we scheduled the time and walked in with problems in our mixes. Fortunately, he didn't charge us for discovering our mistake and let us come back another time. Don't make the same mistake. Use these steps to prepare your music for mastering, and then find and use a mastering house:

1. **Don't mix it "loud."** A mastering engineer will boost your track so it's "loud" (close to 0 dB—the highest limit of a digital track). So, you don't need to make a loud mix. In fact, for mastering engineers to be effective, they need you to bring relatively low-level mixes—ones with "headroom." If you come in with a mix that's too loud, they may send you back to remix it.

2. **Don't shorten or clip the track.** Mastering houses can use the before-and-after silence and noise on a track because it gives them a sound floor to analyze before the music starts. They will clip the tracks to the exact length after they are done working with it.

3. **Make sure you're happy with your mixdown.** Since mastering takes time and costs money, make sure you bring the final mixdown. Test your mixdowns in different environments (such as the car) and with different

devices (to hear how it holds up across different types of speakers). Play it for different people, especially other musicians, and elicit comments. And then settle on your final mixes before bringing them to your mastering studio.

4. **Bring multiple mixdowns.** Although engineers can draw on a surprising variety of tricks to deal with mixdown issues, don't depend on them to fix mistakes such as certain tracks set too low or high. In addition, many mastering houses will ask you to mixdown your songs with the music and the vocals on two different stereo tracks so that they can combine these tracks and ensure that the vocals are heard above the mix. Often they request you bring the following mixes:

o   An instrumental (no vocals) mix

o   A vocals-only mix

o   A combined vocals and instrumental mix with the vocals at the levels you think are right and are happy with

o   Two additional combined vocals and instrumental mixes with the vocals 1 or 2 dB higher and 1 or 2 dB lower (These other mixes also can be used for licensing purposes, for example as the bed of a commercial or video, which we discuss in chapter 13, "Get Heard.")

5.   **Bring the right formats.** Confirm with the mastering house which formats they require. Make sure you bring them what they asked for, whether it's WAV files, CDs, or something else. It's expensive to schedule a session, then show up with music in the wrong format. (Note: the right answer is *never* "MP3 files." MP3 is a lossy, low-quality version of your recording. A mastering house can't do anything with an MP3 file.)

6.   **Plan the track order ahead of time.** The mastering engineer will ask you for the track order, so you should decide on that ahead of time, and bring a list. Debating the order among your band members while the engineer is on the clock is a waste of money.

We recommend that you put your strongest song first. As Bob Boilen, the host and director of National Public Radio's *All Songs Considered*, advises, most reviewers listen to the first song only. If it doesn't grab them, your disc will go into the giveaway pile. If you need help deciding, try them out against your friends, or use services like SoundOut (soundout.com), which lets you try the track against fans of your music genre. They are asked to listen to the song, rate it on a 10-point scale, and write a review explaining their opinion. You'll get a rating for each song, which can give you some objective information about which song people like best.

PREPARE YOUR MUSIC FOR DISTRIBUTION AND RELEASE

Now that you have your music made and mastered, the next step is to prepare it for distribution for the Web, the press, free giveaways, podcasts, and more.

HOW TO ENCODE YOUR MP3S SO THEY CAN BE PLAYED AND HEARD BY THE MOST PEOPLE

Most people never look at the encoding settings when they rip their own CDs to MP3 files and just use the defaults. That's fine for your personal music, but when you want your music to be playable by as many people as possible when you give it out or sell it for distribution, you will need to tweak it.

Here are suggested settings that were born out of trial and error as we encoded hundreds of our own songs (we've released nearly five hundred). If you're curious as to the technical details of how each of these MP3 encoding options work, visit the Web page for this chapter at IndieGuide.com/Music.

1. **Encode the WAVs properly.** Whether you are getting the WAV files from your recording software directly, or encoding them from a CD of your music, you should use the following settings:

   o 16-bit

   o 44.1 kHz

   o Stereo

2. **Change the settings on your MP3 encoder.** You will need to find the options page on the MP3 encoder you are using to adjust the settings.

   For a song that you want to giveaway for maximum playability and size:

   o Constant bit rate (CBR) at 128 KB

   o Joint stereo

For songs that you want to sell at high quality:

o Constant bit rate (CBR) at 320 KB

o Joint stereo

HOW TO NAME YOUR MP3S SO THAT FANS KNOW WHO YOU ARE AND WHERE TO FIND YOU

As we learned as we released songs from our Web sites, the names you give your song files make it easier to organize and can even help lead your fans back to you if they like the music.

Here's a suggested set of rules to use:

1. **Include your band name and the song title in the filename.** Consider using the following naming standard for your MP3 files: "Band Name-Song Title.mp3". Adding your band name to the song file is a quick way to point fans back to who created the song.

2. **Leave out all special characters like punctuation, question marks, apostrophes, and quotes.** Most computers have trouble with these, and there's no reason to introduce any problems.

3. **Replace spaces with underscores.** Some systems have problems with spaces in the name. To overcome this, you can use underscores instead. For example: "Beatnik_Turtle-Pizza_The_Rock_Opera.mp3".

4. **Make sure you spell everything correctly.** Your files may go to thousands of fans. Take a minute to make sure you've spelled everything correctly.

HOW TO RELEASE YOUR MUSIC SO FANS CAN FIND YOU

When fans listen to MP3s of your music, the artist name, album, and song title come up in the player based on ID3 tags. These tags turn out to be critically important for musicians, although some artists skip tagging the music they give out. This is a major mistake: we have songs in our personal music collections that we love, but have no idea who the bands are because they not only failed to include their band name in the filename, they also neglected to use ID3 tags. No MP3 file should be given out without filling the ID3 tags.

These ID3 tags are used by more than just fans or MP3 players. Here's a few of the other surprising uses for ID3 tags:

• The Web site Eventful (eventful.com) will scan your MP3 collection and use the ID3 tags to see if any of the artists in your collection are going to be performing in your area.

• Last.fm uses ID3 tags to identify the artist that is being played and keeps Web pages on every single artist. The more plays an artist has, the more popular it gets.

Here's how to tag your MP3 files:

1. **Decide whether to use your MP3 player, or purchase tagging software.** You can use standard MP3 players like iTunes or Windows Media Player, but there are special tags that the standard players can't always set for you. In particular, it's a good idea to embed the ISRC (International Standard Recording Code; more on this in chapter 5, "Your Rights") into each file, which can't be done with standard players. The more advanced tools like Tag & Rename from Softpointer (softpointer.com/tr.htm) and Jaikoz (jthink.net/jaikoz) can handle it.

2. **Fill in all of the following tags completely:**

   o Album/Movie/Show title

   o Composer

   o Content type

   o Copyright message

   o File type

   o Title/song name/content description

   o Subtitle/description refinement

   o URL frame: copyright/legal information

   o URL frame: official artist/performer Web page

   o URL frame: official audiosource Web page

   o Attached picture: include the album cover or the avatar that represents your band (more on this in chapter 4, "Your Brand").

o ISRC code: note that you can only add an ISRC code using more advanced tagging tools such as the ones we suggested.

o Comment: direct them to your Web site for more music. (For example: "Come to www.beatnikturtle.com for more free music!")

HOW TO CONVINCE FANS TO BUY MUSIC THAT YOU RELEASE FOR FREE

Most artists release free songs in order to get more fans, and more interest in their music. But, of course, this can make fans less likely to buy the same songs.

In today's world, ironically, the more that you give away, the more you tend to get back in terms of attention and fans. But if you want to let your fans know that they should buy the songs you release for free, you might want to consider these simple techniques.

1. **Release samples instead of full songs.** This is a great way to give fans a taste without giving them the song. But keep in mind that when you release samples, the fans are less likely to keep this in their players, and not likely to give it to friends. Using samples is more effective when there's a Buy button right next to the sample. Note that services like iTunes already give samples, so it may be unnecessary for you to create them.

2. **Put an audiobumper at the beginning or end of the track.** When we did our Song of the Day project, releasing one song every day for a year, we put a brief audiobumper, singing our Web site address, TheSongOfThe Day.com. It was unobtrusive enough that people didn't mind having it in their collections, while reminding them where it came from. Of course, the album versions didn't have the audiobumper.

3. **Put out alternate versions or demos.** It's not necessary to give away every version of a song you record. For example, you can give away demos, acoustic versions, or live versions of the songs available while keeping the album version for sale.

HOW TO DECIDE WHICH MUSIC FILE FORMATS TO MAKE
AVAILABLE FOR USE IN SALES, LICENSING, PROMOTION, PR,
AND MARKETING

After putting together hundreds of songs, we learned that when we are creating the files for each song we released, it made sense to create multiple versions so that we had them on hand and ready to go for other purposes. For example, people who made videos with our music wanted WAVs, while fans needed MP3s. While you are putting together your music, consider creating your music in the following formats, and always have them handy and ready to go.

1.   **WAVs.**   Rather than ripping your own music from CDs, get the WAV files directly from your final mastering process so that you have the highest quality WAV files of each song you make. These files are needed for video production, licensing, podcasters, and your own production purposes. Many artists make the mistake of giving MP3s to these creators and don't realize that the songs can sound terrible if the MP3 gets compressed a second time when it's uploaded to sites like YouTube or incorporated into a podcast. Poor sound quality can reflect poorly on you and your music. Once you have the WAVs, keep them handy so that they are available in case someone needs them quickly.

2.   **High- and Low-Quality MP3s.**   You may want to put together both high-quality MP3s for sale and low-quality MP3s for giveaway purposes. See the section "How to Encode Your MP3s so They Can Be Played and Heard by the Most People," on page 38, for how to do this.

3.   **CDs.**   Whether you have a CD that's been burned on your computer or has been manufactured, always have some CDs of your music available so that you can hand them to people. This is especially useful for PR and marketing purposes, and can be more effective than giving someone a card.

LEARNING MORE

Go to IndieGuide.com/Music for a clickable version of every link, Web site, and service mentioned in this chapter, as well as free extra materials to help you put together your music.

THE STRATEGIC GOAL: to build and maintain a team of people who can help you succeed at your music without having you do it all yourself

REFERENCE PAGE: IndieGuide.com/Team

CHECKLIST

What	Description
Manager	The person that handles the business decisions for the band
Booking Agent	The person who books the band and takes booking calls
Attorney	Your legal resource for the band
Accountant/Bookkeeper	Your accounting and bookkeeping resources for the band
Graphic Artist	The person who handles the imagery and graphics for the band
Publicist	The person who runs the public relations (PR) campaigns and takes all calls from the press to arrange interviews
Web Designer/Webmaster	The person who creates and manages your Web, social, and mobile presences
Photographer	The person who handles taking pictures for publicity, the Web, and more
Recording Producer	The person who makes the final call in the recording studio about sound, feel, and arrangements
Recording Engineer	The person who handles the recording process
Mastering Engineer	The person who masters your music
Distributor	The person who handles distribution of your music.
Video Team	A director, cast, crew, editor, and everyone associated with making music videos
Store Clerk (for gigs at stores)	The people who sell stuff to fans at shows. If you sell your album from the stage, congratulations: you're the store clerk.
Roadies	Whoever carries stuff to and from the stage

AND NETWORKING STRATEGY

" 'Do it yourself' doesn't mean 'do it all yourself.' "

—DEREK SIVERS, FOUNDER OF CD BABY AND HOST BABY

WHETHER YOU know it or not, you already have a team behind your music. Beyond the instruments that they play, all the members of your band may have skills that can help you achieve your goals. And even if you're a solo artist or DJ, you have friends, family, and people around you that have skills to help you succeed.

Even labels don't try to do everything themselves. Most keep a minimal staff, and then hire professionals, companies, and services to help them with the roles they need. For example, they hire publicists to handle publicity, graphic artists to handle imagery, developers to help build Web sites, social media experts to help arrange campaigns, attorneys to handle contracts and licensing, and so on.

David Taylor, a songwriter, producer, and music business teacher (davidtaylor2.com), states it this way, "The music industry puts out a product and there's a face on it. Maybe that's the face that *you* see, but the music industry is a compilation of systems and people. If you think this stuff is easy, I want you to watch the end credits of your favorite half-hour television show. First of all, that's just 22 minutes of entertainment. Second of all, it takes all those people to put together those 22 minutes!"

Throughout this book we talk about everything you need to succeed without a label. That may seem like a lot to take on, but, just like labels, you don't have to do it all yourself.

In fact, doing it yourself *doesn't* mean doing it alone.

You've heard the saying before: "It's not what you know; it's who you know." Or, as one of our friends puts it, "It's who you get to know." This is as true in music as it is in any other field. At the end of the day, despite all the advances in technology that have empowered the artist, it's not technology that will get your music noticed, booked, distributed, played, seen, and publicized; it's people.

People make things happen and your goal is to find the right people to help you do it.

WHY TO NETWORK

THE TOP THREE REASONS WHY YOU NEED TO BUILD YOUR NETWORK

1. **Skills and Talents.** One of the goals of networking is to find people with the skills and talents you need. If you think of the types of skills and talents required to create music, get booked, get distributed, get heard, get seen, and get noticed, the following roles—and the skills they require—are the ones you need to cover yourself:

   o   Manager

   o   Booking Agent

   o   Attorney

   o   Accountant/Bookkeeper

   o   Graphic Artist

   o   Publicist

   o   Web Designer/Webmaster

   o   Photographer

   o   Recording Producer

   o   Recording Engineer

   o   Mastering Engineer

   o   Distributor

- Video Director

- Video Camera crew

- Video Editor

- Store Clerk (for shows and events)

- Roadies

2. **Opportunities and Publicity.** Another goal of networking is to find people who have an audience that can get your music in front of new people. These types of people can be harder to network with at first, because people with an audience, especially a large one, are naturally harder to get to know. Some of these people include:

- Journalists

- Music reviewers

- Bloggers

- Podcasters

- Internet and terrestrial radio personnel

- Charities

3. **Customers and Business Partners.** Yet another goal of networking is to find people who will do business with you. They include:

- Bookers

- Venue managers and bar owners

- Video-game creators

- Film, television, and video creators

- Companies that need music

- Theater artists

You might already know some of these people, but if you don't, they may take some time and energy to cultivate. Sometimes they require credentials.

The good news is, once you establish the necessary relationships, they will start coming to *you* with business opportunities.

THE FOUR OPTIONS YOU HAVE TO GET THINGS DONE

Every how-to we cover in the guide comes down to four simple choices. You can:

1. **Do it yourself.** Like many of the musicians we've interviewed for this book, you can do a lot of this yourself. In fact, you're holding in your hand a book that will show you everything you need to know and give you step-by-step "recipes" to follow so you can do it yourself.

2. **Find someone you know to do it for you.** The good news is you're surrounded by people—including other musicians and fans—who can help you. And you'll expand your reach and meet new people who can help as you progress and develop your music career.

3. **Get a company or service to do it for you.** There are more services and resources out there to help musicians succeed than ever in history and for nearly every how-to in this book we'll point you to them. Better still, many of them are free.

4. **Hire a professional to do it for you.** First, with Web sites such as Craigslist (craigslist.org), oDdesk (odesk.com), and Elance (elance.com), you can find and hire people to take on the work. Second, for music-related tasks, keep in mind that there are music industry professionals who are now independent and available for hire.

If you don't do one of the four things above, the work just won't get done. And yet, there are some tasks that you just can't skip—especially when it comes to promoting your band and getting your music heard. Of course, the more people and services you have helping you, the more you can get done at the same time.

NETWORKING STRATEGIES AND TECHNIQUES

WHAT EVERY MUSICIAN NEEDS TO KNOW ABOUT NETWORKING

The word "networking" scares most people. Maybe because they associate it with unpleasant tasks such as finding a job. Or because it can feel like a phony way to befriend someone. But networking doesn't have to be hard, and it shouldn't start with strangers at all. The people that you already know may be the ones who can help you achieve your goals, or they may know people that can get you what you need.

Networking is simple: find out what you can do for people, and help them out.

Most people think that networking is about what people can do for you, but that's backward. Instead, find out what you can do for *them* (even if it's not music-related). As George Hrab (georgehrab.com), a successful indie musician and podcaster, puts it, the secret to getting other people to help you out is "to find talented people and be really, really, really nice to them."

Many people you'll be networking with will have their own Web sites, blogs, and Web presences. Pop their name in a search engine and learn about them before you reach out. This makes it easy to find out a lot about them—their history, bios, what they like, what they dislike, and what they're working on. This makes starting a conversation natural, provides you with ideas on how you can help them, and possibly gives you angles on how you can work together, collaborate, or do business.

When you're genuinely interested in other people and focused on helping them solve their problems, those people will instinctively help you afterward. If you're wondering why this simple technique works—of offering something ahead of asking something in return—we recommend you read *Influence: The Psychology of Persuasion,* by Robert B. Cialdini. But we've had plenty of success following this on our own.

Throughout our music career, we would often look for opportunities to help people who could eventually help us later, by offering them our music, or solving their music needs, since it was easy for us to create, record, and produce. Then, when it came time for us to ask for a favor, they were happy to help us out. For example, our band did this when promoting *The Cheapass Album*—an album of songs based on game titles from the trendy board-game manufacturer Cheapass Games. At the time of the release back in 2004, we discovered a niche podcast created by Scott Alden and Derk Solko, the people behind BoardGameGeek, a Web site that gets over 1.5 million unique visitors a month (boardgamegeek.com). It was immediately evident that the podcast didn't have a theme song. We didn't know Scott or Derk, but we decided to make our own opportunity and e-mailed them to see if they'd let us do a theme song for their show. A few days later, after we sent them our albums, they agreed to let us write a demo and give it a listen.

Within a few weeks, they adopted the song for their podcast. They talked about us in many podcast episodes, which kept our name, our music, and our Web site in front of their listeners. We kept in contact with them and later took it a step further by doing more music, helping them with voice-over bumpers, and creating some off-the-wall public-service announcements. They even interviewed us in one episode. Scott and Derk became a big part of our opportunity network, and we all became good friends. Their podcasts have been downloaded thousands of times, and they continue to be downloaded years later by new visitors.

If all you remember about networking is to solve other people's problems, you can't fail. And as you expand your network, problems get easier to solve, more stuff gets done, and opportunities start coming your way.

THE TOP THREE WAYS TO NETWORK

There are many books on the subject of networking, but below are three simple and effective ways to connect with others to help you and your music.

1. **Get an introduction.** It never hurts to ask someone you know, "Can you introduce me?" when you want to connect with someone you don't know yet. Once you find a connection in common, it's much easier to start a new relationship.

    For example, for years we wanted to be part of the Chicago leg of the International Pop Overthrow (internationalpopoverthrow.com)—a roving festival that showcases power-pop rock bands. We went the traditional route of sending in our CD and press kit and never heard anything back. Months later when the festival came to town, we discovered that our friend Yvonne Doll of the band the Locals (localsrock .com) managed to get in. When we told her we were hoping to be a part of the festival, she arranged to have us meet David Bash, the festival organizer, after her set. He asked for a CD, and the very next day he contacted us to fill in for a last-minute cancellation in the schedule. We had a great show and thanked Yvonne for the introduction. We played the festival many years after that and were included on a couple IPO compilation albums.

2. **Make your goals and problems known so others can offer
help.** No one will know to help you if you don't ask. The people who you
already know might have the skills, opportunities, or connections you
need—or know someone who does.

For instance, when we were putting together the artwork for our second
album, *Santa Doesn't Like You*, we lacked the software and know-how to get
it in the format that the CD printing house required. We were stuck, and were
complaining about the problem at a party. One of guests overheard our
dilemma, and revealed she was a graphic artist and had the necessary software
to create the files. We'd had no idea she could do this. She was just someone we
hung out with in our building from time to time. All she asked for in return was
to get a credit in the liner notes so she could use it as part of her portfolio. We
were happy to do that for her, and we got the album art done in time.

But that's just one example. When we wanted to make a music video but
lacked the equipment, we asked around. Soon, we not only had the equipment,
but we had friends willing to direct and act. Other examples include getting
booked at a college outdoor festival through a friend who worked at the
college and getting press for our TheSongOfTheDay.com project when a
friend mentioned it to his buddies who wrote for a popular Chicago blog
called Gapers Block (gapersblock.com).

3. **Network where you're the only musician so you stand out.** Most
musicians only think to network at music events. But you should look for
opportunities at events where you are the only musician. For instance,
Reggi Hopkins, executive director of the Music Industry Workshop and
the Center for Music Technology, also runs a recording studio. Instead of
just networking at music events, he attended a local business community
event at Chicago's Chamber of Commerce. While everyone else there
mingled in a business suit selling consulting, accounting, or other business
services, he was the only musician. He offered his studio and music to
create one free radio commercial. This brought business to his studio.

We also network at events where we stand out. For example, we've gone
to DragonCon (dragoncon.org), where podcasters, bloggers, filmmakers, and
other creative people hang out. Most of them need music, and being one of
the only musicians attending the events, we've generated new opportunities
and collaboration projects as well as expanded our fan base to an audience
we never would have otherwise connected with.

THE TOP THREE WAYS TO GIVE BACK TO PEOPLE IN YOUR NETWORK AND KEEP THEM INVOLVED

It's important not only to add people to your network but also to give credit to everyone who helps you out on the way to keep them motivated. These techniques are free; use them as often as possible.

1. **Offer cross-promotion and link love.** You have fans; they have fans. Introduce your work to each other. People within your reach are more likely to work with you if they know that they'll get exposure. For example, when we became the house band for a sketch comedy group, the Dolphins of Damnation, at Chicago's Second City Theater, part of the reason the comedy group got the time slot was because the band came with an established fan base. In return, we got to play in front of their fan base and anyone else who came to Second City to see a sketch comedy show.

One of the easiest ways to cross-promote today is through a technique called "link love": link to them so your fans can check out their Web site. For example, we have a special "shout-out" section at our TheSongOfThe Day.com site that lists every podcast that has played one of our songs. It's our little thank-you. The most recent plays get a mention on our front page, with direct links to the episodes so that fans of our music can check them out. And we also tweet to our followers to check out the podcast. This results in more requests to play our music—not just from the same podcasters, but from others who saw that we offered something in return.

2. **Put their name in lights.** Movies always end by rolling the credits of everyone who was involved in making it happen. This is good advice for any musician as well. When people help you, give them credit. It's free, and people really appreciate it. There are many ways you can do this, including the following:

- Blog posts
- Credits on your Web site
- Album liner notes
- Shout outs in a video
- Social media posts

3. **Celebrate and acknowledge successes.** Theater groups throw a cast party at the close of every run. We suggest doing the same for everyone who has helped you out whenever you reach a milestone such as completing a tour, releasing an album, or getting some great publicity. We've thrown parties, held barbecues, and taken people to dinner to show our appreciation and to celebrate. Usually, we end up talking about the next projects we want to work on, because everyone's excited about what they've helped achieve, and they usually want to be involved in the next project.

HOW TO EXPAND YOUR REACH WITH SOCIAL NETWORKS

With today's social networks like Twitter, Facebook, LinkedIn, and Google+, it's easier than ever to reach out and contact others. In fact, these social networks help magnify your reach since you are constantly in contact with all of your networks. We'll talk more about how to set up and use these networks effectively in chapter 8, "Your Web Strategy," chapter 9 "Your Web, Social, and Mobile Presences," and chapter 11, "Your Marketing Strategy."

HOW TO FIND PEOPLE TO FILL SKILLS THAT YOU NEED WHEN YOUR NETWORK RUNS DRY

With the Web, it turns out there's a lot of options for you to connect with people, even if you don't know them personally. When it comes to finding skills, you have a choice:

1. **Go to where the party is.** You can head to the community sites where the people with the skills you're looking for congregate and hang out with one another. For instance, if you're looking for a graphic artist, you may hit the Adobe Photoshop community board (forums.adobe.com/community/photoshop). If you're looking for video help, you may hit the Final Cut Pro board (discussions.apple.com/community/professional_applications/final_cut_studio) or a community and informational site like Creative Cow (creativecow.net). And head to IndieGuide.com/Team for more sites that can help with creative projects.

2. **Go to contracting sites.** You can head to Web sites where the people with the skills you need post their availability for hire. Sites such as oDesk (odesk.com) and Elance (elance.com) specialize in this.

3. **Post an ad.** You can post an ad in your local newspapers or on a site like Craigslist (craigslist.org).

If you're looking to find musicians, see chapter 2, "Your Music," for more options.

THE NUMBER ONE FORGOTTEN NETWORK

Don't forget your fans when it comes to working on your goals. It's easier than ever to reach out to them and ask them to help, and you never know what skills they may have, or whether they are connected to someone that can help you out. And fortunately, fans today want to interact and participate—not just listen.

HOW TO USE YOUR NETWORK TO RAISE MONEY

Crowd-funding sites like Kickstarter (kickstarter.com), Indiegogo (indie gogo.com), and PledgeMusic (pledgemusic.com) can get your network to help finance you. While each crowd-funding site approaches funding in slightly different ways, in general you set a target dollar amount for a project (an album, video, tour) and set a time limit to achieve the goal. You then ask your fans to pledge money, usually offering something like credits in the liner notes, an autographed copy of the album, or tickets to a live show. If the target amount is reached by the deadline, you get the money.

Nataly Dawn of the indie band Pomplamoose (pomplamoose.com) used Kickstarter to raise money for a solo album. In exchange for pledges, she offered a variety of different incentives. For instance, for those who pledged between $10 and $30, they'd get a download of the album before it was released, while those who pledged $3,000 or more would get a concert at their house. By the time the pledge drive closed, she ended up getting 2,315 backers who pledged a total of $104,788 toward her solo album.

Similarly, the indie musician Nick Bertke, better known as Pogo (pogo mix.net), whose videos have generated over fifty million views on YouTube, and who has produced remixes for Disney Pixar, Microsoft, Showtime, and others, also successfully fan funded a solo project. Although he was shooting for $15,000, his 1,178 backers pledged $25,299.

There's a lot to using these sites effectively (and some tax implications as well), so to get the most out of fan funding, head to IndieGuide.com/Team for more information, tips on maximizing the money you can make, and links to other crowd-funding sites.

HOW TO NETWORK IN THE MUSIC INDUSTRY

Conferences, for musicians, used to primarily be about trying to get signed to a label. But this has changed, and there are many ways that you can connect with other musicians, with people in the music business, and with people that have services and Web sites that can help you succeed in music if you are doing it yourself.

Use these options to connect with other musicians and other people in the music business.

1. **Connect online.** Visit Web sites like Just Plain Folks (jpfolks.com), The Velvet Rope Forums (tiwaryent.com/forums/ubbthreads.php), and Harmony Central Forums (acapella.harmony-central.com) to find other musicians online. But there's a multitude of options, more than we can fit here, and we track them at IndieGuide.com/Team.

2. **Connect locally.** It seems that every town has a musicians' hangout, depending on the style of music. We can only help you with our hometown of Chicago, where we live. We hang out at the Old Town School of Folk Music (oldtownschool.org), which has classes on every genre of music you can imagine, not just folk, and is a great hangout to find and meet other musicians. And if you like jazz, the Bloom School of Jazz (bloom-schoolof jazz.com) connects jazz musicians. And Mary Datcher (twitter.com /globalmixx) runs Chicago Collabo, a music-business mixer. Make sure to go out and find your own town's local hangouts.

3. **Connect at conferences.** There's a wealth of conferences that allow musicians to network and get information about the new music business. Explore conferences like South by Southwest (sxsw.com) and NAMM (namm.org). And if you want to connect internationally, try MIDEM (midem.com). But go to IndieGuide.com/Team for links to over a dozen more conferences of all kinds.

LEARNING MORE

Go to IndieGuide.com/Team for a clickable version of every link, Web site, and service mentioned in this chapter, as well as free extras to help you build and manage your team.

CHAPTER 4

THE STRATEGIC GOAL: to create and maintain a consistent identity that you control, and that will be the first thing that leaps to people's minds when they meet, promote, think about, and engage with you and your music

REFERENCE PAGE: IndieGuide.com/Brand

CHECKLIST

What	Description
Band/Artist Name	Your band or artist name should be unique (ideally, one you can trademark), match your Web site URL, and be entirely yours.
Website URL	The URL of your website, used in nearly all of your branded materials.
Fonts	Defined font styles for your website, logos, and imagery so that you can stay consistent.
Music Description	A one-line clear description of your music.
Links to music, videos, and web presences	Prepare links to all of your sites. Consider using URL shortener tools like bit.ly which let you track how many times people click on them.
Logo	A logo for your band. Preferably using line art, in a vectorized layered file so that it can be resized and reused repeatedly.
Color Palette	A set of colors for all of your branded materials, specified in both CMYK and RGB values (preferably, Pantone colors) that match perfectly between computer screens and mass-manufactured merchandise so that making new imagery is simple, consistent, and easily manufactured.
Mascot	An optional character that represents your band. Preferably using line art, in a vectorized layered file so that it can be resized and reused repeatedly. Mascots are used in avatars, merchandise, and imagery for your band.
Avatar	A 100 x 100-pixel profile image for all of your online profiles. Typically using your logo or mascot, but occasionally using a personal picture. Should look good when shrunk to a small size.
Banners	Banners for your band that can be used for advertising on other Web sites.
Band Photo	Formal band photo for press and marketing. Should be a 8.5" x 11" 300 DPI JPEG.
Bios	A one-page, one-paragraph, and one-sentence bio for your band for profiles, press materials, and written pieces about your band.
Tagline	A tagline or slogan to use on merchandise, Web sites, and profiles.
Writing Voice	If you have multiple people that write for you, create a description of your writing voice so that marketing, PR, and other copy is consistent.

YOUR BRAND

*"Musicians are as much personalities
and brands as they are their music."*

—JED CARLSON, COO OF REVERBNATION

TODAY, THE people who will meet you or see you play live are probably a small fraction of the total number of people who will hear your music. The majority are those who will discover you online. To these potential fans, you will only be known through your music, name, and the identity you convey through your Web site, logos, photos, blogs, videos, avatars, and so on. That is to say: they will only know you through "your brand." While you can't meet all of your listeners, your brand will.

Because of this, whether you like it or not, you have a brand to manage. Ideally, you should not even start putting your music out into the world until you've come up with a clear and consistent brand identity. Skip this step, and you'll have a haphazard brand that you don't control. If you have three different logos, a new slogan each month, or have an inconsistent online presence, it will only confuse people and will make it harder to gain fans.

If you don't think you need to think about branding, then ask yourself this: why would anyone buy a T-shirt from a musician? The answer isn't just to "support them," because if that were true, you could just sell plain white T-shirts with nothing on them. It's your brand that gives the merchandise you'll be selling its value. It's your brand that helps create the unique identity and community your fans and team can relate to and rally around. It's your brand that shapes how the press and media see and understand you and makes it easier for them to cover you.

Now is the time to make a brand that really represents you and your music. We'll give you the practical steps to do it in this chapter.

DEFINING YOUR BRAND

WHAT MUSICIANS NEED TO KNOW ABOUT BRANDS

The American Marketing Association defines the term brand as "a name, term, design, symbol, or any other feature that identifies one seller's good or service as distinct from those of other sellers."

But your brand is not just about business and sales—it's part of your art. You can't ignore it. Your artistic identity is tied to your music. The key to effective branding is ensuring that your audience sees the identity you want to project with your art. This is especially important today since most people who experience your music will never meet you.

Whether you're a solo musician or part of a band, there's simply too much information about you and your music for new fans to easily digest. Branding is about distilling your identity into its key components. Some of these components are your name, your images (logo, album artwork), and your text (your story, your tagline). But for musicians, there are considerations that other businesses may not have to worry about. For example, if you choose the right color scheme for your logo, it'll be easier for you to mass manufacture merchandise and have the colors you see on your Web site exactly match what you print on a T-shirt. Another example would be your band name. If you make sure your band name is free and clear before you start using it, you'll be able to trademark it and make it your own.

We'll cover the practical parts of making each element of your brand later. But first, let's talk about the ingredients to what makes a good brand.

THE FIVE QUALITIES EVERY BRAND SHOULD HAVE

As Andre Calilhanna of Disc Makers told us, "Your goal should be to wedge yourself into people's consciousness." To achieve this, these are the five qualities you'll need to make your brand effective and memorable:

1. **Accuracy.** Your brand should match your identity. It should give people a clear sense of what you and your music are about.

2. **Impact.** Your brand should convey its message quickly and easily. When it comes to words, this means brevity. When it comes to graphics, it means having an image that "pops." It should be memorable. The cooler your logo, tagline, and so on, the more likely your fans will promote it and purchase branded merchandise.

3. **Repetition.** Repetition cements your identity in the mind of each person it meets. The more often this happens, the stronger the brand will become in that person's mind.

4. **Consistency.** Because repetition is the key to strengthening your brand, consistency is critical. Changing elements of your brand on a whim ruins the associations you've built up over time in people's minds. Your past branding work goes to waste every time you make dramatic changes.

5. **Pervasiveness.** To ensure repetition and consistency, it's crucial you brand everything: your Web sites, your albums, your videos, your social presences, your MP3s, your press kits, your posters, and so on.

HOW TO CHOOSE A BAND NAME THAT IS UNIQUE AND "BRANDABLE"

More than anything else, your band or artist name will be the way people find you and identify you. The name should represent the type of music you play, your energy, and your style as performers. You want a name that's memorable and unique.

But choosing a name today is more complicated than it was in the past. First of all, all artists are international the moment they get on the Internet. So, your name should be unique throughout the world. Second, it's a name that you will be doing business under, so you should choose a name that no one else is using so you won't be infringing on other people's trademarks.

Here's a set of steps you should follow when choosing your name:

1. **Check a band name database.** Check your name against a band name database to ensure that it is unique. We recommend BandName (bandname .com), although directories at Yahoo! and elsewhere are also worth checking.

2. **Perform a Web search.** Use a search engine to ensure that your name isn't associated with something else that might confuse your brand. This is

why it's best to make up a word, or choose a name that's completely unique, so you can track any mentions of your band. For example, our band name, Beatnik Turtle, is one of a kind; we're the only ones with it.

3. **Check your trademark office.** Check your trademark office to ensure that no one has trademarked your name. There are a variety of databases you can check. For instance, in the United States, you can search the U.S. Patent and Trademark Office (USPTO) Web site (uspto.gov) and use the Trademark Electronic Search System (TESS) (tess2.uspto.gov). Perform multiple searches, including one for the actual domain name you intend to use with the .com or other suffix, as well as similar spellings and variations of the name.

You should know that the USPTO is just one database and it's possible that another country, or even a state, may have something registered on file that's similar to your band name. It's easier to use the USPTO Web site to rule out names if you find a match rather than to assume that if you have matches that the name is clear to use. This is why music labels typically hire a professional trademark searching service or attorney, which may be too expensive for indies simply trying to pick a band name. For more information about trademark law and how to register your name as a trademark, see chapter 5, "Your Rights."

4. **Check a domain registrar.** Search for your name with a domain registrar such as NameCheap (namecheap.com), Go Daddy (godaddy.com), or Dotster (dotster.com) to see if it's available, or head to IndieGuide.com/Brand for a full listing of registrars.

IMAGES, FONTS, AND PHOTO BASICS
WHAT EVERY MUSICIAN NEEDS TO KNOW ABOUT
WORKING WITH IMAGES

Even though musicians normally work with just music, there's a surprising number of images that you need in order to make up your brand. If you don't have a basic knowledge of image and color formats, you may end up with files you can't use, or ones that can't easily be modified. If you work with a graphic artist without this basic knowledge, you may end up with the equivalent of an MP3 file when you really need the source tracks!

Here's what you should know about image structures, layering, and colors.

- **Image Structures.** Computers save images in one of two ways:

  Rasterized Images: rasterized image files use a rectangular grid of pixels to capture the image information. The more pixels, the higher the quality and file size of the image. Digital photos are rasterized. In general, you can reduce a rasterized image in size without problems, but if you expand the size, you'll lose sharpness since the file replicates pixels to fill the extra space.

  Vectorized Images: vectorized image files use geometric objects such as curves and polygons to represent the data. You can resize vectorized images with no quality issues since the image is mathematically re-created to fit any scale. You should create your logo, mascot, or any other line-art image in a vector-image editor such as Adobe Illustrator.

- **Layering.** Many art programs such as Adobe Photoshop and Illustrator, as well as GIMP, allow you to create layers. Layering is the art world's equivalent of multitracking. Each layer is a complete and separate picture. This means you can make layers visible or invisible as you work, before you "mix it down," or flatten them into a final JPEG or GIF image. This flexibility allows you to test out different ideas quickly and easily. If you don't like one element, you can simply hide that layer from view. For instance, the source file for our Beatnik Turtle mascot has the standard turtle as the basic layer, with additional layers for each type of hat he wears. This makes creating different versions with different hats a snap.

  Every image that you make that is more than just a single photo should be in a layered format, which will allow you to easily modify it in the future.

- **Color Formats.** Colors formats turn out to be important for more than just compatibility with different computer art programs. It has a huge effect on how easily you will be able to produce merchandise from your imagery and print colors that match the colors on screen.

  RGB: this is the color standard for computer monitors. It's an additive color system, with a light source behind it. Red, green, and blue are blended to create all the colors of the spectrum. Files saved in RGB format are appropriate for anything that will be displayed on a monitor, including anything intended for the Web.

  CMYK: this is the color standard for printing. It's a subtractive system, which doesn't depend on a backlit light source. It's the format that printers and merchandise manufacturers use. Cyan, magenta, yellow, and black are blended together to achieve full-color printing. If you intend to print any of your brand images—on a T-shirt, for instance—match the RGB number of each color to a CMYK number so that the resulting ink color matches what appears on your screen. Keep in mind that CMYK cannot represent every RGB color, although the opposite usually comes out fine.

Black-and-white Line Art: some print media, such as newspapers, print only in black and white. Giving them your CMYK color logo and letting them do the conversion to black-and-white line art may have disastrous results. A black-and-white line-art version of your logo will also come in handy if you print a CD with one color on the silk screen.

Grayscale: grayscale printing allows shading, which is useful for photos that will appear in newspapers and other black-and-white media. Color images convert more easily to grayscale than to black and white, but those created specifically for grayscale will work better.

HOW TO CHOOSE A VERSATILE COLOR PALETTE THAT CAN BE USED ON THE WEB AND FOR MERCHANDISE

Locking in a color palette is a subtle and powerful way to evoke a mood that mirrors your music. Using the same colors will only strengthen this connection between your music and the identity you wish to convey to the world and will make your brand consistent.

You have two jobs when making a color palette. One is to choose a set of colors that work well with each other. The second is to choose colors that look the same whether they are shown on computer monitors or in mass-manufactured print materials such as T-shirts, CD covers, posters, and so on.

A palette comes in handy when, for example, your logo has three colors and your Web banner has four. Each of these colors will be shown on the screen at the same time. If you do it right, you'll determine a set of colors ahead of time that always work well with each other. Then you can borrow colors from the palette every time you make new images and know that the colors will work well with the other images you are already using.

Getting all your colors to match between screen and print can be made easier by using colors in the Pantone system. This can give you a set of print colors (CMYK) that match to screen colors (RGB). Pantone's color-matching system is widely used by printing houses and other merchandise and clothing manufacturers.

To ensure a consistent color scheme:

1. **If you want to use Pantone, get a Pantone color chart.** Go online and download a Pantone color chart. (You can find links to Pantone resources at IndieGuide.com/Brand.)

2. **Pick your colors.** Pick each color you want in your palette and note the RGB number and the CMYK number. You will want to choose colors that have harmonies with each other. (See IndieGuide.com/Brand for reading material on color topics or talk to a graphic designer.)

3. **Use the RGB colors for online images and CMYK/Pantone colors for printed items.** Use the matching RGB numbers in your art software. Use the matching CMYK numbers when working with printers or merchandise and clothing manufacturers.

HOW TO FIND PRECLEARED AND ROYALTY-FREE PHOTOS, IMAGES, AND GRAPHICS TO USE

Unless you can create everything from scratch, you'll probably be looking for photos, images, clip art, and other graphics to use to start building your brand images. The Internet may be filled with photos and artwork, but most of them are not copyright-free. To do this right, you'll need to use artwork that is in the public domain, has been issued under a Creative Commons license that allows commercial use, or comes from services that produce royalty-free artwork that can be incorporated into your work for a one-time fee.

To find photos and artwork that meet your needs (and are precleared so you can use them), do the following:

1. **Check out free sources.** There are many free sources for photos, images, and graphics. Public domain images are always free, and there is also a great deal of material licensed under Creative Commons licenses that allow for commercial use, while others require you to go back to the creator to get the rights (so you need to check the license carefully). Check out Wikimedia Commons (commons.wikimedia.org) and Flickr Creative Commons (flickr.com/creativecommons) for tens of millions of photos and

images to use. Additionally, U.S. governmental works fall instantly into the public domain. As a result, any images created by NASA (nasa.gov) or other U.S. governmental bodies are available for you to use without permission. For more sites and resources, see IndieGuide.com/Brand.

2. **Research royalty-free sites and services.** There's a wide variety of photo, image, and clip-art services like iStockphoto (istockphoto.com), Getty Images (gettyimages.com), and Clipart.com (clipart.com) that will charge a one-time fee for the use of an image. For more sites and resources, see IndieGuide.com/Brand.

3. **Make sure that you understand the terms, and verify that they are royalty-free.** Be sure to read the agreements carefully before downloading, buying, or using an image. The important thing about these services is they come with a license that allows you to incorporate the image into your brand materials, Web site, merchandise, and so on so you don't have to pay for each use (royalty-free). We'll discuss this more in chapter 5, "Your Rights."

HOW TO CHOOSE FONTS TO MAKE A DISTINCTIVE LOOK FOR YOUR MUSIC

As with your color palette, consistency and repetition call for you to define and limit the fonts you use as well. Consistent fonts among your logo, Web site, press material, merchandise, and albums help tie all your materials and merchandise to your brand. The fonts you choose for your brand may not be as simple of a choice as you think. Your online fonts need to be standard ones that are found on every browser so that they look good on every computer. Of course, fonts within graphic images are readable in any browser since they are really graphics.

1. **Choose fonts for your Web site.** The best online fonts are usually sans serif fonts such as Arial, Verdana, and Helvetica. These are guaranteed to work with nearly every browser.

2. **Choose fonts for your printed materials.** Printed materials are usually serif fonts, since they are designed for easier print reading. Times New Roman is a common choice.

3. **Choose fonts for your logos, banners, and imagery.** Here's where you can go nuts and try all kinds of fonts to make your images pop. You

may want to go beyond the default fonts that exist on your computer and download additional font libraries from the Web. See IndieGuide .com/Brand for links to free and for-pay font libraries. Keep track of any fonts that you download since they may need to be installed on other computers or shared with any graphic artist or print houses you use in the future.

HOW TO MAKE A LOGO

Your logo is the most important image that you have. You will be putting it on your Web site, your albums, your merchandise—nearly everything that you release. We recommend either setting your band name in an unusual typeface or using a combination of typeface and symbols. Whatever you create, it should be distinctive enough for a T-shirt or other merchandise.

The logo you choose will often suggest both the appropriate matching color palette and font. A dynamic logo isn't easy to create, so we suggest enlisting the help of a talented graphic artist in creating it. And make sure everyone in the band approves of the final version—you don't want to change it drastically once you start using it.

Whether you create it yourself or hire a graphic artist to create a logo, these are all elements that you should consider when making the logo:

1. **Use a color palette, and stick with CMYK colors.** As mentioned above, using CMYK colors, especially Pantone colors, will ensure that the colors match what people are used to seeing on screen when you mass manufacture your logo on merchandise.

2. **Choose exciting fonts.** See the fonts section in this chapter for advice on fonts for logos.

3. **Use line art, not pictures.** If you look at logos from most every major brand, they are usually line art because they are simpler, more iconic, more impactful, and, most important, easy to view whether they are resized larger or smaller.

4. **Make the logo a vectorized layered image.** You may be repeatedly resizing and adjusting the logo for specific purposes, so it's necessary to make it a vectorized layered image. Some of the most common formats for logos are AI, PSD, or TIFF formats. If you have a JPEG or GIF, you will have a hard

time resizing or modifying the image. (If you work with a graphic artist, make sure to get the layered and vectorized source files!)

5.   **Consider including your Web site address.**   Logos today often include the URL since this promotes your Web site.

A mascot is a character that represents your band. For instance, the Grateful Dead had its dancing bears, Iron Maiden has Eddie the Head, and Beatnik Turtle has, well, our beatnik turtle. Your mascot is not the same as your logo, although your logo can incorporate your mascot. You don't have to have a mascot, but it turns out to be useful for album artwork and avatars, as well as for merchandising because it gives you more branding images to work with. Like your logo, it's best if your mascot image is line art, since the image will be resized depending on how it's used. Your mascot's colors should be taken from your color palette.

Whether you create it yourself or hire a graphic artist to create a mascot, these are all elements that you should consider when making the mascot:

1.   **Use a color palette, and stick with CMYK colors.**   Again, using CMYK colors, especially Pantone colors, will ensure that the colors match what people are used to seeing on screen when you mass manufacture your mascot on merchandise.

2.   **Use line art, not pictures.**   Mascots are usually line art rather than pictures because they are simpler, more iconic, more impactful, and, most important, easy to view whether they are resized larger or smaller.

3.   **Make the mascot a vectorized layered image.**   You will be repeatedly resizing and swapping elements in and out of your mascot—probably even more than your logo. Make sure that it's a vectorized layered image (often AI, PSD, and TIFF formats). If you have a JPEG or GIF, you will have a hard time resizing or modifying the image. (And, again, if you work with a graphic artist, make sure to get the layered and vectorized source files after they create a mascot for you!)

HOW TO MAKE AN AVATAR OR PROFILE IMAGE THAT CAN
BE USED IN SOCIAL NETWORKS, MESSAGE BOARDS, AND WEB
PRESENCES

YouTube, Twitter, Facebook, discussion boards, and so on allow you to upload a profile image, or avatar, to represent you. It can also be used for other image identifiers such as the ID3 image tag embedded in an MP3 (we discuss this in chapter 2, "Your Music").

In general, these avatars are square and small, so your logo might not be in the right shape, or may not be clear enough when it's shrunk down to size. You can either create a special, stripped-down logo or use your mascot image. Or if you're a solo artist, you can use a headshot. The main point is to create a profile image that can consistently be applied across Web presences. That way when people see your videos on YouTube, your comments on Facebook, or chat with you on an instant messenger, the avatar is the same. If you want to see some examples of avatars, see IndieGuide.com/Brand.

To create an avatar, do the following:

1. **Create a unique square image for your avatar based on your colors, logo, and mascot, or headshot.** You should try resizing it to as small as 25 x 25 pixels, and as large as 100 x 100 to make sure that it looks right.

2. **Create a version in GIF, PNG, or JPEG format.**

3. **Use the file on all of your profiles.** You should also consider creating an account on Gravatar (gravatar.com), which makes your avatar available to many of the sites you may be using, and which helps keep things consistent.

HOW TO MAKE PROMOTIONAL BANNERS THAT
CAN BE USED ON OTHER WEB SITES

If you plan on advertising your band, you should consider creating banner images. These images are also useful for people writing stories about your band on a Web site or blog. They are also good for your fans and team to use to help promote you around the Web and on social networks.

To make banners for your music, do the following:

1. **Create banners with the following sizes in JPEG format:**

   o 468 × 60 pixels

   o 234 × 60 pixels

   o 125 × 125 pixels

These are the most common ones, but there's a long list of others, and it changes over time as the Web evolves. For a full list of sizes and samples of other standard-size banners used in Web ads, go to IndieGuide.com/Brand.

2. **Create a page on your Web site where people can get these images.** Create a page on your Web site where all your banners are located to make it easy for people to share your banners. To make it even easier, you can include an embed code underneath them (or use a photo-sharing service that makes this functionality for you). For examples of an embed code, go to IndieGuide.com/Brand.

HOW TO MAKE PHOTOS OF YOUR BAND READY
TO USE IN PRESS, POSTERS, AND BIOS

Although your logo will represent your band and its music, people will still want to see the people behind the band. Your band photo will be used as the representative shot of your entire group in your press kit, in articles the press writes about you, on your Web site, in your booking kit, and on other promotional materials such as posters and flyers.

Your band photo needs to be a group shot of all the members. Naturally, it should be clear, and well composed, since this photo will represent your band to the world and will likely be printed in newspapers, magazines, and blogs when you get publicity.

While you might want to get professional shots of the band, some of the most effective band photos are just candid shots taken by friends. Journalists will often look at the band photo before listening to the music, and it can color their perceptions of what they hear.

To create good band photos, do the following:

1. **Take a lot of photos and pick the one that you think best represents you and your music.** You might need to go through many photos to find ones that meet your needs. It helps to have a handful that you like, so that journalists and Web sites have a choice of which photo to use.

2.   **Use the right size and format.**   Formal band photos for press and booking kits should be 8.5" x 11" in size. The photos should be in JPEG format at 300 dots per inch (DPI).

3.   **Clear the rights to the images.**   Make sure that you have the rights to use the images since photographers own the photos that they take. If it's a friend, have them e-mail you permission to use. If it's a professional, work with them to clear the rights.

4.   **Put the photos on a page of your Web site for people to use.**   Just like the banners above, make these photos easy to find, especially for journalists and bookers who use them for publicity purposes. To make it even more likely others will use the photos, include an embed code underneath them or use a photo-sharing service to create this functionality for you. For examples of an embed code, go to IndieGuide.com/Brand.

HOW TO HIRE A PHOTOGRAPHER AND OWN
THE COPYRIGHT TO THE PHOTOS

Even if you hire a photographer and pay them to do a photo shoot, the photographer will own the photos, and can charge you for every future use. This is not just expensive—especially if you want to use it as an album cover—it can be a nightmare to keep track of who owns each photo that you want to use.

Here's how to find and hire a photographer and come out owning the photos:

1.   **Find a photographer using referrals or Web sites.**   Referrals are still the best way to hire photographers, but if you need help, we suggest using your favorite search engine or Craigslist (craigslist.org).

2.   **Request that the work be done as a "work for hire."**   Some professional photographers will not give you this option, or will charge you extra for it, so you might need to shop around. Since you will be using these photos for many different purposes, it's worth doing a bit of extra legwork to own the rights when they are done.

3.   **Have the photographer sign a contract.**   The contract should specify that it is a "work for hire" and that all copyrights are assigned to you or the name of the business entity of your band. It's customary to credit the photographer, and this is something that you should grant if asked, but the

copyrights should still be assigned to you. (If you would like links to "work for hire" contracts and clauses, see IndieGuide.com/Brand.)

4.   **When done, get the raw files.** Make sure to get the full-size versions of all photos, not just thumbnails. And if the photographer happens to be old school, get the negatives.

HOW TO HIRE A GRAPHIC ARTIST AND OWN THE COPYRIGHTS TO THE IMAGES

Using a graphic artist is more than just finding the right person to work with. You need to make sure that you get the right files back and that the copyright is assigned to you. Otherwise, you will run into trouble the next time you need to use the images. If the graphic artist keeps either the copyright or the file formats, they can lock you in, and your relationship with them should be on an even footing.

Here's how to find a graphic artist, tell them what you need, and come out owning the copyright and correct files:

1.   **Find a graphic artist.** The best way to find a graphic designer is by referral. But because design is a job that can be done no matter where in the world the graphic artist is located, you can hire someone over the Internet to solve your needs. Be sure to check their portfolio and see if you like their work. Consider using the following options to find a graphic artist:

   o   Hire one at sites like Elance (elance.com) or oDesk (odesk.com).

   o   Crowdsource many designers at sites like crowdSPRING (crowdspring.com) or 99 Designs (99designs.com).

   o   Make a contest for prize money on sites such as Worth1000 (worth1000.com), where you get to see the efforts of multiple artists and choose the one you like the best.

   o   View artists' work at sites like DeviantArt (deviantart.com) and contact one there and see if that person does freelance work.

2.   **Request that the work be done as a work for hire and specify that you will own the copyright to the work.** This is especially important when it comes to logos, since you should own yours fully and completely. This should be non-negotiable when it comes to all of the important image

files that you make for your business. Find someone else if your graphic artist refuses to do this for you.

3. **Have the graphic artist sign a contract.** The contract should specify that it is "work for hire" and that all copyrights are assigned to you or the name of the business entity of your band. (If you would like links to "work-for-hire" contracts and clauses, see IndieGuide.com/Brand.)

4. **Check in at different points during the project.** There are often adjustments that you'll need to make as graphical work is being done, and it helps to check in at least halfway through the process to make sure that it's meeting your needs.

5. **When done, get the vectorized layered files as well as the final versions.** Make sure to get the source files that were used to create the JPEG, GIF, or PNG. These are usually AI, PSD, or TIFF files. This will allow you to take the work to other graphic artists or adjust them yourself in the future.

TEXT, BIOS, AND DESCRIPTION BASICS
HOW TO WRITE A MUSIC DESCRIPTION THAT MAKES PEOPLE WANT TO CHECK OUT YOUR MUSIC

You will need an accurate description of your music that grabs people and makes them want to check it out. This is never easy for any band. However, one of the best ways to describe your music is to talk about it in terms of well-known bands that are related to or influence your music.

Here's how to write a compelling description:

1. **Compare yourself to three well-known bands.** This lets you lure the fans of the other bands and get their interest. You can also leverage the marketing efforts of those more popular bands. When people search for those bands—whether through search engines or through dedicated music services such as iTunes or Last.fm—your music can come up as a recommendation. Even better, the people who like the other bands will be just the sort of people who are most likely to become new fans.

2. **Make a description of your own.** This one should emphasize your style, genre, and instrumentation. It should also be short. Again, it's better to go for an accurate description of your music. Ariel Hyatt, the founder of

Ariel Publicity (arielpublicity.com), told us that her favorite description was from the bluegrass, rock, country, blues, jazz, and Cajun/zydeco band Leftover Salmon. Their pitch was that they played "polyethnic Cajun slamgrass." It was accurate, summed up their energetic live show, and did it all with three words.

THE THREE FORMS OF A BIO THAT EVERY MUSICIAN SHOULD HAVE HANDY

You need an interesting and compelling way to introduce your band to people—how it started, the music you play, what you're doing, and any accomplishments. This is usually done in a bio and is used in your press and booking kits, as well as on your Web site.

You should always have three versions of your bio ready to go:

1. **A One-page Bio.** The one-page bio should cover all the points listed above. You'll want to incorporate your short music description within the first or second sentence. The purpose of this bio is to give your audience or the press some detailed background on you and your music.

2. **A One-paragraph Bio.** This is a short bio that describes you and your music succinctly so it's easy to get a picture of who you are quickly. You'll want to incorporate your music description within the first or second sentence. The purpose of this bio is to use it as an aid for the press and other Web sites so they can borrow from it to describe you to their audience in a quick way. It's also good for those Web sites and social networks that provide a profile page so you can explain who you are.

For example, this is our one-paragraph bio for Beatnik Turtle:

Formed in 1997, Beatnik Turtle is a horn-powered geek rock band that has released nearly 500 songs/20 albums in part by succeeding at their self-imposed challenge of releasing a song every single day for a year, throughout 2007, at TheSongOfTheDay.com. They have written music for TV shows, commercials, films, podcasts, theater (including Chicago's world-famous Second City) and have licensed music to Disney/ABC Family and AtomFilms/Viacom. They've also written two books on being an indie band, *The Indie Band Survival Guide* and *The DIY Music Manual*.

3. **An Elevator Pitch.** This is a sentence or two that describes you and your music to someone within twenty seconds or less. It's usually used when you meet someone who asks you about your music. For example, our elevator pitch for Beatnik Turtle is, "We're a horn-powered geek rock band in the tradition of They Might Be Giants that has released twenty albums." The purpose of explaining your bio in a quick way is to get them interested enough to ask more questions and to check out your Web site for more. The most common response we get is: "Wait, *twenty albums*?" which gives us a great opening to talk about our Song of the Day project and Web site. At that point, they are hooked and we have them wanting to find out more.

If you need assistance in writing your bio, there are a variety of writers and biowriting services you can hire. For more information on this, examples of good bios from other musicians, and ideas on how to write yours, see IndieGuide.com/Brand.

HOW (AND WHY) TO CREATE A CONSISTENT WRITING TONE AND VOICE

If you're not a solo artist and have more than one person writing about your music and interacting with your audience, keeping the writing voice and tone consistent is more important than it may seem. This is especially true if you use publicists to write press releases about you or have different band members posting tweets and speaking for the band on social-networking sites. The wrong tone to your public writing can cause problems with your public image. For example, if you are making new age music, it probably doesn't help you to write in a hateful or argumentative voice. And by the same token, a spiritual tone might not work for a punk band.

To keep it consistent, do the following:

1. **Create a style guide.** Make a brief guide on how to write for the band or artist, specifying tone and style. In Beatnik Turtle's case, we chose a voice for the band that was a little tongue-in-cheek and self-deprecating. Since our lyrics are typically upbeat and humorous, we felt our writing should be as well.

2. **Identify any topics that should be avoided.** If there are hot buttons or topics that should be avoided, make that clear.

3. **Provide some samples.** Ideally, the writing in your brand materials should evoke a singular tone and remain consistent throughout your story, Web site, newsletters, Web presence, blogs, and any other text you share. Provide a sample to give anyone writing on behalf of the band an idea of what to write.

4. **Note the exceptions.** Of course, your writing voice can change depending on the audience you're addressing. For instance, we adopt a more professional tone in our press and booking materials, since we want potential bookers and music journalists to know that we take them seriously. We also write more formally on our blog so that our readers understand that we are sharing genuine information.

5. **Pass the writing by an editor.** You should put any serious writing through another person to edit it or make sure that it works.

HOW TO WRITE A TAGLINE/SLOGAN FOR YOUR BAND THAT CAN BE USED ON T-SHIRTS, WEB SITES, AND MERCHANDISE

Not every group uses or needs a tagline, but they come in handy. This is especially true if you can create one that really captures the essence of your band and music. Your slogan is most likely to be used on the Web, but it can also become part of your logo, be included in your e-mail signatures, or be used on promotional materials. Web services such as YouTube, Twitter, and Facebook typically provide fields for short taglines that are perfect for slogans. If you don't have one, you'll have to leave these empty or make up something on the spot, leading to inconsistent branding.

Here's how to create one that works:

1. **Keep it short.** Keep it to no more than ten words. Five or fewer is best. You may want to use your music description.

2. **Intrigue them.** Brad Turcotte of Brad Sucks (bradsucks.net) has a motto of "A one man band with no fans." While his slogan doesn't tell much about his music, it has caused a lot of people to want to check him out and even want to become fans just to prove it wrong.

3. **Try it out.** Bounce your idea off of others to see how it works. You may also want to ask your fans to help create one for you.

PUTTING IT ALL TOGETHER

HOW TO BUILD A BRAND TOOLBOX

By having all your brand images and text accessible in the cloud, you'll save yourself time when you need to access them such as when you need to create merchandise, deal with the press, make album art, and more.

Do the following to have a brand toolbox handy:

1. **Prepare the materials.** Have the following handy for all of your publicity, promotion, and brand needs.

   o Name/Website URL

   o Color palette

   o Fonts

   o Logo

   o Photos

   o Mascot

   o Avatar

   o Banners

   o Music descriptions

   o Tagline/slogan

   o Bio/story

   o Writing-voice style guide

   o Blurbs, testimonials, and press clippings

   o Link to music (see chapter 2, "Your Music," on how to prepare songs for distribution)

   o Links to videos

2. **Use shared storage sites.** Google Drive is a perfect place to store bios, press releases, testimonials, and other text. It also has a way to upload and share files. Dropbox (dropbox.com) and Box (box.com) are also good services that provide storage and sharing for any type of file.

3. **Make sure to store the final versions of images as well as the raw data files.** Don't just have the JPEG and GIF files handy. Keep the source files accessible so that you can work with clothing and merchandise manufacturers or graphic artists when you need something changed quickly.

LEARNING MORE

Head to IndieGuide.com/Brand for clickable versions of every link, Web site, and service mentioned in this chapter, as well as free extras to help you build your brand.

CHAPTER 5

THE STRATEGIC GOAL: to understand and leverage the rights you have as a musician so you can promote, license, sell, and protect your creative works

REFERENCE PAGE: IndieGuide.com/Rights

CHECKLIST

What	Description
Legal Business Entity for Your Band	Establish a legal business entity for your band for tax reasons and legal liability protection.
Band Agreement	Create an agreement outlining who owns the intellectual property, equipment, profits and losses, and ownership of the business so these issues can clearly be spelled out ahead of time, and to help reduce disagreements.
Performing Arts (PA) Copyright Registrations for All Released Music	Register all released song compositions with the copyright office for full statutory protections in case of copyright infringement.
Sound Recording (SR) Copyright Registrations for All Released Sound Recordings	Register all released sound recordings with the copyright office for full statutory protections in case of copyright infringement.
Performance Rights Organizations (PROs) for Song Compositions	Register twice at song-composition performance rights organizations as both a songwriter and a publisher to get the full amount of royalties you are owed when your song composition is performed.
Performance Rights Organizations (PROs) for Sound Recordings	Register twice at sound recording performance rights organizations as both a featured performer and sound-recording owner to get the full amount of royalties you are owed when your song recording is performed.
ISRC Codes	Get ISRC codes for all sound recordings so that the sound recording PROs can easily track when your recording is performed.
Split Sheets for Compositions	Fill out a split sheet for each composition so ownership is documented.
Trademarks for Your Brands	If you want additional legal protection, register your band name and brand materials so you alone can use these materials and sell them in the marketplace.

YOUR RIGHTS

*"Obscurity is a far greater threat to authors
and creative artists than piracy."*

—TIM O'REILLY, FOUNDER AND CEO OF O'REILLY MEDIA

MUSICIANS, COMPARED to other types of artists, have their rights defined by some of the most convoluted laws ever created. Copyright laws come into play when you write a song, when you cover a song onstage, when you record a song of your own, and even if you hand your song to a filmmaker to use for free. Each of these activities has entirely different legal issues associated with it. Worse, these issues only become more confusing since the laws behind them were originally intended to protect record labels, music publishers, and other middlemen—not indie musicians making music today or using the Web. We're going to give you a step-by-step overview of using the laws to both protect and promote your music. You'll soon understand why it's generally safe to play cover songs in bars, but why you owe money if you record a version of someone else's song. You'll learn how to register copyrights of your own music, how music licensing works, the importance of merchandising rights, how to trademark your band name, and how to work with attorneys to protect your interests.

And we'll do our best to eliminate the legalese and explain it in plain English. Our goal in this chapter is to introduce you to these topics and give you a basic understanding of the law and the terminology. But many of these topics will spiral beyond the scope of this book. In fact, entire books and law school classes are dedicated to them. But you don't need to be an expert; you simply need to know enough to know when to go to an expert and to be able to ask the right questions and understand some of their lingo. Of course, if you have any specific questions, we recommend contacting your attorney or accountant.

BUSINESS FORMATION

THREE REASONS WHY YOU SHOULD ESTABLISH YOUR BAND AS A LEGAL BUSINESS ENTITY

As Tony van Veen, CEO and president of Disc Makers and CD Baby, says, "Half of 'music business' is 'business.'" Once you start making money off of music, you're running a business. And whenever business and money are involved, legal issues tend to follow.

Some of the reasons to start a business include:

1. **Tax Reasons.** When you make money, the government wants to know so it can get its share. Technically, when you make income—even when someone downloads a song from iTunes or pays the cover to see your band—this is something that should be tracked.

2. **Tax Benefits.** Establishing a business in the eyes of the government can usually afford you certain tax benefits such as writing off money you spend on the business—instruments and equipment, services from professionals or companies, meals, and so on—that can offset the money you make.

3. **Avoiding Legal Liability.** A big advantage to starting a business is to shield you from personal liability that your business may cause. That means if your band goes broke and owes money to other people (producers, distributors, etc.), it's the business that can go bankrupt, not you. The same protection applies if someone sues the band. You won't have to lose your house or car if the business is sued—all that's at stake is what the business owns.

THE NUMBER ONE REASON WHY YOU SHOULD HAVE A BAND AGREEMENT

Many bands do well without any formal legal agreement among the members, handling issues, business deals, and money case by case. However, an informal approach doesn't protect you from yourselves (a band member suing the band or leaving the group) or others (one of your songs infringing on another songwriter's copyright).

If you choose to establish a formal business, you'll end up putting together a legal agreement that outlines in advance how the business will operate and everyone's rights and responsibilities. Even if you don't establish a formal business, having an agreement at the outset can help set expectations and avoid disputes. This only becomes more important (and complicated) when multiple people are in the band.

THE TOP TEN CONSIDERATIONS YOUR BAND AGREEMENT SHOULD COVER

At a minimum, agreements should cover the following:

1. Band name, brand ownership, and trademark ownership

2. How band decisions are made and who's authorized to enter into agreements on behalf of the band

3. How profits, losses, and expenses are handled

4. Band-equipment ownership

5. Ownership of sound recordings and songs

6. How publishing revenue is administered and distributed

7. How merchandise and merchandising rights are handled

8. What happens when additional band members join

9. What happens when band members leave

10. How disputes are handled

This is by no means a complete list. You'll want to talk to your attorney to create an agreement that covers all your needs.

HOW TO ESTABLISH YOUR BAND AS A BUSINESS

If you take what you're doing seriously, set up a legal structure such as a partnership, LLC, or corporation for your band. Outlining what everyone's rights and responsibilities are in an agreement is part of the process of forming a business. Doing this will solve many of the issues that we'll be talking about throughout this chapter.

There's a lot to this step since it involves individual facts and circumstances, so it therefore goes beyond the scope of the guide. However, the steps in establishing your band as a business are as follows:

1. **Research how to set up a business for musicians.** This is not something to go into blindly. We recommend the book *Music Law: How to Run Your Band's Business*, by Richard W. Stim.

2. **Talk to your accountant.** They know about the tax and accounting structures behind each business type that you could set up and can help steer you to the best choice for your financial situation. They can also help you with tax filings at the end of the year if they help you create the business.

3. **Talk to your lawyer.** They know the paperwork and understand tax law and legal process. For tips on working with attorneys and how to make the best use of their time (so you save money), see the last section in this chapter.

4. **Set up your business.** Fill out the paperwork carefully, and keep in mind that you will need to set aside some money for filing fees. Then, remember to keep up with the paperwork throughout the year.

TOP TOOLS FOR ORGANIZING YOUR BAND'S BUSINESS

There are a variety of tools and Web services that can help you manage your band as a business. These stem from customer-relations-management software that's geared toward musicians, like Bandize (bandize.com) and The Indie Band Manager (indiebandmanager.com), to small business financial software like Quickbooks (quickbooks.intuit.com), Sage 50 (peachtree.com), and Mint (mint.com). For more small business tools geared toward musicians and finance, see IndieGuide.com/Rights.

COPYRIGHT

THE TOP THREE THINGS EVERY MUSICIAN NEEDS TO KNOW ABOUT THE LAW AND TECHNOLOGY

Copyright protects the authors of original works of music, text, graphics, videos, or other art forms. As an indie band, you will likely be creating all these types of works. While some think of copyright as a single right, it isn't. It's better understood as a collection of many more specific rights—all of which can be divided, sold, retained, or amended as you see fit.

When musicians have copyright questions, they often want clear, black-and-white answers. The truth is, the law is still evolving, and it's often at odds with technology. The law doesn't map well to the needs of a post-Internet indie band for a variety of reasons:

- **The law is about getting permission; the Web is about copying and sharing.** The purpose of copyright is to help you control your work, but the purpose of the Web is to easily copy data from one computer to another.

- **The Web is global; the law is not.** While this guide will focus on U.S. law, the instant you put your music and other intellectual property on the Web, it's available to a global audience—with different laws and attitudes toward intellectual property.

- **The law is old and changes slowly; technology changes rapidly.** The law usually evolves by forcing old rules onto new situations. Because of this retrofitting, most terms that lawyers use to describe music are out-of-date. For instance, the law calls any recording a "phonorecord," although most music never makes its way onto a phonograph of any kind.

That said, because copyright affects just about everything a musician does, it's best to understand the basics.

HOW TO COPYRIGHT YOUR MUSIC

Copyright protects "original works of authorship" whether they are literary, artistic, or musical. All the music you create, any videos you make, and any text you write on your blog or Web site is copyrightable. You don't need to register your music with the U.S. Copyright Office to get copyright protection. Copyright now occurs *automatically* once you follow these two steps:

- **Create and express something original.** Only an original work can be granted copyright protection. Additionally, copyright doesn't protect the ideas underlying your work, just the unique way you expressed them. For instance, with music, the subject of the lyrics would not be granted copyright protection. In disputes, however, the courts decide what's original.

- **Capture it in a fixed, tangible format.** With text, this is as easy as writing down your words, but with music, you have more options. You could write it down in notation or record it in some way such as on your computer, with a video camera, or even on your phone's voice mail. Playing a song live, however, would not give you a copyright, unless you record it.

Once those two requirements are met, you instantly hold the copyright in that original work that you've captured, and it's your property for your entire life plus seventy years after your death. If you've created a business entity and made it the copyright owner, then the copyright will last ninety-five years from publication. This means that, like any property, you'll want to make sure your work is in your will so your children, your children's children, and your children's children's children can continue to license uses for your song and reap any revenues it generates.

THE TOP NINE THINGS YOU CAN DO WHEN YOU OWN THE COPYRIGHT IN SOMETHING

When you own the copyright in some text, video, image, or audio, it's your property. And as with property, you can do pretty much anything you want with it. For instance, you can

- perform and display it;
- copy it;
- sell it;
- rent it (license);
- give it away for free;
- make modifications;
- translate it;
- create derivative works; and/or
- divvy up any of these rights to different people.

If anyone exercises any of the above without your permission, you can enforce your rights and sue for infringement. Most of the time, however, you'll be looking for ways to let others use your work in exchange for money, licensing it to them for specific purposes.

DEBUNKING THE TOP SEVEN MYTHS OF COPYRIGHT

Unfortunately, there are a lot of myths about copyright—from the idea you can "copyright" your work by mailing it to yourself to "the right of fair use" protecting you from infringement claims. The list below sets seven of these myths straight.

1. **You don't have to register your music with the U.S. Copyright Office to get a copyright.** Registration doesn't "give" you the copyright—music is automatically copyrighted once recorded in a tangible form. Registering your music with the copyright office does give you some benefits, however, which we discuss later.

2. **You don't have to register your work in every country to protect it.** Thanks to international treaties and the Berne Convention, once you copyright something in one country such as the U.S., Canada, or Europe, it's protected in most countries around the world.

3. **Mailing a CD to yourself doesn't copyright your music.** Mailing a CD to yourself to get a canceled date stamp on the envelope will not give you the copyright, since copyright occurs at creation. If you did it to prove you created the work at the time of the postal date, don't bother: you're better off registering your work with the U.S. Copyright Office instead since that will stand in a court of law and gives you other benefits.

4. **You don't need to use the © symbol to protect your copyright.** You were required to use the symbol before 1979, but you no longer need to include a symbol or any notice of copyright to ensure your rights. Of course, providing notice of copyright is always a good idea.

5. **You must pay licenses to record cover songs, even if you're not making money from them.** Recording someone else's song requires a license. This license is needed even if you're just giving the cover song away for free.

6. **"Fair use" isn't a right and does not automatically protect you from infringement claims.** Fair use is simply an affirmative defense to

infringement. It's not a right. The fair-use defense allows news reporting, commentary, teaching, and criticism (the reason you can quote a movie or a song in a review, for example). The courts get to decide what's "fair" based on the facts and a complicated legal test, and proving it in court can be expensive.

7. **Copying any amount of someone else's copyrighted compositions or sound recordings can be infringment—even if it's just a few measures or seconds.** No bright-line rule or exception to copyright law clearly explains when "copying" crosses the line into infringement. The rule of thumb is, the more you copy, the more likely you're infringing. It's best to create original songs or to properly license those songs or samples you don't own.

WHAT EVERY MUSICIAN SHOULD KNOW ABOUT THE TWO TYPES OF COPYRIGHTS IN MUSIC: THE COMPOSITION AND THE SOUND RECORDING

If you write music the old-fashioned way—on sheet music—then your composition is copyrighted the moment you write the words and music on paper. Writing down your original composition in this way gives you a copyright to the song. Most likely, though, you'll create your music by recording it onto your computer or some other sound recording device. If you do, you actually create two copyrights in one: one for the musical performance that was captured (the "sound recording") and one for the words and music (the "composition").

While it's hard to think of the recording as separate from the composition, under the law, it is. The Beatles' record company owns the rights to the recording of the Beatles' version of "Yesterday," but it's John Lennon and Paul McCartney who own the composition. As owners of the composition they get royalties when musicians record cover versions—not the record company.

1. **The Sound Recording.** The sound-recording, often referred to as the "phonorecord" in legalese, can be owned by a person, a group of people, or even a legal business entity such as your band. For signed bands, the owner is usually the record label, since it needs to have the exclusive rights to these recordings in order to make and sell albums, or to license the recordings. As

an indie band, you can make money off the sound recording, just as a label would.

2. **The Composition.** The ownership of the copyright in the composition is split in two:

o **Author.** The author is the songwriter (or songwriters) who writes the words and music to the song and has the right to grant permission as to how the song can be used.

o **Publisher.** The publisher works for the author and handles all the business work the composition generates, such as copyrighting the song, convincing others to perform it, licensing the song for use in film and television, and collecting the royalties.

The law sees the author and the publisher as a team—two sides of a single coin working together on behalf of the song. Most musicians do a good job of tracking who wrote what in the song and the percentage of ownership, but they rarely define who the publisher is. This is a problem since the law states that the two roles split any income a song makes fifty-fifty. To earn all the royalties a song generates, someone has to fill the publishing role. For an indie band, the publisher is usually the person who wrote it, or the band if it has created a business and wants to own the publishing share.

THREE WAYS YOU CAN DIVIDE UP
THE AUTHOR/PUBLISHER ROLES

Some of the more common options for dividing up the roles of author and publisher are the following:

1. **Songwriter as Author, Songwriter as Publisher.** Each songwriter creates his or her own publishing company to receive 100 percent of the royalties for a song—50 percent for being the author and 50 percent for being the publisher. If there's more than one songwriter on a song, each songwriter has his or her own publishing company, so the author share of 50 percent is equally divided between the songwriters and the publishing share of 50 percent is equally divided between the publishers.

2. **Songwriter as Author, Band as Publisher.** Rather than have the songwriters in the band earn all the licensing royalties, some indie

bands have opted to share the publishing rights. The songwriters split the author share according to their author-ownership percentage, while the band's publishing entity receives the full amount of the publishing share. For this method, the band needs to form a publishing entity. This publishing share is then divided among the band members based on their agreement.

3.   **Band as Author, Band as Publisher.**   Some bands decide to give the band both the author and publisher shares. To do this, the band needs to form a publishing entity and have an agreement among themselves stating that no matter who writes the songs, the band gets the income from both the author share and the publisher share. This is then split according to the band agreement.

Although these are the most common choices, you can negotiate any other arrangement you choose. Some bands split based on who performed on the song. Whichever method you choose, the point is to get your agreement down in writing. If you register your music with the copyright office, you'll need this ownership information on hand. If you want to create your own publishing company, you can find the steps and tools at IndieGuide.com/Rights.

HOW TO DETERMINE SONGWRITER OWNERSHIP PERCENTAGES AND KEEP TRACK OF WHO OWNS WHAT IN YOUR MUSIC

For every sound recording you make—whether it's a studio, acoustic, live, or demo recording—you will need to keep track of the author, publisher, and sound recording owner for each composition and recording. This is especially challenging when defining the sound recording owner since recordings may be created over time on multiple computers or at different recording studios. Typically, a band agreement helps define some of these roles. Still, to avoid disputes, we recommend you do the following:

1.   **Decide ownership percentages.**   In general, there are two ways to determine and divide up ownership percentages of who authored what in a song:

   o   Divide authorship equally among all those in the room at the time of creation; or o   Divide authorship into percentages based on who contributed what part and how much of the song.

You can negotiate anything; just make sure you have an agreement in place so it's clear to everyone.

2.   **Write it down in a song and sound-recording split agreement.** Once the authorship and sound recording ownership percentages are worked out, write it down so you can avoid disputes in the future. We recommend using a song and sound-recording split agreement to record who's filling these roles for any particular sound recording you make. A downloadable version is available at IndieGuide.com/Rights.

WHAT EVERY MUSICIAN SHOULD KNOW ABOUT WORK FOR HIRE AND COPYRIGHT

When someone pays you to create a song for them, they may ask you to sign an agreement with a work-for-hire provision in it. If you agree to this, you give up your copyright interest in the composition or sound recording and make them the owner in exchange for payment. If you're ever hired to write a theme for a podcast, commercial, film, or TV show, you'll want to be aware of this provision since it'll affect all the rights you have that we discussed above. In fact, because they own the copyright, if you want to highlight the work you made on your Web site or portfolio, you will need to ask them for permission to use the work you made. This is something you will want to negotiate.

Note that you will want to use work-for-hire provisions yourself when you hire photographers, designers, graphic artists, or anyone else that does creative work for you. Unless you put work-for-hire provisions in the contract that you use when you hire them, they will own the copyright in everything that they do. See IndieGuide.com/Rights for links to work-for-hire contracts that you can use for people doing creative work for you.

THE SEVEN REGISTRATIONS YOU SHOULD DO FOR EVERY COMPOSITION AND SOUND RECORDING TO ENSURE YOU'RE PROTECTED AND PAID WHAT YOU'RE OWED

For every composition and sound recording you create, you have the option to register your work in the seven ways listed below. Doing so can either protect you or get you paid when your song is performed.

If this seems complicated, it's because the system is made for labels and music publishers rather than musicians who do everything themselves. But if your music is out there and getting played on radio, television, satellite radio, webcasts, or even services such as Last.fm, Spotify, and Pandora, you need to register them properly so that you can get paid for all the royalties that you are owed.

We'll discuss how to do the seven registrations below, but use the following table as a checklist.

What	Description
Copyright for the Composition	Register the copyright of the composition with the copyright office so that you can get statutory protections for it before you release it.
Copyright for the Sound Recording	Register the copyright of the sound recording with the copyright office so that you can get statutory protections for it before you release it.
The Songwriter at a Performance Royalty Organization (PRO)	When your composition is performed on stage, on the radio, or on television, you're entitled to a royalty. The performance royalty is split in half, 50 percent for the songwriter and 50 percent for the publisher. Register the songwriter of each composition with a PRO so that you can collect that half of the royalties.
The Publisher at a Performance Royalty Organization (PRO)	When your composition is performed onstage, on the radio, or on television, you're entitled to a royalty. The performance royalty is split in half, 50 percent for the songwriter and 50 percent for the publisher. Register the publisher of each composition with a PRO so that you can collect that half of the royalties.
The Sound-Recording Owner at Sound-Exchange	When your sound recording is played by streaming services, you're entitled to a royalty. The performance royalty is split in half, 50 percent for the sound-recording owner and 50 percent for the featured artist. Register the sound-recording owner of each composition with SoundExchange so that you can collect that half of the royalties.
The Featured Artist at SoundExchange	When your sound recording is played by streaming services, you're entitled to a royalty. The performance royalty is split in half, 50 percent for the sound recording owner and 50 percent for the featured artist. Register the featured artist of each composition with SoundExchange so that you can collect that half of the royalties.
An International Standard Recording Code (ISRC) for Each Track of the Sound Recording	Services like SoundExchange use the ISRC code (www.usisrc.org) to recognize when a sound recording is being played. Register the ISRC code for every sound recording that you release. (Note: A single composition may have many different recordings: live, demo, remixes, and more. Each of these should have a different ISRC code registered.)

HOW TO REGISTER THE COPYRIGHT OF YOUR COMPOSITION
AND SOUND RECORDING WITH THE COPYRIGHT OFFICE

Registering with the U. S. Copyright Office is optional. You don't need to register your songs with them to get a copyright or even to collect royalties. Registering your composition with the copyright office makes a public record of your copyright claim. It's a way to declare to the world that you've created a song and confirms the date of creation by a recognized authority. The office won't listen to what you sent or compare it to other works in their system. Instead, all registering your copyright does is to create a file in the copyright office's database outlining the details of your claim of copyright. Your physical submission ends up in that huge warehouse from the ending of *Raiders of the Lost Ark*. It's only later, if you run into a copyright dispute, end up in court, and need to prove when you wrote the song, that they retrieve the file. Given that it's the copyright office providing the evidence, the court will give a lot of weight to what was registered.

Registration provides additional benefits, such as the right to file an infringement suit against someone. Also, registration that's done before an infringement claim can result in additional money awarded to you should you win—possibly including attorney's fees.

To register your compositions with the copyright office, follow these steps:

1. **Decide what songs and sound recordings you want to register.** You will need to have the songs and sound recordings on hand either because you'll need to upload them during the electronic registration process or to mail them in after you've completed the process.

    If you have to choose between registering compositions or registering sound recordings of the compositions, you'll actually get greater protection registering the composition. This is because you can get many sound recordings out of a composition, but when you register a sound recording, all you're registering is that one instance of the song.

2. **Determine if you can create a compilation.** Each song or sound recording you want to register costs money—$35 if you do it electronically, $65 if you use paper forms (note that these fees are likely to increase). If you have a lot of songs you want to register, you can save money by bundling your songs into a single compilation. An easy way to think of this

is registering your album as opposed to each song on the album individually. There are rules to doing this, however, and a few things must be true:

   o For unpublished works, you can bundle songs together if (1) the copyright claimant (the person filing the registration) is the same for all the songs that make up the bundle and (2) the authors of each song are the same on all the songs that make up the bundle or, if different, at least one of the authors is the same in all the songs that make up the bundle.

   This may sound confusing, but basically what it means is you can put a bunch of unpublished songs you wrote on one CD, give it a title like "My Songs Collection 1," and send it in. They'll register your CD and in the process register all the songs that make up the collection.

   o For published works, you can bundle songs if (1) they're all published together on the same date within the same published collection (like how most musicians release songs—on an album) and (2) this published collection has the same copyright claimant (the person filing the registration).

3. **Register at the copyright office.** In the United States, you can register compositions as "works of the performing arts" and sound recordings as "sound recordings" for $35 each through the electronic registration system (copyright.gov/eco). If you'd rather submit paper forms (Form PA for compositions, Form SR for sound recordings), the fee is $65 for each submission. (Note that these fees are likely to increase.) In Canada, you can register at the Canadian Intellectual Property Office (cipo.gc.ca). Follow the instructions at either site to complete the registration process.

4. **Upload or submit a hard copy of your music.** Once completed, the system may ask you to upload your music electronically or require you to send in a hard copy through the mail.

5. **Save your application and proof of registration.** Save your application (it should be saved automatically if done electronically) and any paperwork the copyright office sends you (such as a certificate offering proof of registration) for proof.

HOW TO COPYRIGHT TEXT, ARTWORK, PHOTOS, IMAGES, GRAPHICS, AND VIDEO WITH THE COPYRIGHT OFFICE

As an indie musician you're doing it all—creating text, artwork, photos, graphics, and video for your brand, a Web site, albums, merchandise, and more. Just as with music, copyright for all these mediums is automatic once you create anything original in a fixed, tangible format. However, if you want to ensure additional protection, you can register them with the copyright office as well. You can do this electronically (which is cheaper) or through the mail with paper forms (Form TX for text, Form VA for visual arts such as photos, images, graphics, and videos).

HOW TO REGISTER WITH A PRO FOR SONG-PERFORMANCE ROYALTIES

Typically, once you've made your music available to the public (releasing an album for sale), you're allowed to register with a performance royalty organization (PRO). Becoming a member at any of these PROs allows you to register information about your songs (usually online) so the PRO knows which songs to track in their surveys. To ensure you get any money that might be owed to you, here's how to join a song-performance PRO.

1. **Choose your song-performance PRO.** For simplicity, song-performance PROs like to encourage, and often require, membership in only one organization. Each PRO calculates royalties differently. Some also offer perks such as discounts for music equipment at music chain stores, career assistance, and health insurance benefits, so you'll want to choose the best one for your needs. In the United States, there are three general PROs you can join: ASCAP (ascap.com), BMI (bmi.com), and SESAC (sesac.com). You can apply to join ASCAP and BMI, but to join SESAC, you must be invited and meet their requirements. In Canada, you can join SOCAN (socan.ca). Note that there are PROs in different countries as well as ones for specific genres of music such as CCLI (www .ccli.co.uk), which specializes in Christian music. For a more complete list of PROs, see IndieGuide.com/Rights.

2. **Register as both the songwriter and the publisher.** Each PRO has its own registration method and (nominal) application fees, so you'll need to visit their Web sites and contact them to register. If you only register as an

author/songwriter, you'll only get half of the money that is due to you, which is a common mistake made by musicians. If you're acting as your own publisher (which most indies are), you'll want to register with your PRO as both the author/songwriter and publisher for each of your songs. This will guarantee you receive two checks if any of your songs are picked up in the PRO's performance surveys.

For more tips on how to make money from performance royalties, see IndieGuide.com/Rights.

HOW TO REGISTER WITH A PRO FOR SOUND-RECORDING-PERFORMANCE ROYALTIES

To ensure you get any money that might be owed to you for the performance of your recordings digitally on services like Last.fm, Pandora, Spotify, and satellite radio stations, do the following:

1. **Choose your sound-recording-performance PRO.** In the United States, the PRO to join is SoundExchange (soundexchange.com). Since sound recording rights are different from the song rights, you can join this PRO in addition to one of the song-performance PROs like ASCAP or BMI.

2. **Register as the sound-recording copyright owner and featured artist.** Sign up as a sound-recording copyright owner and designate the featured artist for the sound recording—your band—since royalties are split between the two. If you don't register both, it will result in lost royalties. SoundExchange will adjust these splits if there is more than one featured artist, or if you wish to provide a cut to your producer or another band member. For more information on these issues and to learn more about registering your sound recordings, see the SoundExchange Web site (soundexchange.com).

For more tips on how to make money from performance royalties, see IndieGuide.com/Rights.

HOW TO REGISTER ISRC CODES FOR YOUR SOUND RECORDINGS (AND WHY)

To maximize the chance of getting paid, you should also register for an International Standard Recording Code (ISRC) for each of your sound recordings. PROs use the ISRC codes to determine if your music has been played.

Follow these steps to register an ISRC code for each recording:

1. **Apply for an ISRC registrant code at isrc.org.** Go to isrc.org and go through the ISRC registration process. If you don't have an ISRC registrant code, you will say no to the registrant code part of the questionnaire, and they will ask you to register one. There is a one-time fee, currently $75, to become a member. Alternatively, you can use a currently registered authority to register ISRC codes for you. Note that many CD duplication houses will register ISRC codes on your behalf for your recordings.

2. **Register ISRC codes and track them.** Once you have a registrant code, register ISRC codes for each of your songs, and keep a record of the data so that you can use it with sites like SoundExchange (soundexchange .com).

3. **Keep in mind that new recordings, or changes to current recordings, can require getting a new ISRC code.** See the U.S. ISRC FAQ page (usisrc.org/faqs/assignment.html) for multiple situations where you'll need to get a new ISRC code for a recording if it's modified. For example, you will need to do this if a sound recording is remixed or edited, if the length changes by more than ten seconds, if a previously released sound recording is used in a new recording, and for other reasons.

USES, LICENSING, AND MAKING MONEY

THE TOP SIX WAYS YOU CAN USE THE COPYRIGHTS IN YOUR COMPOSITION (AND LICENSE THOSE USES TO OTHERS)

When you own the rights to your composition, you can license them for various uses. You can do this for free or charge a fee or royalty. There are a variety of ways you can exploit your copyright and make money from your song, and we'll go over the most popular uses below.

License your composition to be

- used in a sound recording;

- available as a digital download;

- used in an audiovisual work (video);

- played publicly;

- sampled; and/or

- printed, along with your lyrics.

Anytime a song is licensed, it's the author/publisher team that grants it and receives the royalties. The sound recording owner only comes into play if the user licensing the song also wants to use that specific sound recording. If so, then a separate license will be negotiated with the sound recording owner (which we'll talk about in the next section).

We'll go through each one and the implications below.

1. **License your composition to be used in a sound recording.** Authors/publishers must grant permission whenever their song is released as a recording for the first time. After your song's been published and thus made publicly available, the law allows anyone to record a version. However, you're still entitled to a royalty for each recording copy made, whether physical or digital. This is known as your "mechanical" right.

The royalty rate is set at 9.1 cents per copy for songs under five minutes. For songs over five minutes, the rate is 1.75 cents per minute. For example, if your song is over 6 minutes, but under 7 minutes, then it's 6 x 1.75 cents, or 10.5 cents in total; if your song is over 7 minutes but under 8 minutes, then it's 7 x 1.75 cents, or 12.25 cents in total, and so on (see copyright, gov/carp/m200a.pdf for more information). These rates are adjusted every few years by the Copyright Arbitration Royalty Panels (CARP), so to get the most up-to-date rates see copyright.gov/carp. You can always charge less than this rate (including nothing at all), but you can never negotiate anything higher. These royalties are owed to you whether the copies are intended to be sold or given away for free. It doesn't matter if the copies are for promotional purposes, a charitable cause, or handed out as a gift. As long as a copy is made, you are technically owed these royalties, unless you waive them.

Most songwriters don't realize that when their band duplicates a thousand CDs containing songs they wrote, those songwriters are entitled to a royalty for each copy made—to be paid by their band! When you sign an agreement with a CD printing house, that agreement typically has you avow that you have all the necessary permissions for all the songs on the album the house is copying—including permissions from the authors/publishers within your band.

Of course, paying your band's songwriters $910 for the right to use the songs on your band's album, on top of all the money spent to make the CDs in the first place, may not only break your band's bank, it may even break up the band. But it goes beyond CDs: releasing songs digitally also results in mechanical royalties being owed. This includes uploading MP3 and WAV files to your band's Web site and each subsequent download (whether free or paid). The author/publisher should get a royalty for the upload and the download.

Most bands often skirt this issue by having the authors/publishers waive their right to these royalties or by working out a deal with them to get paid after the album has recouped the initial outlay of funds. This is yet another reason why a band agreement can help solve these issues long before they even arise.

2. **License your composition to be available as a digital download.** Allowing your songs to be downloaded as an MP3 on your Web site triggers an additional songwriter right—the "performance" right. This is in addition to the mechanical right. Although your band's songwriters may waive these rights so you can upload them, you will have to obtain this license for cover songs. We'll talk about this additional license in the section later on allowing your song to be played publicly.

3. **License your composition to be used in an audiovisual work (video).** Authors/publishers can grant permission to allow their song to be tied to a visual image and license its use for a royalty. Examples include songs used in

o films and film trailers;

o television shows;

- o   television commercial campaigns;

- o   documentaries;

- o   music videos; and/or

- o   YouTube videos and Web series.

Using a song in such a way is known as a "synchronization" right, since the user of the music is syncing the song to the visual image. If the user also wants to release audiovisual work to the public in the form of a DVD or digital download, the author/publisher can grant a second license, called a "videogram" license. Unlike your mechanical right, your synchronization and videogram rights are not limited by statute. You can negotiate any price or deny the use of your song altogether. It's completely up to you.

4.   **License your composition to be played publicly.**   Once you release a song to the public, the law allows anyone to play it. There are no royalties for private performances of the song, such as when you listen to an artist's album in your car, but when it's publicly performed, that's a different story. A song can be performed publicly at or through

- o   broadcast media such as TV and terrestrial radio;

- o   public establishments such as restaurants, bars, shopping centers, hotels, theme parks, airports, etc.;

- o   "noninteractive" digital-stream broadcasters that don't allow listeners to control the music that's being played, such as satellite, cable radio, webcasts, or Web-simulcasted radio stations; and/or

- o   "interactive" digital-stream Web sites that allow listeners to skip, rewind, pause, or control the song or playlist such as the music player on your Web site or services like Spotify.

In general, companies that use music enter into subscription arrangements with PROs to report what music they play over their airwaves or in their establishment. By doing so, they cover themselves for the copyrighted music that they play. For establishments such as a bar, paying a general license fee to a PRO covers whatever bands perform live onstage as well as songs publicly broadcasted throughout the place—including the jukebox, the televisions, music on hold, and whatever the sound guy plays before and after the band.

In the United States, each time a song is played publicly, the author/publisher is entitled to the mechanical statutory rate (for example, this is currently 9.1 cents per play for songs under five minutes). It's this royalty that PROs collect and distribute. Song performance PROs such as ASCAP (ascap.com) and BMI (bmi.com) collect money from radio, television, live music venues, and businesses that play music (based on rates set by statute) and then distribute the royalties to the songwriters. When these PROs pay out, they split the money: half goes to the author or authors of the song and the other half goes to the publisher of the song. These PROs are only focused on the song itself, not the recording, so if you have two versions of your song getting airplay—your own sound recording and someone else's cover of your song—you can get paid whenever either one is performed.

Sound recording PROs like SoundExchange (soundexchange.com) monitor digital public performances of songs through services like Last.fm, Pandora, Spotify, or satellite radio, and then distributes the royalties. When this PRO pays out, it splits the money: half goes to the copyright owner of the sound recording and the other half goes to the featured performer who played on it. So you should register as both when it applies.

But just because your song is played doesn't mean you'll get paid. There's too much music for even the PROs to keep track of. Where economically sensible, PROs conduct surveys for a complete count of what exactly has been played, for instance by gathering playlists from radio stations. Otherwise, they conduct sample surveys to give an approximation of what songs have been played and how frequently.

Unfortunately, such methodology does not work well for indie musicians. The more plays, the greater the chance of being represented in these statistics. However, as we will discuss in chapter 13, "Get Heard," most of the mainstream media that PROs monitor are gated off or extremely difficult for indie bands to get played on. It comes down to luck as to whether any of your performances get caught in one of their surveys. If you're lucky enough to have that occur, however, the check can be quite sizable— anywhere from hundreds of dollars to thousands. More likely, however, you'll only get a letter at the end of the year stating that their sampling showed that none of your songs were performed during the last twelve months.

So, for us indies, receiving performance royalties is rare—even if you can point to exact instances where your music was performed in public (although some PROs have set aside royalties for members who get played in media and venues that are not included in their surveys). Ironically, when you perform your own songs live, you should get compensated for the performance of these copyrighted works. Unfortunately, PROs in the United States do not survey venues where indie bands typically perform. Instead, they put money from these venues into a general license fund that is then distributed to PRO members based on featured performances on radio and television—where most indies never get played.

Still, the relative cost of joining these PROs is minimal. If you expect to have your songs performed by others beyond your own band, then it's worth joining and registering your published songs with one of them. While it's possible you won't receive any royalties, not registering guarantees that you won't.

Note that just as your band's author/publisher is owed mechanical royalties for any CDs you press, so too is the author/publisher owed performance royalties for any digital downloads played from an interactive music player on your Web site. The same advice we gave in dealing with mechanical royalties within your band so you can print CDs applies here as well: you will need to handle or waive the performance royalties technically owed to the songwriters.

5. **License your composition to be sampled.** The sampling right to a song is not as straightforward as the other rights we've discussed previously. In general, when a sample of a song is incorporated into another's work, it's the sound-recording owner who gives permission and gets a royalty, since it's the recording that's being used as an instrument. However, depending on the length and use of the sample, the author/publisher may also be asked for permission as well. Typically, to avoid any legal issues, artists and labels that use samples in their music err on the side of caution and get a license from both the author/publisher and the sound-recording owner.

6. **License your composition lyrics to be printed.** Authors/publishers must be asked permission whenever the music or lyrics of their song are printed. The author/publisher can license such use for a royalty. The

music and lyrics can appear in magazines, books, on Web sites, and even in greeting cards. Although anyone can perform or record a published song as long as the statutory royalties are paid, the printing rights are different and not subject to the same limits. If you print the lyrics of your songs in the CD booklet or on your Web site, your band's author/publisher is owed a royalty. The same is true for cover songs. Even if you've gotten a mechanical license to record the song, you'll still need to negotiate a separate license for the right to print the lyrics.

THE TOP FIVE WAYS YOU CAN USE THE COPYRIGHTS IN YOUR SOUND RECORDING (AND LICENSE THESE USES TO OTHERS)

When you own the rights to your sound recordings, you can license them for various uses. This is in addition to any rights you have in the song. You can do this for free or charge a fee or royalty. There are a variety of ways you can exploit your copyright and make money from your sound recording, and we'll go over the most popular uses below.

License your sound recording to be:

- released;

- used in an audiovisual work (video);

- played publicly;

- sampled; and/or

- used in some other way not mentioned above.

Anytime someone wants to use a sound recording, he or she must ask the sound-recording owner for permission. The author/publisher team is always excluded in sound recording license analyses (if they aren't the sound-recording owner, too!). However, as outlined in the previous section, any licensed use of the sound recording usually results in a separate license being needed for the song, since, by definition, using the sound recording is using the song.

We'll go through each one and the implications below.

1. **License your sound recording to be released.** The sound-recording owner must approve any release of the sound recording and is entitled

to a royalty for each copy made. This includes the use of the sound recording by others such as on compilation CDs or sound tracks. It also includes any digital downloads whether from your Web site or someone else's podcast. This is called the "master use" right. The master use right is similar to a mechanical right with one important exception: no compulsory license option forces the use of the sound recording. Unlike a published song, which can be played by other musicians, the use of a sound recording depends solely on the permission of the sound-recording owner. And unlike with a mechanical royalty, no statutory rate is imposed on how much the owner can charge.

2.   **License your sound recording to be used in an audiovisual work.**   Sound-recording owners can license their master to be used with a visual image such as in a film, documentary, music video, television show, or commercial. Similar to the above, this licensing is not compulsory, and the rate is negotiable.

3.   **License your sound recording to be played publicly.**   Before the Internet, there were no performance rights in a sound recording. When terrestrial radio started, the powers that be negotiated and decided that radio would not need to pay any license fee for the use of the sound recording over its airwaves. They reasoned that radio was a promotional arm for the record labels; record labels wanted to sell records, cassettes, and CDs, and radio was one "safe" way to have the public sample the music that was available for sale without giving the public control over the sound recordings. Unfortunately, this is not true for the Web and other new broadcast mediums such as satellite and cable radio. Sound-recording owners—which are mostly record labels—lobbied Congress to create a performance right for the sound recording. Their efforts have been successful, but in a limited way: only "noninteractive" digital-stream broadcasters must get permission. "Noninteractive" is a legal category that simply means any technology that mimics terrestrial radio. If the listener can interact, the law doesn't see this as a sound-recording performance since it's the equivalent to a track on a CD. Any service that meets the noninteractive definition must license the use of the sound recordings they play. Basically, this boils down to satellite radio, cable radio, and people streaming audio

on their Web site. It also covers any terrestrial radio station that chooses to simulcast its signal over the Web. Once again, knowing where and when your sound recording was played is a challenge. Therefore, the U.S. Copyright Office designated a new PRO, SoundExchange, to help sound-recording owners collect and distribute royalties. We'll discuss how to register your sound recordings with SoundExchange in a later section.

4. **License your sound recording to be sampled.** Sound-recording owners must be asked permission whenever their sound recordings are sampled or otherwise used as a loop, groove, or instrument. Once again, the sound-recording owner can deny use or license the master-use rights for a royalty. As with all sound-recording owner rights, there is no standard fee or process to obtain permission.

HOW TO PROTECT YOUR RIGHTS IN MUSIC LICENSES: FOUR SMART NEGOTIATION POINTS TO USE

The rights we listed above for the song and sound recording are the more common ones you'll run into, but they're not the only ways they can be licensed. Other uses for music include ringtones, musical greeting cards, musical toys, or even the creation of that singing plastic fish on the wall of your dad's den. You can license your song for any of these uses, and new uses for music seem to be invented every day. Your licenses for such novel uses of your music—or any use that's not limited by statutory rates, such as sync and videogram licenses—should be as follows:

1. **Nonexclusive.** This way you can continue to license the song to others at any time. Exclusivity should cost a higher royalty rate.

2. **Limited for a Specific Use.** Don't grant more rights or uses than the user wants at that moment. That way, the users have to come back for additional licenses should they ever need to use the song in different ways in the future.

3. **Limited by Territory.** Worldwide rights should earn higher royalty rates than rights in one territory.

4. **Limited in Duration.** Never grant rights "in perpetuity," which would allow the licensee to use your song forever.

Taking these factors into account can help you reserve the rights you have to your song so that, if a new technology comes along, the licensee will need to come back to you to make a new deal.

HOW TO USE YOUR RIGHTS TO *PROMOTE* YOUR MUSIC

Uploading music to your Web site and shackling its use doesn't encourage people to discover it. The best way for people to discover what you're about is to hear your songs. Unfortunately, the default setting of copyright is "You can't copy without permission." So unless you state otherwise on your albums or on your Web site, fans who share your music with friends are infringing on your rights.

One way to encourage people to share your music is to issue your music under a Creative Commons license. That way they can share it freely. Creative Commons (creativecommons.org) is a nonprofit organization that provides free tools to help authors, musicians, and other artists create simple licenses that change their copyright terms from "All Rights Reserved" to "Some Rights Reserved." The organization has drafted a number of premade and linkable licenses that are free to use and customize depending on your needs. These Creative Commons licenses tell the world which rights you're willing to grant and which rights you wish to retain—whether for your music, Web site, photos, artwork, or other creations. If a user wants to use your music for a purpose not expressly given by your Creative Commons license, then the user needs to contact the author/publisher and sound recording owner as outlined above.

Depending on the Creative Commons license you choose to use, the license does not preclude you from licensing your music for money elsewhere. For instance, Jonathan Coulton released "Re: Your Brains" and "Code Monkey" during his Thing a Week project under a Creative Commons license. Although the license allowed his fans to download and share his music, it restricted the sharing to only noncommercial use. So, when a video game maker, Valve, wanted to use his song "Re: Your Brains" for its game Left for Dead 2, they had to obtain the necessary commercial rights. The same thing happened when a television production company wanted to use "Code Monkey" as the theme song for a show with the same name: they still had to obtain the necessary rights from Coulton. In fact, the company will need additional licenses if the show makes it to DVD. Also, since the show aired on the G4 network, its airplay is monitored by Coulton's PRO. If the song was detected in its survey, Coulton probably had a sizable check sent to him.

Here's how to license your music under a Creative Commons license:

1. **Make sure you have permission.** When you issue such a license, you need the permission of both the author/publisher and the sound recording owner. They all have to be on board with this decision, otherwise you won't have the necessary rights to issue the Creative Commons license. And they should be aware that the license is granted in perpetuity—you can't revoke it once you've released your songs under this license. We suggest that you read it carefully and be comfortable with the terms before using it. However, if you license your music this way, it can help in promoting your music and could lead to opportunities like those mentioned previously.

2. **Visit the Creative Commons Web site and choose a license.** There are a variety of licenses to choose from (creativecommons.org). The license we recommend and use at TheSongOfTheDay.com, is their music-sharing license, also known as the Attribution-NonCommercial-NoDerivs (or, "no derivative work") license. Licensing your music this way allows anyone to use and copy your songs as long as they attribute them to your band, don't modify them, and don't use them for commercial purposes. Any person who wants to use your song or sound recording for a commercial reason such as on a TV show, in a film, or on a Web site with advertising must license it from you the usual way.

3. **Hyperlink or post the license at your site.** Creative Commons generates both a "plain English" license that anyone can understand and a "lawyer-readable" contract. These agreements sit on their site and can be hyperlinked. Alternatively, you can post the license at your site.

WHAT ALL MUSICIANS NEED TO KNOW ABOUT ACTING AS THEIR OWN PUBLISHER AND LICENSING THEIR MUSIC

Getting licensing deals for your music when you own all the rights can result in a significant amount of money. When our band licensed some of our music to ABC Family/Disney for use in a nationwide television campaign, we were able to negotiate two separate licenses: one for the right to sync our composition to video images in the advertisement and another for the right to use our sound recording. Had we been signed to a label, we would have only received the sync deal. However, acting as our own publisher, we ended up receiving all the money. Similarly, when Jonathan Coulton licensed his music to Valve and G4 he acted as his own publisher and got similar deals.

Being your own publisher and finding licensing opportunities that generate income requires that you spend time actively researching and contacting potential music buyers. This area goes beyond this guide, but if you're interested in music publishing and want to know more about what publishers do, we recommend *Making Music Make Money: An Insider's Guide to Becoming Your Own Music Publisher,* by Eric Beall.

However, opportunities can come to you. With more and more media companies now surfing iTunes, MP3 blogs, podcasts, and the Web looking for a song title or music that fits their needs, they end up doing direct licensing deals with indie musicians. For instance, Brad Turcotte of Brad Sucks believes this is exactly what happened when VH1 licensed his song "Sick as a Dog" for a scene in a television show where someone was puking. Companies don't care if you're a "known artist"; they just want a song that fits their needs. If you want to make it more likely that you get one of these opportunities, make sure to ID3 tag your music so that they can find you (see chapter 2, "Your Music," for steps on how to do this) and so that your contact information is available wherever you have a presence.

HOW TO LICENSE YOUR MUSIC THROUGH MUSIC AGGREGATORS AND LICENSE AGENCIES

Sometimes production and advertising companies rely on music aggregators to find music. There are a variety of services that you can use to increase your chances of getting your music licensed or to learn about the music they're seeking so you can write new music or match your preexisting music to the opportunity. In fact, some of these services have opened up their catalogs in novel ways to get your music in places online that make it easier and easier to license. For example, Vimeo, a video-content host, created the Vimeo Music Store (vimeo.com/musicstore) for indie and mainstream filmmakers to easily license music for their films at the click of a mouse.

In general, there are three types of music aggregators:

- **Music Production Houses and Licensing Agencies.** These are services that hire songwriters and musicians to create original music in a variety of styles, which they in turn sell or license to others. Because their clients are often in radio, television, and film, they create a variety of versions of each song, chopping them into fifteen- and thirty-second clips and making instrumental versions. Depending on the music aggregator, the music is either licensed per use, covered by a yearly subscription arrangement, or sold royalty-free.

It takes some work to build a relationship with these types of music aggregators. They often negotiate a work-for-hire arrangement with musicians, paying in advance in exchange for the song and sound recording. Others work out deals that allow the songwriter to retain some of the rights and receive additional royalties when a song is licensed. Typically, performance rights for the author/publisher are not affected, but the music aggregator may want part of the publishing rights. Songs are licensed to these catalogs exclusively, as the music aggregators need to ensure that the song and sound recording are only available through their library.

Brett Ratner, an indie musician, also writes and records music for the music aggregator Wild Whirled Music (wildwhirled.com). Wild Whirled has paid agreements with nearly a hundred songwriters, like Ratner, who specialize in writing and recording different genres of music. The company's music has been used in countless television shows, films, and advertising campaigns. For instance, many of Brett's original alternative-country songs have been used on the television show *My Name Is Earl*.

Some music aggregators such as Wild Whirled do not take unsolicited submissions of recordings. Instead, they assign musicians in their roster to write songs to match what they're looking for. Others, such as NOMA Music (nomamusic.com), Audiosocket (audiosocket.com), or the virtual record label Magnatune (magnatune.com) do accept submissions, but the final decision as to whether you are added to their catalog is up to them.

• **Music Matching and Licensing Services.** Like dating services, these companies try to match the specific musical needs of media and production companies with musicians who already have the type of music they need or who don't mind writing new music. Requests are posted on these companies' Web sites for musicians to upload their music or create new material for consideration, usually for a fee. The aggregator then filters the submissions, passing along the closest matches to the production company for consideration.

An example of this is Taxi (taxi.com). They make "wanted" listings available to their members for a yearly fee of approximately $300. Submitting a song for consideration costs a small fee to encourage musicians to discriminate rather than upload their entire catalog for each listing. Taxi's staff then reviews each submitted song and decides which ones to send on. They'll even critique the song and the recording for the musician. If the music user chooses your song, Taxi puts them in touch with you to work out a licensing deal.

• **Noncurated Licensing Services.** These services allow any musician to upload his or her music to their site for potential licensing. However, unlike the above services and agencies, these services do not actively promote your songs; instead, they promote the collection that is available and allow media companies to browse and decide what they want. An example of this type of service is Pump Audio (pumpaudio.com/artists), which offers musicians a 35 percent cut of any royalties it receives from your music.

Similarly, many music distributors offer these licensing opportunities as well. For instance, CD Baby offers its musician clients the option of giving it a percentage of any license royalties in exchange for CD Baby's listing the musicians' songs in its catalog of what is available for licensing to television producers and filmmakers.

If you're interested in using music aggregators and licensing agencies, follow these steps:

1. **Make sure you have permission.** You will need to sign an agreement with any music aggregator and therefore need the permission of both the author/publisher and the sound recording owner for any song you want to license. All parties need to agree with this decision, otherwise you don't have the necessary rights to enter into any agreement.

2. **Choose the type of music aggregator that's right for you.** Each music aggregator has its own terms and conditions. You will need to read and be comfortable with the terms, the royalty splits, and other obligations. Keep in mind that most of the royalties at issue are not limited by statute and that these licensing deals can be substantial. If they are exclusive arrangements, you're obligated to pay these third parties a share of any licensing revenue you may create through your own efforts. When it comes to your rights, you always want to weigh the pros and cons and talk to your attorney.

3. **Follow the instructions.** Once you agree to the terms and conditions, follow the instructions to take the next steps, whether uploading your music or submitting your music to a particular wanted ad.

WHAT MUSICIANS NEED TO KNOW ABOUT MUSIC PUBLISHERS AND MUSIC ADMINISTRATORS

Another way to get your music out there is to negotiate a deal with a professional music publisher who will actively lobby television production companies and other commercial music users to license your music. These publishers are essentially agents for your songs. They spend their entire day promoting, marketing, and pitching the songs in their catalog to others in the hopes of getting someone to license them.

Typically, music publishers work song by song, although some may want to publish your entire music catalog. Since their job is to match existing music to the needs of their customers—the music users—a lot depends on your style, genre, lyrics, the quality of the sound recording, and, of course, luck.

When you negotiate a deal, you will want to be aware of the rights and provisions the publisher wants for promoting your music. The following provisions might be part of the deal:

- Granting them all or part of the publisher's share of the music

- Granting them all or part of the songwriter's share of the music

- Asking for administrative fees for every deal they negotiate

- Requiring that the musician pay a monthly or yearly fee in exchange for promoting the music

- Asking for exclusive rights to the music

If you want to engage a music publisher, your goal is to grant as little as possible so you can make as much as possible off of the royalties. Note that if a publisher asks for monthly or yearly fees to promote the music, be wary since music publishers can't guarantee results (they aren't the ones making the licensing decisions; they only pitch the songs). In general, successful and respected publishers are selective as to which artists they take on, since they have a reputation of providing good music for licensing. Finally, if you are not a well-known artist and they charge fees, they may press you hard to sign up because the fees keep them in business, not their cut of royalties for successfully placing artists' music. They may spend more time finding musicians, in order to collect their fees, than generating licensing opportunities for your music.

You should research any publisher that you consider signing up with, including searching them on your favorite search engine (usually adding the word "scam" by their name) and asking their current and former clients about them.

Another option for music licensing is to use a music administrator. Unlike a music publisher, music administrators do not actively try to get a song licensed. They simply handle the business side of things, should you make a licensing deal happen on your own. You pay them fees in exchange for handling this work rather than a cut of royalties.

HOW TO MAKE MONEY WRITING SONGS FOR OTHERS (AND NEGOTIATE YOUR RIGHTS)

Rather than exploit your existing songs, you can always take commissions for writing songs. Music made to order for television shows, films, commercials, the theater, and video games is big business with professional songwriters, who usually create such music under work-for-hire agreements. While writing themes for television shows and films may seem out of your arm's reach, you can still write music for podcasters, Web series, YouTubers, indie and student filmmakers, or other Web site owners. Often, these music users just take whatever music is handy, infringing on copyrights simply because they don't know where else to start. As a musician, you can not only help improve their production values but also keep them out of legal trouble. At the same time, you'll be getting your music heard while promoting your band.

If you want to write songs for others, here are some of the top things to keep in mind:

1. **Advertise that you will write songs on commission.** Create a page on your Web site offering to write songs for others. Advertise it to your fans and team through your blog, social networks, and newsletters. For instance, our band has been writing songs, themes, and other incidental music for years under Beatnik Turtle's "songs-on-demand" service. We write themes,

beds (instrumental music you can talk over), and bumpers (audioclips used between scenes or segments of shows).

2. **Determine what rights you (and they) want to license.** Typically you will want to keep the rights to the composition and sound recording and give them a license to just the rights they need.

> o   **If You're Writing Music for Free.** If you're writing music for a particular purpose and license it to the customer for free, you have more say in what rights you keep and what rights you license. You should license only the rights the customer needs to produce his or her work. And you should always ask for attribution (a credit in the film, a mention on the podcast, a link back to your Web site, and links to where people can buy your music). If it's a podcast, we've found that once you produce music for podcasters, they often end up featuring you and your music prominently on the show, sometimes highlighting a track on an episode or even interviewing you down the road. You can always negotiate for these things as well.
>
> For instance, with podcasters and YouTubers, our band generally keeps the rights to the music and grants a nonexclusive license solely for the intended purpose—to use as the podcast's theme song, to use in this short film posted on YouTube, and so on. We then allow derivative works so the customer can cut, speed up, talk over, and incorporate the song into their work. Then we expressly state that all other rights not discussed are reserved. That way, if they have a new use, such as putting their work on a CD or DVD to sell, they need to come back to us for permission. In exchange, they give us attribution, a link back to beatnik turtle.com, and links to where our music is sold.
>
> o   **If You're Writing Songs for a Fee.** If you are writing for a fee, we suggest entering into a more detailed agreement to clarify which rights the music user is getting. For example, when we're hired to write music for a commercial endeavor, such as a theme for a television show, we always draft a contract and make it clear what they can and can't do with the song and sound recording. Typically, we grant more rights (including derivative rights) and are more flexible since they're paying us.
>
> o   **If Your Client Asks for a Work-for-Hire Agreement.** Some clients will want a work-for-hire agreement to give them the greatest

flexibility, since it gives them full ownership to the music. You should only grant it for an extra fee. And note that you should get exceptions in the agreement so that you have the right to post it on your Web site as part of your portfolio, or put it into a music video promo of your services. Otherwise, you'll have to negotiate the rights with them every time you want to use their song.

3. **When you get a request, detail the working relationship in writing before you do anything.** For minor deals, a simple agreement in an exchange of e-mails might be fine for licensing your music. For more complicated deals, especially financial agreements or work-for-hire arrangements, you should have a signed contract that covers the rights more explicitly, since you don't know how the composition or sound recording might be exploited and used in the future. And, of course, for large deals, it's worth the financial cost to bring in a lawyer.

HOW TO GET MUSIC INTO VIDEO GAMES

Video games have a great deal of music needs. From video game sounds when you perform actions in the game to background music to cut-scene music, it's a big part of the experience of a game.

But although the video game industry is exploding, and every video game needs music, it's been a rather closed industry. Most video game houses use the same musicians that they already have worked with over and over to meet their needs, making it hard to break into the business. That said, there's a lot of video game development going on, including a vibrant indie game industry, and all of the video game makers need music. Connecting with developers and video game houses is the key.

George Sanger (fatman.com), also known as the Fat Man (who is actually rather skinny!), is one of the most legendary video game musicians in the business. Sanger and his team have written music for over two hundred and fifty video games. His team normally charges per minute of finished audio for the game, a standard way to charge for this industry. When dealing with clients, the key is to establish how much audio is required. He suggests: "Especially the inexperienced guys aren't going to think about how much music they need. Ask them how many hours of gameplay they expect a person to put in. So let's say they say seven. Okay, so a person is going for a seven hour drive. How many tunes should they have on their iPod? Repetition is a big problem in game audio."

If you'd like a background on the history of video game music, we recommend Sanger's book, *The Fat Man on Game Audio: Tasty Morsels of Sonic Goodness.*

Here's how to work within the video game industry:

1. **Network with video game designers.** Besides going to conventions such as the Game Developers Conference (gdconf.com), you can use game-developer-resource sites like Gamedev (gamedev.net) or IndieGameMusic (indiegamemusic.com) to connect with developers looking for music. Or go to IndieGuide.com/Rights for more links to video-game-resource sites to connect with developers.

2. **Negotiate your contract.** Negotiating points include the following for video game licensing: how much money per minute of music delivered; whether the music is work for hire; whether the rights revert back to you after a number of years; and whether you make money on royalties based on sales. When negotiating, be prepared to explain music licensing for the sound recording and composition to your customers. When it comes to licensing, Sanger suggests: "This is something that indie musicians need to know. [The video game developers] have no idea what they are asking." Although some houses ask for the music as a work for hire, the key is that most want the music royalty-free so they can pay once and not have to worry about it afterward.

3. **Promote your work for future deals.** If the music is a work for hire, you should include in your contract the rights to use the songs as a promotion. You should also ask for rights to images from the game (the same ones that they use to promote it themselves) to help you get more jobs in this industry. Otherwise, you will have a harder time making promotional materials for your Web site and portfolio.

CLEARING RIGHTS

HOW TO CLEAR COVER SONGS FOR PLAYING LIVE

Generally, when you play a cover song live—whether onstage or an in-studio radio performance, you can perform any published song you want. Copyright law grants you the right to perform any published song, and the author/publisher doesn't get a say in the matter. Lynyrd Skynyrd can't stop you from playing "Free Bird," even though they, and everyone else in the room, may

THE INDIE BAND SURVIVAL GUIDE

want to. The owner needs only to be paid the statutory rate. Chances are, however, that you've never paid a cent to the owners of "Free Bird."

Are you in trouble? Yes. And no.

You're not in trouble because the venue or radio station you're playing at has picked up the bill. They've already paid a PRO to cover the right to perform any music in their place publicly—check the front window for a PRO license sticker. So next time you perform onstage and launch into "Free Bird," it's the venue that's paying for your performance—not you.

If the venue doesn't have a license with a PRO (and some don't), then when you play "Free Bird," it's actually you who's *technically* liable and needs to pay the royalty owed to the author/publisher. Now, being liable and being sued are entirely different things. More likely than not, rather than go after a musician, the PROs go after the venue, since it knows exactly where the venue is (and it can't run). If you discover that a particular venue isn't paying a licensing fee, then PROs probably want to know. Be sure to leave the tip anonymously, though, since you'll still want to play the venue.

HOW TO CLEAR COVER SONGS FOR RECORDING

The law allows anyone to record a song previously made available to the public. In other words, no one can stop you from recording a cover version of a well-known song—you just need to pay for the mechanical right to copy the song. The maximum rate publishers can ask for is the statutory rate (for example, this is currently 9.1 cents per play for songs under 5 minutes). It doesn't matter if you intend to give your version of the song away for free or use it as a promo; the compulsory license must be paid for each copy. A copy of a song is a copy, and to avoid an infringement claim, you're supposed to obtain a license.

Note that although a mechanical license allows you to record a cover, it does not allow you to make significant changes to the song—a derivative version. What constitutes a derivative version as opposed to a cover version is up in the air, but in general it means you can change the style and genre to make it your own, but can't change the basic melody or a substantial part of the lyrics. Also, obtaining a mechanical license does not allow you to do anything with the original sound recording of the song. That's a different license, obtained from the sound-recording owner.

You must clear cover versions ahead of your release. It's not something you can do after the fact (since after the fact you will be in violation of the copyright). To clear a cover song for your album, follow these steps:

1. **Determine how you will make your cover song available to the public.** You will need to pay a separate license fee for each method you make your song available:

    o   Digital download

    o   Physical (CDs, vinyl, cassettes)

    o   Ringtones

    o   Interactive streaming

2. **Determine the number of copies you'll make of the cover song.** You will need to pay a fee for each copy.

3. **Know the royalty fees you'll need to pay.** For CDs, you'll need to pay a royalty for each CD you make (whether it's for sale or given away for free). If you make 1,000 CDs of an album containing one cover song that's under 5 minutes in length, you will need to pay $91 (1,000 CDs times 9.1 cents per song). For digital downloads, the rates are the same; however, they're calculated by downloads, not pressings. Plus, you'll need to estimate how many you think you'll sell. For example, if you had one cover song under 5 minutes in length available and you estimate it'll be downloaded 300 times through a digital retailer, the amount you would owe would be $27.30 (300 album downloads times 9.1 cents per song). Additionally, if your cover songs are available as singles, the same rate applies to all downloaded single tracks of the song.

4. **Clear the rights yourself or use a service to help you.** Try one of the following methods:

    o   **Contact the publisher of the composition and work out a deal yourself.** To do this, you'll need to figure out the publisher of the song and follow the steps as outlined by the copyright office (see copyright.gov/circs/circ73.pdf). You can find the publisher's contact information by checking the U.S. Copyright Office online database, searching the Internet, or checking the CD booklet if you have the album of the song on hand. You can also check the ASCAP,

BMI, or Harry Fox online databases (discussed below). Once you have the publisher's contact information, you can contact them. Keep in mind publishers are limited by the statutory rate, so that's the maximum they can go. If you get anything under that rate, you've gotten a bargain.

o **Use a rights-clearing service.** Harry Fox (harryfox.com/public/ songfile.jsp) is a royalty and collection agency for mechanical rights that works on behalf of many song publishers when their songs are covered by artists and reproduced physically or digitally. Basically, their Web site service, Songfile, streamlines the process of getting a license. You will have to pay Harry Fox a processing fee for its service (currently $15) as well as the license fee, which they pass on to the publisher. Harry Fox has some limitations, including the fact that it can only issue licenses for the U.S. market and can only grant digital download licenses in one-year increments (so you have to renew each year). There are also some limits to the number of copies Songfile can license as well: for physical copies, the minimum is 250 and the maximum is 2,500. For downloads, the minimum is 150 and the maximum is 2,500. If you are making anything less or anything more than these limits, you'll need to go to the publisher directly to negotiate. Another service you can use is Limelight (songclearance.com), which works on behalf of the person requesting to clear the song. Similar to Harry Fox, for a fee (currently $15 plus the license fee), you can use Limelight's service to clear a song and streamline the process. Limelight will only issue licenses for the United States and has a minimum limit of 25—whether for CDs or digital downloads. Although many publishers are affiliated with Harry Fox and Limelight, not all of them are, so after you do your initial Songfile search, you may have to contact the publisher and work out a deal on your own (see previous section).

HOW TO CLEAR COVER SONGS FOR A VIDEO

Although the law makes it relatively easy to clear cover songs for recording and distribution, clearing cover songs for a video is handled differently. There is no mechanism like Harry Fox or Limelight for handling synchronization licenses since the law doesn't set a rate for this use. Because of this, whenever you want to post a video of your cover song, you'll need to contact the author/publisher and negotiate a deal.

HOW TO RECORD OTHER PEOPLE'S SONGS FOR FREE

Not all songs require licensing. You can skip the entire step of asking and paying for permission if one of the following two things is true:

1. **The song is in the public domain.** Songs in the public domain are works that are no longer protected under copyright either because they were published before 1923, have fallen out of copyright for some other technical reason, or have been purposely declared a public work by its author through a Creative Commons license (such as a CC0 license—creativecommons.org/about/cc0). If the song you're recording is in the public domain, you don't need anyone's permission. For example, our band did this when we recorded a series of traditional Irish pub songs for our album *Sham Rock* such as "Tell Me Ma," "Beer, Beer, Beer," and "Whiskey, Yer the Devil" (bit.ly/bt-irishsongs). Since these songs are in the public domain, we didn't need to license any rights. Of course, our versions of the song and the parts we added—our unique guitar, horn, and lyrical arrangements—are copyrighted by us, as are the sound recordings. If another band wanted to do a cover of our cover using our arrangements and the parts we added, they would need our permission.

   To find out whether a song is in the public domain, you'll need to do research—by checking your favorite search engine and Public Domain Info Online (pdinfo.com), which is a site that catalogs songs in the public domain.

2. **The song is licensed "for commercial purposes."** If the song you want to cover is released under a Creative Commons license that allows it to be used "for commercial purposes," then you won't need to pay a license fee if you choose to cover the song and release it for sale. Note that you will need to abide by any other terms of the Creative Commons license, such as attributing the song to the author.

HOW TO CLEAR RIGHTS FOR SAMPLES AND LOOPS (AND HOW TO GET SOME FOR FREE)

Whenever you incorporate any samples and audioloops in your music, you need permission from the sound recording owner. There are a few ways around this—namely, using precleared and royalty-free samples and loops as discussed in chapter 2, "Your Music."

If you can't or don't want to use precleared and royalty-free samples and loops, then you'll need to do the following:

1. **Contact the copyright owner of the sound recording and work out a deal.** You will need to research and find out who owns the sound recording. Often this is the record label that issued the song. Unlike recording cover songs, the law does not require the copyright owner to license the audio for a set fee. In fact, the owner can deny you permission, and if this happens, you're out of luck. If the owner does grant you permission, be prepared to pay large fees, since the law doesn't limit the royalty fee, so there's no limit to the amount the owner can charge for a sample clearance license. The clearance may cost you anywhere from a few hundred to a few thousand dollars. Additionally, the owner may ask for a percentage of the income derived from your song and a bonus payment when a certain threshold of copies sold is exceeded.

2. **Contact the publisher of the song and work out a deal.** Clearing samples can be a nightmare since you not only have to get the sound-recording owner's permission (step 1 above), but, technically, you should get the permission of the author/publisher, too. This means you'll have to pay a fee for the use of the composition on top of the use of the recording especially if the sample or loop is identifiable (it's a recognizable "hook" or it's a lengthy sample). Since using a sample or loop of someone's song isn't the same as recording a cover version of that song, your use is considered a derivative work. That means the author/publisher can deny you permission to use the song, which means you can't use the sound recording either. If the author/publisher does grant you permission, be prepared to once again pay large fees, since, like the sound recording, the law doesn't limit the royalty fee.

HOW TO CLEAR VIDEO OWNED BY OTHERS TO USE IN YOUR VIDEOS

Many musicians sync their music to copyrighted video footage from films and TV on YouTube to make videos for their music. But, just like music, permission is needed when you don't own video clips and want to use them in your videos.

Once again, copyright law doesn't require the copyright owner of a video clip to license it for a set fee. This means if you want to use a video clip you don't own, you'll need to contact the copyright owner and work out a deal. Keep in mind the owner can deny you permission. Most likely, however, the owner will ask for a large fee in exchange for the use of the video. Fortunately there are videos in the public domain, videos that are issued under Creative Commons licenses, and services that produce royalty-free video footage that can be incorporated into your videos for a one-time fee. We discuss these options in chapter 14, "Get Seen."

HOW TO CLEAR PHOTOS, IMAGES, AND GRAPHICS OWNED BY OTHERS SO YOU CAN USE THEM

Don't get caught using other people's copyrighted images in your own materials. Many musicians use copyrighted images on their Web site and merchandise or use copyrighted photos on their albums and posters. Just as you need to get permission to use and cover other people's music and videos, so too do you need permission for the use of photos, images, and graphics you don't own.

There is a difference between those who create images and those who create video, however—perhaps because of the amount of effort that's needed to film video. While video can be expensive to secure the rights to, photos and artwork can be licensed for less. For instance, we found a photo of sheep grazing in a field in New Zealand on Flickr that we wanted to use for album art. We e-mailed the photographer, explained that we wanted to use it for the back of our album and the number of copies we were going to make, and were pleased when he said all he would want in exchange was credit on the album.

Although we suggest in chapter 4, "Your Brand" that you use images that are your own, in the public domain, issued under Creative Commons licenses, or issued through services that produce royalty-free graphics, sometimes you want to use an image that is copyrighted. To do this, you need to ask permission. The same principles that apply for video as stated above apply for getting permission for images (they can deny you permission; there's no limit to the fee they can request).

MERCHANDISING RIGHTS

WHAT EVERY MUSICIAN NEEDS TO KNOW ABOUT
MERCHANDISING RIGHTS

As we'll mention in chapter 6, "Your Albums, Merchandise, and Sales," merchandising—the business of using your brand iconography to sell products—can be a major part of your income. From a copyright perspective, merchandising involves two owners:

- The owner of your copyrighted brand images and text.

- The merchandising-rights owner—the person or company who has the contractual right to sell products with your copyrighted brand images and text.

Your band agreement should outline who or what owns your band name, brand, and merchandising rights, although, to the extent that your products have lyrics from your songs printed on them, use may actually fall under the author/publisher's printing rights. Permission must be obtained or worked out before using any lyrics. Song titles, on the other hand, can't be copyrighted and are fair game.

Music labels often try to take a cut of merchandising rights. Bands that hold on to these rights typically sell them for an advance (and possible royalties) to a merchandise company that handles everything from design to order fulfillment. However, these one-stop shops only purchase the merchandising rights from national or major-label acts. As an indie band, these rights are yours, and doing the merchandise yourselves means that all the profits will be yours as well. One notable exception: often venues want a cut of any merchandising revenues earned in their establishment. Any such cut should be negotiated ahead of time, with an agreement in writing.

TRADEMARK

WHAT EVERY MUSICIAN NEEDS TO KNOW ABOUT TRADEMARK

Since musicians now reach a global audience, protecting your band name and brand is more of an issue than ever. The law that helps protect your brand is known as trademark law. Since brands are valuable and take a long time to build up, trademark law sprouted up to limit confusion in the marketplace of who was doing business as whom.

A trade or service mark (for simplification, we'll stick with the word "trademark" since they are essentially the same) is a distinctive word, phrase, symbol, or design that uniquely identifies your product or service to the world and separates you in the mind of the public from competing products or services. For a musician, trademarks include your band name, logo, tagline, or mascot. Most of these marks come out of the public domain or common language, even if the mark is made up, like Starbucks or Enron. For instance, our band Beatnik Turtle is a combination of two very known words: "beatnik," which refers to the pre-hippies of the 50s and early 60s, and "turtle," which is an amphibian. It doesn't really mean anything when put together. But over the course of fifteen years, twenty-plus albums, Web sites, countless live shows, the book you're holding in your hand, and years of fan and media interaction, the two words have come to mean our band and particular brand of geek rock.

Given the value of your name and brand, you'll need to determine who in your band is the trademark owner. Typically, band agreements turn the band name, brand, and trademark over to the band as an entity.

THE TOP FIVE THINGS TO KNOW ABOUT TRADEMARK LAW

There are a few things to know about trademark:

- **Trademark law is not copyright law.** Unlike copyright law, which protects your copyright for your life plus an additional seventy years before your work falls into the public domain, trademarks—even famous ones—can fall into the public domain if not diligently protected. After all, if you're taking a word or symbol out of the public domain but aren't actively using and protecting it to ensure that it identifies your product or service, then someone else should be able to use it. This is why famous brands such as Coca-Cola, Budweiser, and McDonald's have to aggressively protect their trademarks from any use that might confuse and "dilute" the value they've built in their marks with the public. Only through active maintenance of their marks does the law allow companies to keep them.

- **The first person to use the mark usually gets the rights to it.** Under the law, the first person to publicly use a mark for a specific product or service in commerce automatically owns it. To claim a trademark, you need to be the first indie band or musician in the world to use your name, logo, tagline, or mascot online in some public manner. Proof of your first public use can come from your Web domain name, your Web site, a newspaper ad or poster announcing a live show, and so on.

- **The value of your trademark grows over time.** The more you repeatedly and consistently use your trademarks over time, the stronger your trademark rights become and the stronger the protection the law gives you.

- **You can end up sharing a similar mark with others as long as it's not in the same trade or service.** When you claim a mark, you're doing so as a musician. This doesn't mean a person or company can't use the same marks with a different product or service that's not in your same space, however. In general, you only have the rights to those marks for music purposes. They can use a similar mark as long as it doesn't confuse people in the market. The problem is, with the world getting more and more connected, the marketplace is getting smaller.

- **Famous brands are one exception to sharing a similar mark.** If your mark is too similar to a mark outside music that's very famous, however, you'll likely be infringing and may be contacted to stop using it. For instance, if you name your band Google, it's likely that Google would successfully prevent you from operating under this name, even though you're a band, not a search engine. This is true even if you named your band The Google, G00gle, Gooooogle, or even Gue Gull, since these are similar sounding or looking. Courts make these fact-based decisions, and there are always exceptions for attorneys to argue over, but our general advice is to avoid any name or mark similar to ones already in use. If you're still stumped about what name or mark would be considered fair game, consult your attorney.

- **You need to protect your mark.** Once you have a mark, you need to protect it from dilution and confusion in the marketplace just as aggressively as the famous brands do. If another band starts using your name or any other marks of yours, you have the right and obligation to prevent them from doing so (and force them to change their name). This is true even if the other band plays different music from yours. The public—and your fans—may become confused about which band is which when it comes to shows, albums, and merchandise, and the longer you let the other band's use of the mark stand, the more strength they will have to defend it in a court of law.

Unfortunately, enforcing your rights usually costs money. You'll want to hire an attorney to send a cease-and-desist letter to any infringing party and either negotiate a compromise such as allowing them to choose a different name retaining some element of their former name or to prevent them from engaging as a band under that name. You'll also want to register your trademark.

HOW TO TRADEMARK YOUR LOGO AND NAME (AND IN WHICH CLASSES)

Like copyright, a trademark is automatically generated as long as it's distinctive and you use it, so you don't need to register with the U.S. Patent and Trademark Office (uspto.gov) or the Canadian Intellectual Property Office (cipo.gc.ca). However, doing so will give you additional rights, including a public record that can act as a deterrent to other bands searching for a name of their own. Whether you choose to register your mark is typically a matter of cost. Unlike registering a copyright, registering a trademark is expensive.

As an indie musician you do it all: you sell products (which are covered under trademark) and perform music (which is covered under a service mark). Every product and service is designated into a particular class of goods and services. So, you should consider registering your marks under the following classes:

- **Class 9.** The sale of digital media (CDs, downloadable audiofiles, etc.) under your band name

- **Class 16.** The use of your band name in posters, pamphlets, newsletters, and other promotional materials

- **Class 25.** The use of your marks on T-shirts and other merchandise

- **Class 41.** Entertainment services including the use of your name in conjunction with performing as a band

Keep in mind that each trademark you register (name, logo, tagline, mascot) and each class you register it in costs money. Registering under each class can cost between $275 to $375 for the application alone depending on the method (electronically or paper). This does not include attorney costs or other filing fees that may come up during the process. If you have to choose just one, we recommend trademarking your band name in Class 41.

HOW TO REGISTER YOUR TRADEMARK WITH THE TRADEMARK OFFICE

Trademark registration is more complicated than copyright registration, but both the U.S. Patent and Trademark Office (USPTO) and the Canadian Intellectual Property Office have detailed online registration systems that walk you through the process. You can register on your own, but we recommend using an attorney, who can help determine if you're application will likely succeed and if it's worth doing since, if your registration is rejected, you will lose the application fee. Unlike the U.S. Copyright Office, the USPTO employs examiners to review your application, perform their own trademark search, and send you an "action letter" asking for additional information if they find an issue with your application. Once your registration is approved, you can use the registration symbol, ®. Until then, it's against the law (though you can use ™ or SM).

CONTRACTS AND TRANSACTIONS

TOP FOUR TIPS TO SAVE MONEY WHEN ENGAGING ATTORNEYS

One of the more common legal items you'll be dealing with day to day is contracts. Musicians enter into signed agreements all the time—for recording studios, gigs, CD duplication, equipment rental, and more, not to mention most of the online services we talk about in the guide. Most of the contracts you deal with can be handled on your own, but when the deal is especially big, it's something you're not too familiar with, or you need to create a contract to use, having an attorney look things over is a good idea.

Attorneys can cost a great deal of money. But when it comes to preparing, reading, and reviewing contracts, they don't necessarily have to. When you hire a lawyer, you're hiring their expertise and time. To the extent you can do some of the legwork upfront, prepare for your meetings, and know what you want them to do, you can speed things up and save yourself some money. Follow these tips:

- **Be specific with what you want the attorney to do.** As Dan Hetzel, an entertainment attorney based in Chicago, says, "Just like when you take your car to the mechanic, if you don't know what you want them to do, you're at their mercy to figure it out." Tell the attorney exactly what you need him or her to do—such as review the agreement, prepare an operating agreement, and so on.

• **Be up front about time and budget.** There's also nothing wrong with telling them how much money you have budgeted to get something reviewed. It's also okay to set boundaries on their time. Once hired, they're working for you. Rather than have them spend an hour drafting you an e-mail about what to look out for in the contract, tell them you want a phone call and get all the details in half the time.

• **Be prepared and give them context to save time.** Give the attorney enough of the backstory about the agreement and what you have questions about. Tell them what it is you want out of the deal and what you're worried about so the attorney knows what your goals are and the attorney can review the agreement with your thoughts and concerns in mind.

• **Bring all the paperwork.** If you're setting up a business, there's a lot of paperwork that can be completed by either you or the attorney. To cut costs, have the attorney focus on the legal work (preparing the operating agreement, for instance), not gathering all your paperwork. Bring all the necessary paperwork to the meetings.

OTHER ISSUES: TAXES, INSURANCE, WORK VISAS, AND MORE

Many legal and business issues go beyond the scope of this guide. Links to government, legal, and business resources are posted at IndieGuide.com. We once again suggest reading *Music Law: How to Run Your Band's Business,* by Richard Stim, for more information, as well as consulting your attorney and accountant.

LEARNING MORE

If you are interested in learning more about copyright, including its history and how the Internet is changing the law, we recommend *Free Culture: How Big Media Uses Technology and the Law to Lock Down Culture and Control Creativity,* by Lawrence Lessig, professor of law at Stanford Law School and founder of the Creative Commons organization. The book is freely available under a Creative Commons license at free-culture.cc. Also, if you want to learn more about the intricacies of getting permission from copyright owners for audio, videos, photos, images, graphics, and more, we recommend a detailed book on the subject, *Getting Permission: How to License and Clear Copyrighted Materials Online and Off*, by Richard Stim.

Also, head to IndieGuide.com/Rights for a clickable version of every link, Web site, and service mentioned in this chapter, as well as free extra materials to help you handle music rights, licensing, and contracts.

PART TWO
GET SALES AND
PLAY LIVE

THE STRATEGIC GOAL: to make albums, create merchandise, and set up distribution and sales channels

REFERENCE PAGE: IndieGuide.com/Sales

CHECKLIST

What	Description
Albums	Produce albums ready for sale. Use the album checklist so that you don't miss any steps.
Physical CDs	Manufacture CDs for live music sales, promotion, publicity, or radio play.
Print-on-Demand CD/DVD Distributor	If you don't manufacture CDs or DVDs, have a print-on-demand store for fans that want to buy discs rather than digital downloads.
Music Download Cards	Download cards can be used to sell unique codes to allow digital download sales at shows.
USB-Flash-Drive Albums	Flash-drive albums can allow bands to sell digital music at shows or other appearances.
Online Physical CD Sales Distributor	A distributor that will handle sales, and shipping, for physical CD sales.
Digital Distributor	Use an aggregator that will distribute your albums to all the digital distribution outlets.
Ringtone Sales Distributor	A distributor that will handle ringtone sales.
YouTube Sales Distributor	If you are a YouTube partner, use a distributor that allows you to sell music, merchandise, and tickets to YouTube visitors.
T-shirt/Merch On-Demand Sales	Sites like Cafepress (cafepress.com), Spreadshirt (spreadshirt.com), and Zazzle (zazzle.com) handle on-demand, $0-inventory merchandise sales.
T-shirt Manufacturer	A mass manufacturer of T-shirts for making an inventory to sell.
Poster Manufacturer	A printer to make an inventory of posters for sales or promotions.
Sticker Manufacturer	A printer to make an inventory of stickers for sales or promotions.
Book Manufacturer	An on-demand, or mass manufacturer of books for sales or promotions.
Fulfillment Vendors	For any inventory sales, you must handle taking orders yourself or use a fulfillment vendor to take orders and handle shipping.
Online-Ticket-Sales Vendor	An online store for handling your ticket sales.
Sponsors	Find brands or stores that will pay your band to feature them.

MERCHANDISE, AND SALES

*"The easiest sale to make is to someone who bought
from you in the past and yet, the most common mistake
musicians make—where they leave money at the table—
is by not having enough stuff to sell their fans."*

—TONY VAN VEEN, CEO OF DISC MAKERS AND CD BABY

PROBABLY THE top questions musicians have after they make their music is: How can I sell my songs on iTunes, Amazon, Rhapsody, or any of the other digital music services? How can I make my own CDs? And what about ringtones? Fortunately, these are some of the easiest problems to solve. Many businesses behind these services have been around for a decade or more, and they are mature companies with high-quality offerings.

They are also surprisingly inexpensive. In just a handful of album sales, usually ten or fewer, you'll already have covered the cost per album of worldwide digital distribution and will start making a profit on your music sales. Of course, doing it right takes a lot of work, and we will cover exactly how to prepare an album for digital distribution, disc manufacturing, and more in this chapter.

PREPARING YOUR ALBUMS FOR CREATION, DISTRIBUTION, AND SALES

ALBUM CHECKLIST

After putting together twenty albums with our own band (with more on the way) we learned to make a checklist to make sure that there was nothing we missed. Use the following to make sure that you've done everything necessary before even contacting the digital distributor or CD manufacturer.

1. **Choose an album name.** While this is an obvious step, it needs to be done first. You will need this to coordinate the album art, press releases, and all the communications about the album.

2. **Clear the legal rights.** This usually takes longer than you'd think, so see "How to Clear the Legal Rights for Your Albums" in this chapter and start this as early as possible.

3. **Finish the master.** As discussed in chapter 2, "Your Music," solidify the running order, master the album, and obtain the master CD for your use.

4. **Get a bar code.** If you want to sell your album in any store or online digital retailer such as CD Baby, you'll need to have a unique universal product code (UPC), or bar code. Most manufacturing houses will provide one for a fee. If you need other options, go to IndieGuide.com/Sales for links to places that will provide one.

5. **Set the dates for the album release (and album-release party).** The release date is yet another item you need to determine as early as possible. This lets you schedule the manufacturing of your CDs, set the release date for the digital distributors, and work with publicity to announce the album.

6. **Prepare the liner notes.** Before you sit down to make the liner-note art, you should get together all the text. See the section "Top Things to Add to Your Liner Notes and Album Art" in this chapter so that you don't leave anything out. Don't miss the people you should thank, copyright information, or track information. And when you're done, proofread it!

7. **Prepare the art.** See the section "How to Prepare Artwork for an Album" in this chapter for detailed steps on how to prepare artwork.

8. **If you decide to manufacture CDs, choose the type of CD you will make, and how many.** See the sections "The Three Types of CDs Available for Manufacture" and "How to Decide How Many CDs to Make" to help you with these decisions.

8. **Submit the materials to the CD manufacturer or digital distribution site and track the process.** Also, you should get a proof of the CD if they offer it. Many CD manufacturers charge extra for a full production proof, but they are usually worth the money. The last thing that you want to do is repeat a mistake a thousand times.

HOW TO PREPARE ARTWORK FOR AN ALBUM

The album art that you have to prepare depends on your choice of CD packaging. This can be a standard plastic case with a four-panel booklet or just a sleeve. You also need to decide whether to use color or black and white. The CD printing house or digital distributor will give you the necessary templates. Note that the album cover is the most important part of your art, since this is the only image retained by online retailers and MP3 programs such as iTunes.

We recommend the following:

1. **Use a template, and make sure to account for bleeds.** Use a template from your disc manufacturer or digital distributor. Usually, most templates suggest a bleed area of one-eighth inch past the trim lines so that your image will look normal in case of small paper cutting discrepancies. The templates will have a clearly marked bleed region that you should fill with your images, or at least a solid color.

2. **Use a palette of colors that go well together, using CMYK values in your art program.** Remember that *printed* colors are sometimes different from *on-screen* colors. We learned this the hard way when our album *Sham Rock*, which was a cool neon green, ended up looking more yellow—not at all the effect we were going for. Also remember that home printers are very different than commercial printers. You can't assume that a proof created on your home printer will turn out the way you want when it goes to a commercial printer. To avoid all of these mistakes, change your album art to CMYK (the color values used by commercial printers) and then print it to see how the final product will look.

3. **Get permissions for any copyrighted materials that you use in your artwork.** Remember that all photographs, including ones made of your own band by other photographers, are owned by the photographer, and you will have to work out the rights if you want to use them on your album.

4. **Put a bar code on the back cover, usually in the lower right corner.** When you obtain your bar code, it should be given to you as an EPS file.

5. **If you wish, use the compact disc logo on your CD.** You can use the logo if your CD conforms to one of the standards owned by Philips. Your CD printing house can tell you which standard has been met and should have the image available for you (it's also easy to find on the Internet). Using the compact disc logo tends to make your CD look more official, but there's no other good reason to use it if you don't want to go to the trouble.

6. **Don't put any Web site URLs on the album cover or in the title.** Sites like iTunes now have rules where they will not display any covers with Web sites on them. Avoid this, and leave it out of your cover art.

7. **Check and then double-check the spelling and grammar of all the text on the CD art, and then make a printed proof.** We suggest actually printing a proof and putting it in a jewel case and showing it to as many people as you can. We have a compilation CD from a small label that says "Masteqrs of Reggae" on the side. Don't make the same kind of mistake.

Once this art is complete, you should carefully save the finished layered art files (not just the output file) in multiple locations and back it up in a safe location. You may need it again for a reprinting of your disc.

When doing the art, the printing package will determine whether the silk-screening process will give you a few choices for colors: a few discrete colors, three color printing (which has a limited color range), or even full color printing. Follow the guidelines of the printing house carefully. The template requirements for these different options can be very specific. In particular, layering may make a big difference when discrete colors are used in silk-screening, because the layers tend to cover each other up. Also, each panel may have different characteristics; it's not uncommon to do a full-color front panel with a black-and-white inside panel. You or your graphic artist need to take this into account. Keep in mind that not all images convert well to black and white from color, so if you need to do so, making a proof is an especially good idea.

HOW TO CLEAR THE LEGAL RIGHTS FOR YOUR ALBUMS

Before you can produce your album, there are legal issues to clear. Digital distribution services as well as CD manufacturers will require you to sign a release form declaring that all the music on your album is original and "owned" by you. If all your music is original, you'll check that box and move on. However, if you record any cover songs or incorporate any copyrighted samples or loops, you have to provide proof that you received the proper permissions. That's where the next steps come in.

1. **Cover the mechanical royalties on any cover songs that you release.** See chapter 5, "Your Rights," on how to clear rights for cover songs. Note that you have to pay for every copy of a cover song that you manufacture. Even if you only sell two copies, if you make a thousand discs, you have to pay mechanical royalties for a thousand copies at the time that you make them.

2. **Get permission for any non-royalty-free samples or loops.** As mentioned in chapter 2, "Your Music," royalty-free samples are fine, but any that aren't must be cleared and paid for. Note that there are usually two copyrights you have to clear: the composition copyright for the song and the copyright for the use of the sound recording.

3. **Clear the legal status of all the artwork.** Just like you need permission to use cover songs, you'll need permission to use any graphics, fonts, or photographs you don't own. One way around this is to use precleared and royalty-free artwork.

4. **Clear the legal status of all the text, including cover song lyrics.** If you use any text that is copyrighted by others, you need to clear it. This usually only comes up if you intend to print the lyrics to a cover song. (And it's the reason why lyrics to cover songs are usually not included in the liner notes on albums.) If you're not sure about this, just skip printing the lyrics.

5. **Get permission for guest musicians (if needed).** Ever see a sentence in a CD's liner notes that reads: "So-and-so guest musician appears courtesy of so-and-so label"? This is usually due to exclusivity clauses in the label's contract that bind the musician to the label. To the extent that you collaborate or work with a musician signed to a label, you may need the label's permission for them to participate. Make sure to ask any guest musicians affiliated with labels if this is something that needs to be done.

HOW TO GET IMAGES THAT ARE PRECLEARED
AND ROYALTY-FREE

There are a surprising number of photos and images that you can use for free and without paying a license to the owner (a royalty fee). Some options include the following:

- **Photo and Clip-Art Library Subscriptions or CD/DVDs.** You can subscribe to services that will give you access to tens of thousands of images, such as Clipart.com (clipart.com), Getty Images (gettyimages.com), or iStockphoto (istockphoto.com). In addition, you can purchase archives of stock photos or clip art on CD or DVD.

- **Photo-Sharing Sites.** Many photo-sharing sites, such as Flickr and Photobucket, allow you to copy photos, but most of them don't allow you to use their images for commercial purposes. Note that if you use images from members of these sites, the license they have will determine whether you need to ask permission. See chapter 5, "Your Rights," for more information.

- **Government Archives.** Anything created by the United States government, such as space photos taken by NASA (nasa.gov) or other governmental departments (see usa.gov for a listing), is in the public domain and copyright-free, thanks to taxpayers.

TOP THINGS TO ADD TO YOUR LINER NOTES AND ALBUM ART

When we made our first CD, we rooted through the liner notes of all the discs in our collections for ideas and eventually made a big checklist that we are sharing here. Write your liner notes in a word processor first, rather than directly into the art, because you'll want to revise it, share it with others for feedback, use the spelling and grammar checkers, and print out copies for proofing before converting it to 8-point type.

This part has no formal rules, of course, and you don't need to include liner notes at all if you don't want to, but most musicians have fun with them. Keep in mind that everything you write can be reused for your Web site.

Some things you might want to include in the liner notes, and in some cases various other places on the album art, are

- name of the band/artist;

- name of the album;

- lyrics;

- track titles and listing;

- song lengths/total playing time;

- beats per minute (BPM) info for each song (useful for DJs);

- copyright information for

  o the author/publisher of each song;

  o the affiliated performing-rights organization for each song;

  o the sound recording;

  o the art and photos;

  o cover songs, audioloops, samples, reprinted lyrics, artwork, photos, etc.;

- musicians for each track;

- instruments on each track;

- credits for producers, engineers, artwork designers, and photographers;

- mastering and recording studios used;

- band Web site and contact information;

- where and when the album was recorded;

- where the album was mastered;

- other albums and merchandise for sale and where fans can purchase them; and/or

- thank-you messages.

We suggest repeating the copyright, credits, and especially contact information on the back cover as well as in the liner notes. Also, your on-disc text should repeat this information in case the CD is separated from the case.

WHAT MUSICIANS SHOULD KNOW ABOUT SOUNDSCAN AND ALBUM SALES

SoundScan is the U.S. music industry's primary method for tracking music sales. For example, the Billboard Hot 100 charts are all based on Sound-Scan numbers. The system is maintained by Nielsen, the same company that releases television and radio statistics. You need to decide if you care enough about these statistics to limit where your music is sold.

SoundScan statistics are reported by online digital distribution stores such as iTunes and Rhapsody, as well as by physical CD stores such as Best Buy. Unfortunately, plenty of ways to sell music are not tracked by Sound-Scan, most notably the indie musician's most successful sales method: selling at concerts.

The traditional music industry finds SoundScan statistics useful to determine which bands have gotten a significant sales volume. But for indie bands, these statistics are more useful for gaining legitimacy in the eyes of journalists. Since SoundScan is a third party, their impartial information can prove that people really are interested in your band. If you really care about SoundScan numbers, limit your sales to channels that report in order to get your numbers as high as possible. Otherwise, you'll start regretting those show sales because, as far as SoundScan is concerned, they never happened. There are sometimes ways around this, though. CD Baby, for example, provides a method to sell music at concerts using credit cards, and those sales are tracked.

You need a UPC bar code for your album if you want your sales to register with SoundScan. Even if you're selling your music digitally, SoundScan requires the UPC to track the sales, because that's the unique code they use to identify each album.

Keep in mind that it's difficult to make enough sales to register as more than a blip on SoundScan. So it's usually not worth it for an indie musician to bother with the system, especially if he or she isn't interested in entering the traditional music industry. After all, music-buying customers don't really look at those numbers. If you do care, evaluate each of the album and music sales sites in the next section for whether they report to SoundScan.

WHAT MUSICIANS SHOULD KNOW ABOUT ALL-IN-ONE INCLUSIVE MUSIC SALES SOLUTIONS

Although it seems that handling sales of ringtones, getting on iTunes, and selling physical CDs online are different problems, some distributors handle all of these services for you in a single place. We cover each topic separately below, but keep in mind that you can handle this in two ways: you can pick and choose individual solutions for each issue that you are trying to solve, or you can see if any of the all-inclusive services offer what you need. The larger players like CD Baby (cdbaby.com), ReverbNation (reverb nation.com), TuneCore (tunecore.com), Nimbit (nimbit.com), Topspin (topspinmedia.com) or Bandcamp (bandcamp.com) all handle many different aspects of your sales. If you decide to use one of these services, we suggest that you compare their latest offerings and price differences side by side, so that you can make the best choice possible.

CREATING PHYSICAL ALBUMS

THE THREE TYPES OF CDS AVAILABLE FOR MANUFACTURE: MUSIC CDS, DATA CDS, AND HYBRID CDS

When you decide to make a physical album, keep in mind that you have more choices than just a standard music CD. Although the right choice is nearly always to create a music CD, here are the three types available to you.

1. **Music CD.** This should be your first choice since this is playable in any regular CD player.

2. **Data CD.** While a data CD can't be played in regular CD players, you can use them to distribute a great deal of digital music, photos, videos, and other files. Unfortunately, this isn't very useful for PR or radio campaigns, but it is quite useful as a physical product to sell if you have a lot of albums or files to offer your fans.

3. **Hybrid CD.** This type of CD can be played both as a regular music CD, but can also be popped into a computer to let users copy sound files or run a program. This can make for a more valuable sale for you, since it can offer extras a buyer couldn't get otherwise.

HOW TO DECIDE HOW MANY CDS TO MAKE

Do you want five CDs? One hundred? Five hundred? One thousand? Five thousand? Answering this question about how many to make depends on your goals. Are you going to promote your release to the press? New media? Are you going to target college radio or commercial radio? Or are you going to focus on podcasts and music blogs? Knowing the answers to these questions will help you determine how many CDs to make.

To determine the size of the print run that makes economic sense, you should do your best to estimate the number of copies you'll need in each of these categories.

- **Your Press Campaign:** determine the number of press outlets, both new media and traditional media, to which you plan to send a CD.

- **Your Radio Campaign:** determine the number of discs you plan to send to radio stations.

- **Promotional Copies:** estimate the number of discs you'll need for promotional purposes such as giveaways, contests, fan thank-yous, etc.

- **Free Copies:** determine the number of discs that you'll pass out to your fellow band members, family, friends, street teams, etc.

- **Copies for Sale:** estimate the number you believe you can sell for a profit. If you have past sales figures, use these to project the number you expect to sell. Consider the CD sales you'll have at shows, online, consignment, and any other physical CD distribution.

Add these together, and use this as a guide for your CD run.

THE FIVE METHODS MUSICIANS CAN USE TO CREATE CDS

Once you know what type of CD to make, and how many, there are a surprising number of options for mass-producing CDs:

1. **Make it yourself.** You can always use your own computer to burn CDs and print covers and liner notes. This method is certainly easy for demos and very small runs of discs, but it's surprisingly expensive per disc because of the cost of toner for home printers, blank media, and empty CD cases. It's also time-consuming to do (just imagine using scissors to cut perfectly square foldouts for the CD case twenty times in a row) and usually results in a low-quality product that is not appropriate for PR campaigns, radio, and CD reviews.

2. **Buy a bulk duplication machine.** If you need to be able to make large numbers of CDs on demand, bulk duplication machines may be an option for you. These machines will usually both duplicate CDs and print reasonable quality images on the CD face. To price this method out properly, consider the cost of CD-Rs and toner, both of which are usually expensive since most duplication machines insist on proprietary supplies for their devices. This cost can make this kind of machine a poor investment on a per-CD basis. In other words, if you end up printing a lot of copies of one album, you may have been better off going with a CD manufacturing house unless you plan on making a lot of different albums and EPs. See Disc Makers (discmakers.com/duplicators) for a sampling, or see IndieGuide.com /Sales for more links.

3. **Print on Demand.** Print on demand services like CreateSpace (createspace.com) and Lulu (lulu.com) charge no money up front. This allows you to make a profit on every sale. The print-on-demand disc is a good quality CD-R that can be used for PR, radio, or anything else. If all you're trying to do is sell physical CDs online, there's no initial cost. If you are trying to make discs for PR or reviews, you can also make a short run with these services (and the prices get cheaper the more you make). On a per-CD basis, this is still an expensive option, but it is usually comparable to what you would pay for toner and materials if you did it yourself on your own computer, except that print on demand usually makes a better-looking product. However, if you think you'll need one hundred CDs or more, consider the next method instead.

4. **Duplication.** Duplication creates CD-Rs, and is cost-effective between one hundred and five hundred CDs. The packaging looks great—it's usually identical to the replication option—and the finished product can be used for any purpose. CD-Rs don't last as long as a replicated CD (although they'll last a couple years or so), and the cost per CD is usually two to three times higher than replication.

5. **Replication.** Replication is created from a glass master CD and creates the highest-quality product. Most CD houses don't even offer replication unless you're going to print a thousand CDs or more (although some are starting to provide it at five hundred). Although this method has the highest up-front costs, it also has the lowest cost per CD with the best result.

HOW TO CREATE CDS WITH YOUR HOME COMPUTER

Most computers with a CD burner have CD duplication software on the system itself. This makes it simple to make a CD at home. You can use these steps to make your discs look as professional as possible.

1. **Consider buying inkjet-printable CDs and an inkjet printer that can handle CDs.** Inkjet printers are very inexpensive, and while you'll have a large choice of different CDs that you can use for burning CDs on your home computer, an inkjet-compatible disc works the best if you are trying to make a music CD as a finished product. It doesn't impress anyone to hand them CDs carrying the name of your local office supply store on the disc, with your band and album title written with black magic marker.

2. **Buy a box of jewel cases.** If you have a PR or radio campaign, you will want your CDs to be inside jewel cases, which you can buy at any office supply store.

3. **Print out the tray card at home, or use a service.** You can print your CD tray card at home or use services like Print It Fast Online (printitfaston line.com) to print tray cards only.

4. **Use your CD program to create the CD.** If you have a CD burner, you may have CD-burning software already on your computer. Or use programs like Roxio (roxio.com) or Nero (nero.com) to burn an audio CD with your music.

HOW TO CREATE AND SELL REAL CDS OR DVDS FOR $0 AND NO INVENTORY AND MAKE MONEY ON EVERY SALE (PRINT ON DEMAND)

Although many fans prefer digital distribution, there are still some that want to buy CDs (or DVDs for music videos) instead. If you don't want to lay out the money for a print run, you can prepare the same materials and just sell them on demand. You'll make money on every sale. You can use make small runs of high-quality discs for live shows or PR campaigns. And the best thing is that your product will always be in print.

To make print-on-demand CDs or DVDs, do the following:

1. **Choose a print-on-demand house.** Choose a site like Lulu (lulu. com) or CreateSpace (createspace.com), or check out IndieGuide.com/Sales for links to more options.

2. **Prepare your CD the same way that you would for a normal print run.** Follow the instructions in the "Album Checklist." Just use the templates from the print-on-demand house for your art and on-disc print.

3. **Link the store to your Web presences.** Make your fans aware that you now sell CDs or DVDs from all of your Web presences. Include links and any store widgets (if provided) to maximize sales.

HOW TO MAKE A CD OR DVD PRINT RUN USING A CD PRINTING HOUSE

Once you've decided to make a CD or DVD print run, use these steps to create a run of your own discs.

1. **Choose a printing house.** You need to choose a house first, since that will influence the art templates you will need to use, as well as some of the other steps that are particular to the house. If you choose a manufacturer close to where you live, you can save money on shipping. Otherwise, using companies like Disc Makers (discmakers.com), DiskFaktory (www.diskfaktory.com), and NW Media (nwmedia.com) offers not just manufacturing but many other services that may help you with your album's release.

2. **Follow all the steps in the "Album Checklist" on page 129.** If you'd like a handy checklist to help you keep track of what you do here, go to IndieGuide.com/Sales and download the Album Release Checklist, which has reminders for you to use. This same checklist is used for the digital music sales, so it serves both purposes.

3. **Work with the printing house to create the discs.** Follow the instructions at each printing house carefully. They often will be happy to talk to you on the phone to make sure that your print run goes smoothly.

4. **Execute the seven recommended registrations to maximize your royalties.** See chapter 5, "Your Rights," for details on how to execute the seven recommended registrations before your album release. As a reminder, register the songs twice with the copyright office (forms SR and PR), twice with the composition performance rights organization (once as publisher and once as songwriter), twice with the sound-recording performance rights organization (once as sound-recording owner, and once as featured performer), and get an ISRC code for each song.

5. **Register the CD with Gracenote, freeDB, and, optionally, AllMusic.** See the section below, "How to Register Your CD So When People Rip the Music, the Song Names Come Up Automatically and the Ripped MP3 Files Have the Correct Track and Artist Info" for details on Gracenote and freeDB. Then, optionally, go to AllMusic (allmusic.com) for details on how to register your CD with them. Note that some disc manufacturers will do this for you.

WHAT EVERY MUSICIAN SHOULD KNOW ABOUT CD CASES

Whether you make CDs on your own or have a CD printing house do it, the CD case that you choose is important. The CD libraries used by journalists, reviewers, and radio stations are based around the size of a standard CD jewel case. Although there are slim cases, folders, and other interesting choices, none of those work nearly as well in a CD library.

Then again, every rule is made to be broken. George Hrab, an indie musician whom we've mentioned previously, has done a fantastic job packaging his CDs, making each album unique. For example, one of them comes in a tin box, another in an embossed paper sleeve, and another in a large DVD-style box. Each one stands out as a piece of art, giving his fans a genuine reason to buy the physical disc as merchandise, not just as a music holder. His covers also tend to pique reviewers' curiosity enough to get them to pick one up simply because it's different. His sales have benefited from this unique approach.

HOW TO REGISTER YOUR CD SO WHEN PEOPLE RIP THE MUSIC, THE SONG NAMES COME UP AUTOMATICALLY AND THE RIPPED MP3 FILES HAVE THE CORRECT TRACK AND ARTIST INFO

Ever wonder how the album name, band name, and song names get filled in automatically when you load a CD into your computer? The Gracenote MusicID service (gracenote.com) and freeDB (freedb.org) are the engines behind this. Both do exactly the same thing, but Gracenote's service costs money for the software developer to license. The companies that run these databases get listeners to do the hard work for them.

This registration turns out to be more critical than it at first seems because if a fan rips your CD, the resulting MP3 files won't have the track titles or band name unless they fill it out themselves. And since most music players have a simple submission button that allows you to upload this information to the database, you will want to submit the information yourself since fans are not always the best spellers, and they sometimes get the information wrong.

To do this yourself, do the following:

1. **If you use a duplicator, see if they will automatically enter the data for you.** Many duplicators will handle entering data for you. Check your duplicator to see if this is a service they provide.

2. **Do it yourself.** For Gracenote, the most common program to use to submit the data is iTunes. Just put in your disc, enter all of the track information and CD information, and then use the Submit button in the Advanced menu. See the Gracenote FAQ for a guide on how to do this (gracenote.com /about/faqs/#upload).

For freeDB, see freedb.org/en/applications__freedb_aware_ applications.9.html for a full list of freeDB-aware applications you can install.

For more detailed information on how to do this yourself, see IndieGuide .com/Sales.

HOW TO MAKE MUSIC DOWNLOAD CARDS

Music download cards are useful for both sales and giveaways. The biggest problem that musicians deal with in face-to-face situations is how to hand their music to people. Cards are the lowest-cost way to allow music downloads, providing a single-use code that can be entered online for a download of the album or song.

To make download cards, do the following:

1. **Choose a download card provider.** Services like Disc Makers (discmakers.com) and Nimbit (nimbit.com) provide download cards. For a free option that takes a bit more do-it-yourself setup, use Cash Music (cashmusic.org). And for links to more options, see IndieGuide.com/Sales.

2. **Consider customizing the cards.** Instead of a business card, you have the option of using download cards instead, which allows you to hand music to anyone that is interested in your contact information. The designs you can use for these cards are quite flexible, so be creative.

HOW TO CREATE AND SELL YOUR MUSIC ON
USB-FLASH-DRIVE

USB flash drives allow you to transfer files between computers using a small device, sometimes also called a thumb drive. These flash drives are easily large enough to hold not only music albums, but also artwork, lyrics, photos, videos, and more.

Although flash drives cost more than CDs and download cards, you are giving a better value to the fan, and the flash drive itself is an item that your fans can use after they've transferred the files.

To make flash drives for sale, do the following:

1. **Choose a USB flash drive provider.** Besides buying cheap USB drives yourself, you can also use services like Disc Makers (discmakers.com) to create them for you.

2. **Consider custom drives.** There's a wide range of USB drives that you can make because USB drives are a promotional item for businesses, not just bands. Sites like Premium USB (premiumusb.com) or Custom USB (customusb.com) have USB drives in all shapes or sizes that allow you to make a desirable item that fans really want to purchase—beyond just getting the music. Set a premium price on it, and you can really use this to improve your sales.

For links to more USB options, see IndieGuide.com/Sales.

SELLING YOUR PHYSICAL ALBUMS

HOW TO SELL YOUR CDS/DVDS ON CONSIGNMENT

Most music stores, especially the mom-and-pop stores, will let you sell your CDs on consignment. This means that they will pay you after the album is sold, rather than before. Consignment helps you even if you don't sell a single CD, because it will help get your band name in front of more people. If music fans start seeing your CDs at stores around your area, they will begin to think that your band is significant (at least in the area) and are more likely to recognize your name the next time they see your poster.

To sell CDs on consignment, do the following:

1. **Identify the music stores in your area that sell on consignment.** Keep in mind that even some very large retailers, like Best Buy, can have a consignment shelf.

2.   **Set a price, work with the local stores, and keep a list of where you sent the CDs.** The list will allow you to check back and see if you have any sales.

3.   **Offer a copy of your disc to the people running the store.** If any of them like your music, they'll probably promote it to people walking in the door. In fact, offer one to the store itself to play on the PA. People who work in music stores are not doing it for the money; they love music and usually recommend their favorites to customers.

HOW TO GET YOUR PHYSICAL ALBUMS AND DVDS DISTRIBUTED IN STORES AROUND THE WORLD

Most distributors are aimed at labels, rather than independent bands. They dislike having to deal with the small volume that indie bands generate. But there are now ways you can get your CD distributed through stores, including Wal-Mart, Best Buy, and other large retailers.

To get distribution, do the following:

1.   **Sign up with a CD retailer that works with a distributor.** Sites like CD Baby (cdbaby.com) allow you to make your CD available to stores around the world. Once you sign up, your product will appear in their distribution databases, and if the stores request your CD, they will handle the distribution.

2.   **Work with stores to generate demand.** If you are touring, you can generate demand and then inform local music stores that they can get your product through the distributor that you hook up with.

HOW TO SELL YOUR PHYSICAL CDS/DVDS ONLINE

While some people want digital music, some still prefer physical CDs. Online CD stores are the best way to handle this distribution, unless you want to set yourself up as an online merchant and deal with packing, shipping, and handling orders. When you evaluate online CD stores, imagine that you're a fan, not a musician. Ask yourself where you'd go to buy music. If the online store's front page mostly brags about being a great place for bands to sell music rather than looking like a store, avoid it. They're probably just there to take your money.

If you use a store that seems indie-friendly, read the agreement carefully.

Do not sign up for any services that take any rights to your music. The music store is there to sell your music, but they should not get any more rights to it than a grocery store gets to the breakfast cereals it sells. Also, there's no limit to the number of CD stores that your music can be sold in. Don't agree to an exclusive deal unless you get a clear benefit from it.

To sell physical CDs or DVDs online, do the following:

1. **Choose an online CD store.** Selling CDs online can technically be done by any store that handles "fulfillment." But it's best to do it using services that handle CDs in particular because you'll be in a music store rather than just featuring it from your Web site. Try services like CD Baby (cdbaby.com), Nimbit (nimbit.com), BandCamp (bandcamp.com), or Amazon (amazon.com). Or see IndieGuide.com/Sales for links to more options.

2. **Link the store to your Web presences.** Most of the best music stores will allow you to drop in links or even widgets into your Web sites.

After doing this, consider reading the section below on using online stores effectively for ideas on how to improve your sales at both physical and digital storefronts.

HOW TO USE ONLINE STORES EFFECTIVELY

Once you decide which online stores to use, adopt the following techniques to get the most out of your new storefronts.

1. **Mention bands that sound like yours in the description.** If the terms of use will allow you to, list major bands with a similar sound in the album description so that searches for the other bands will wind up on your page.

2. **Add quotes from good reviews.** Make extensive use of good reviews in the description. The movie-listings page of your newspaper is full of quotes from reviewers for a reason: they work.

3. **Offer samples.** Make song samples available if the store allows it. If they don't, put song clips on your site, then link to those clips from the description in the online store. Studies show that samples greatly improve sales.

4. **Link from your site.** Put links to all your online album storefronts on every page of your band Web site to drive traffic and make it as easy as possible to buy your music.

5. **Link back to your site.** Link back to your own Web site from your storefronts so that customers can find more information about you and your albums.

DIGITAL DISTRIBUTION AND SALES

HOW TO SELL YOUR MUSIC ON ITUNES, AMAZON, AND THE REST OF THE DIGITAL DISTRIBUTION OUTLETS

Selling your music online is surprisingly inexpensive and gives you world-wide digital distribution on each of these music services. But, as usual, there's more to the process than it seems. Perhaps the biggest irony of digital music stores is that, even though they've opened their shelves to indies, they dislike dealing with them directly. You must use a digital aggregator service to get your music in stores like iTunes. These services can come and go quickly, though, so we suggest you use them with caution.

Take the following steps to get your music on digital distribution services:

1. **Choose which type of service to use.** There are two main types of services for digital distribution:

   o Subscription-based services, in which you keep the full profit of every sale but pay a yearly subscription (and sometimes an initiation fee). Some examples of the subscription services are TuneCore (tunecore. com) and ReverbNation (reverbnation.com). The upside of these services is that you keep the entire profit, and the downsides are the yearly fees as well as the fact that it tends to cost more if you want to be in more sales outlets.

   o Sales-cut services, where you pay a single initiation fee, and they take a cut of every sale. Examples of the sales-cut services are CD Baby (cdbaby.com) or Nimbit (nimbit.com). The upside of these services is that there are a large number of outlets that your music will be in for a single low fee. The downside is that they will keep taking a cut of every sale, and this can be a drag on your profit.

If you expect a reasonable number of sales, the subscription-based service will give you more profit after you make up for the slightly higher sign-up fee and the yearly renewals. If you expect less sales across multiple years, the sales-cut services will get you more exposure for less money and allow you to sell in more services, and the lack of renewal fees will save you in expenses. Check out the latest pricing and compare each based on your expected sales, and you'll be able to make decisions about which will work best. You can also use a service like RouteNote (routenote.com), which lets you choose which model you want, and switch between the two models.

There are a lot of services beyond the ones mentioned in this guide that will distribute your music. For a full listing, head to IndieGuide .com/Sales for links to the latest digital distribution outlets and pricing comparisons.

2. **Use the "Album Checklist" on page 129 to prepare your album for digital distribution.** Use the checklist above for both physical and digital production.

3. **Follow the "How to Use Online Stores Effectively" checklist on page 146 to get the most out of your sales.**

Both types of digital aggregators are inexpensive. By the time you've sold around ten albums, you've already made up for the cost and you'll be able to make a profit on every sale.

HOW TO SELL DIGITAL MUSIC DOWNLOADS DIRECTLY

Just like you can sell music through digital aggregators, you can also sell music MP3 downloads directly, which can give you a much larger cut of the sale. Although these options are better for you as a musician, keep in mind that music fans will be more reluctant to work with new merchants. In general, they are more likely to want to buy music from stores they know.

Still, with the higher margin, these stores are worth looking into. Use the following steps to sell digital downloads.

1. **Choose a service.** Stores like CD Baby (cdbaby.com), VibeDeck (vibedeck.com), Nimbit (nimbit.com), and BandCamp (bandcamp.com)

handle direct music sales to customers. But there are numerous options, so go to IndieGuide.com/Sales for the latest services that handle music sales.

2. **Use the "Album Checklist" on page 129 to prepare your album for digital distribution.** Use the checklist above for both physical and digital production.

3. **Follow the "How to Use Online Stores Effectively" checklist on page 146 to get the most out of your sales.**

HOW TO MAKE RINGTONES OUT OF YOUR MUSIC AND SELL THEM
Ringtones sprung up from nothing years ago to turn into a multibillion dollar business. A big reason for the business' success is that the wireless carriers already had their customers' payment information, and the charge could just be added to their bill. It became a perfect impulse buy.

The good news is that any musician can sell his or her music on ringtone services, although keep in mind that the carriers take a big percentage of the transaction: it can be 50 percent or more.

To sell ringtones, do the following:

1. **Choose a ringtone distributor.** Using sites like TuneCore (tunecore .com) can get you into the iTunes ringtone store for a yearly fee. And sites like Myxer (myxer.com) allow you to make ringtones from your music, as well as allow you to sell mobile downloads of all sorts (such as wallpapers), where the basic account is free. It is also possible to use Web sites to just turn your music into a ringtone without selling it, although these sites can come and go. Because of this, see IndieGuide.com/Sales for more links.

2. **Promote your ringtones.** Besides promoting sales from your Web presences, sites like Myxer allow you to set up an SMS text code to give away free ringtones for promotion.

HOW TO SELL AT YOUTUBE
YouTube, with its partner program, allows musicians not only to share in the ad revenue for any videos in the channel but also to put up links and set up a store to feature merchandise.

If you have not become a YouTube partner (and it's up to them which artists they choose to work with), you should simply put links to the stores on your Web site or other sales outlets.

If you have become a partner, do the following:

1. **Work with YouTube-accepted music and merchandise partners.** Topspin (topspinmedia.com) is the first service that performs this currently.

2. **Work with YouTube-accepted ticket-sales partners.** Songkick (songkick.com) is the first service that handles ticket sales through YouTube, but there are indications that more will work with them in the future.

Although there are only two services that provide this now, more are expected. To keep up with the latest services and news about selling on YouTube, see IndieGuide.com/Sales.

MERCHANDISE CREATION, DISTRIBUTION, AND SALES

WHAT MUSICIANS SHOULD KNOW ABOUT ON-DEMAND MERCHANDISE SALES SOLUTIONS

Whether you want to sell T-shirts, posters, stickers, or other merchandise like mugs, watches, and so on, there are services that will handle all of these merchandise options for you, often for free. Sites like CafePress (cafepress .com), Spreadshirt (spreadshirt.com), Printfection (printfection.com), and Zazzle (zazzle.com) can easily make all types of merchandise for $0 up front. You will be able to make money on every sale with no inventory required and you can inexpensively order a handful of items so you can sell them at shows or events. Of course, if you know you can generate a lot of sales, then you should skip print-on-demand solutions so that you can mass-produce inventory and make a much larger margin on your sales.

HOW TO SELL T-SHIRTS FOR $0 WITH NO INVENTORY

Previously, to make T-shirts and other merchandise, you would have had to print a minimum number to qualify for a volume discount at a manufacturer. Then you would have had to keep that inventory on hand or pay for storage, then sell enough items to make back your original investment before actually making a profit. If there's one thing that's difficult for indie bands, it's predicting how many people will want to buy their merchandise.

One positive trend for us has been the rise of print-on-demand services. Typically, there is no initial cost, so these services have turned merchandise sales from an inventory-based business with a lot of money required up front to being an on-demand business with no initial costs. These services usually will let you print your images on any product options they offer. Once a fan buys an item, the print-on-demand manufacturer manufactures it on-demand and ships it directly to the customer.

Your profit depends on the price that you set. The print-on-demand store will charge a base price that builds in their profit, and whatever you charge above this will be your net profit. Shipping is paid by the customer, so your profit per item is predictable.

Print-on-demand services have a lot of benefits:

- No (or low) up-front costs are required.

- No inventory is required.

- You will profit on every sale.

- The service will handle ordering and fulfillment.

- You can try as many designs and shirt colors as you want and sell only the successful ones.

- A range of products can be made available using the same image, so you can generate a storefront with clothing, coffee mugs, lunch boxes, calendars, and other merchandise, available in just a few clicks.

- You can print some samples for yourself for a reasonably inexpensive price and show them to fans or wear them onstage and see what people would like to buy.

- Once you see which designs sell online, you can then make an inventory of real printed items knowing that they will sell.

A few of the downsides are:

- The profit margin is far lower, so if you can sell a lot of units, volume manufacturing makes more sense.

- If you want to sell the merchandise at your shows, you'll need to buy it in advance and at cost, which is higher than had you ordered at a volume discount.

- Some of the services' financial arrangements are unusual, such as having a minimum required profit before they pay you.

Volume manufacturers give you a more consistent-looking product than the print-on-demand services. But, fortunately, it's simple to buy a single item from a print-on-demand service to see how it will look.

To sell print-on-demand T-shirts (and other merchandise) do the following:

1. **Create images to use as T-shirt designs.** Most of the sites allow you to upload many images to use for merchandise. Try your logo, your mascot, and other designs. It's free, so go ahead and try a bunch of designs.

2. **Choose a vendor.** Popular vendors include CafePress (cafepress.com), District Lines (districtlines.com), Spreadshirt (spreadshirt.com), Printfection (printfection.com), and Zazzle (zazzle.com). Each of them has a different profit margin and payment terms. Note that some require minimum balances before they pay out, and they can sometimes forfeit your balance if you don't reach the minimum in a certain time limit. Read the terms carefully: it can severely affect your profit margins.

3. **Promote the items on your Web presences.** Most vendors have widgets and specialized storefronts that easily allow you to promote your items in your Web site and other Web presences. These are easy to add, and can really boost your sales.

4. **Make samples.** Use the print-on-demand sites to make samples you can wear or display at your gigs. You can also make inexpensive shirts for special events.

HOW TO MAKE T-SHIRTS (SILKSCREEN SHIRTS AND PHOTO-PRINT-STYLE SHIRTS)

A T-shirt with your logo on it not only makes for something unique to sell, it's also great advertising. Of course, to sell a lot of T-shirts, you should have cool designs that people will want to buy. The easiest way to find out what people want is to use print-on-demand sites first—which cost nothing—and then invest in an inventory when you find out what works. Naturally, you can also survey people you know to see what they think.

Once you know what kinds of designs will sell, bulk T-shirt vendors can make your profit margin on T-shirts much higher. For example, if your print-on-demand store charges you $17.99 per sale, and you set a price of $24.99, you'll make $7 per sale. A well-priced mass manufacturer can give you more than twice that profit.

Be creative when it comes to your designs. Some ideas include your logo, shirts based on original songs or song lyrics, album covers, or mottos. Many musicians include their Web site address on the T-shirt as well. Remember that fans buy shirts that say something about themselves. Although your logo and brand should be a part of your shirts, it's less important than the overall design.

Here's how to do a run of T-shirts:

1. **Create images to use as T-shirt designs.** Keep in mind that there are multiple types of bulk T-shirts that you can make, with different processes. So for silk screen, there may be just a few colors that you can work with. Image-based printing may allow for more colors and designs. Work with the store if you have questions.

2. **Choose a vendor.** Work with a local T-shirt store if you have one in the area. Not only will you have no shipping costs, but they often have graphic designers on hand, you can see physical proofs, and people who work at T-shirt stores tend to be in or know of other bands. National T-shirt services include One Hour Tees (onehourtees.com), Bandwear (bandwear.com), or Bandmonster (bandmonster.com). You can also go to IndieGuide.com/Sales to get links to more options.

3. **Promote the items on your Web presences.** Some of the T-shirt vendors handle fulfillment (taking orders and shipping) and have widgets and specialized storefronts. Put these on your Web site and other Web presences.

HOW TO MAKE POSTERS

Commercial printers have gotten so advanced that it's become easy to make high-quality posters, even in very low quantities. This not only allows you to make many different poster designs for your fans on demand, but you can also make one-off posters for your individual gigs.

However, if you want to make bulk posters, you may want to use a bulk vendor, which can get your per-unit price much lower. The choice of which kind of vendor to use will depend on your needs.

If you want to make a high-quality poster, a good design professional knows how to use proportion, balance, color, and aesthetic principles to evoke an emotional response. If you have the resources, consider bringing in a pro. For a good, easy-to-read introduction to the topic, check out *The Non-Designer's Design Book*, by Robin Williams (no, not that one).

The factors of your design may influence which printing vendor you choose and, conversely, which printing vendor you choose may influence your design. Specifically influenced will be the following:

- **Size:** while there is no single standard size for posters, each vendor will usually have standard-paper-size choices. Check with your printing vendor for page sizes, templates, and information on how close to the edge they can print, so that you can make the best choices for your posters.

- **Finish:** there are a wide variety of finishes available for posters, from glossy to matte to uncoated. Your finish will depend on the artistic design that you want to achieve.

   A common option available at many bulk poster shops that works well for inexpensive print runs on inexpensive paper is an aqueous-coated finish. In fact, this is the only option at some bulk printing vendors.

- **Paper (or "Stock"):** depending on the vendor, the choices can range from low-end newsprint all the way up to canvas and fine-art print papers. Paper comes in a range of weights, textures, and finishes, all of which influence how well they work with different printing techniques. Again, your designer and printing vendor can guide you in paper selection. There is sometimes no choice of paper, just as for finish, available at inexpensive bulk-run poster shops.

To make posters, do the following:

1. **Choose a printing vendor.** Working with a local printer is best, so that you can deal with them directly, and have no shipping costs. You can use your favorite search engine, or if you work with a professional designer, they may be able suggest a printer.

   Otherwise, your vendor choices range from on-demand vendors, which allow you to make poster designs available for even single orders to any of your fans, up to bulk printers, which allow you to create an inventory ready to sell. On-demand vendors include CafePress (cafepress.com) and Zazzle (zazzle.com). Zazzle has a particularly good set of size and paper choices to work with.

For bulk vendors, you may want to try a local shop so that you can save on shipping, and work directly with the printer. Disc Makers (discmakers. com), Bandmonster (bandmonster.com), or Bandwear (bandwear.com) are all music-focused options as well, but there are many in this category, and you can go to IndieGuide.com/Sales for more options.

2. **Create a poster design.** Use the templates from your poster vendor and design your poster. There are numerous options for the size of poster you can make, and it's not as standardized as you think. Think ahead, make your choice for the size, and then get the template so you can put together the design.

3. **Promote the items on your Web presences.** Some of the poster vendors handle fulfillment (taking orders and shipping) and have widgets and specialized storefronts. Put these on your Web site and Web presences so that you can promote your posters.

HOW TO MAKE STICKERS

Stickers are more effective than they have ever been in the past because you can feature your Web site address and even QR codes, which easily bring up your information in mobile devices. That address can lead users to everything that your band has to offer. Those stickers also reinforce your brand and are great merchandise items for sale. The best thing about stickers is that they are cheap enough to give away. They work well as incentives if you want to give a freebie for buying an album or signing up for your mailing list.

As you design your stickers, just ask yourself if you think that it says something about your fan's identity (and not yours!). Is the design something your fans will find cool sticking on the back cover of their laptops?

To make stickers, do the following:

1. **Choose a sticker vendor.** Similar to all of the other merchandise production, it's a good idea to work with a local sticker vendor because you can work with its designer, and you can eliminate shipping costs (although stickers are small, so shipping costs are sometimes quite low or even free).

THE INDIE BAND SURVIVAL GUIDE

Fortunately, stickers, like other merchandise, can be made on demand. Some of the same on-demand vendors for T-shirts and other items will handle them, including CafePress (cafepress.com) and Zazzle (zazzle.com).

Services like Sticker Guy! (stickerguy.com), Disc Makers (discmakers.com), and Bandwear (bandwear.com) handle bulk sticker ordering. A full listing of sticker vendors can be found at IndieGuide.com/Sales.

2. **Design the stickers.** Similar to posters, you will need to choose the sizes of stickers that you want to make (and keep in mind that there's an incredible range of sizes for stickers) and then design your stickers in the art templates that your vendor will provide. Whatever your design, you will likely want to include your Web site as part of it so that your fans know to find you and check it out.

3. **Give them out or sell them.** You can certainly sell stickers, but they are also excellent promotional items, so think about giving them away as an extra for signing up for your mailing list, as a CD insert, or as a freebie to bring people to the merch desk. If you are selling stickers on demand, make sure to integrate the store into your Web presences.

HOW AND WHY TO MAKE BOOKS AND E-BOOKS

Books and e-books are now within reach of anyone. And since books can also be merchandise items just like anything else, you should keep them in mind as a sales item. For instance, Jonathan Coulton worked with one of his fans, Lee Peralta, to create a coloring and activity book based on Coulton's songs. And George Hrab self-published a 168-page collection of essays, stories, and illustrations in his *Non-Coloring Book*.

Books are available in all sizes and formats through print-on-demand vendors. Keep in mind that e-books use slightly different templates and are aimed more at text than images.

Here are just a few simple ideas for books that your fans will want to buy:

- Take pictures of your fans, as well as the band, during a CD release party. They are more likely to want the book if they're in it!

- Make a behind-the-scenes book about your band.

- Put together a book of lyrics, album covers, and info about the music.

Templates for books are easy to get, and can offer a mix of images and text. To make a book or e-book, do the following:

1. **Choose the e-book or book vendor.** Vendors like Lulu (lulu.com), CreateSpace (createspace.com), and Lightning Source (lightningsource.com) all handle books on demand. If you want help putting it together, BookBaby (bookbaby.com), which is a branch of the CD Baby family, also has services to help you deal with the production side of print on demand as well as e-book publishing. See IndieGuide.com/Sales for more book printing options.

2. **Design the cover, the inside, and any photos and images.** The design of a print-on-demand book, or e-book, is different than any of the other merchandise options out there. In particular, keep in mind that the cover of a book will be displayed in many different storefronts in small and large sizes. It should be promotional and enticing to your customer base. But the inside of the book needs to read well and be clear. Similar to the other design options, you will get templates for all of the art.

3. **Promote and sell the book.** Promoting a book is similar to promoting an album. Your Web presences should feature it, and, using print on demand, you can easily make several for your merch table.

HOW TO MAKE BRANDED MERCHANDISE OUT OF ANYTHING FOR $0 WITH NO INVENTORY AND MAKE A PROFIT ON EVERY SALE

You can literally slap a brand on everything you can imagine and put it up for sale: clocks, license plate holders, iPad cases, Christmas ornaments, and even G-strings (before you ask, yes, we've made some with our logo on them). Since most of the stores that handle this also sell the items on demand, you can create these items with absolutely no up-front costs and no inventory required. It all starts and ends with the images that you use, which is why you will want to make as many images as you can to make cool merchandise.

One musician who used this branding technique well is Frankendread, a Caribbean musician from Chicago. He tours the country and plays many outdoor festivals. He decided that one way to make some extra money would be to sell bottled water, since most festivals occur in the summer and audience members get hot. However, selling bottled water wasn't enough for him. Being creative, and understanding the importance of branding, he found a vendor who would allow him to brand the bottles with his logo.

Mark Gunn and Andrew McKee of the Brobdingnagian Bards (thebards .net) did something similar and branded bottles of soap bubbles. Although they did this on a whim, they discovered that many of their fans saved the bottles for years as prized mementos. So keep in mind that offering unusual merchandise can help you stand out from the crowd.

Once you have these for sale, just like the T-shirts and stickers, you can also create a storefront for your fans to use and make a profit out of every sale while you see what they are interested in buying. If you see something is particularly popular, think about creating an inventory of the items so that you can make a higher margin.

Do the following to make all kinds of merchandise available:

1. **Choose a vendor.** Check out Cafepress (cafepress.com) and Zazzle (zazzle.com), or Printfection (printfection.com) for print-on-demand services. For a volume manufacturing solution, try Bandwear (bandwear.com) or other services aimed at corporate clients such as PRstore (prstore.com) or Branders (branders.com).

2. **Use vendors' templates and try out many different images.** Most of these vendors will show you electronic mock-ups of the items for sale so you can play with many different options.

3. **Integrate the widgets and stores into your Web presences.** The on-demand vendors have widgets and stores you can use to promote your merch.

HOW TO SELL YOUR MERCHANDISE ONLINE

If you go with a volume manufacturer for your merchandise, you may want to sell it to your fans from your Web site, rather than just at shows. This is called fulfillment, and any business on the Web that is trying to handle the sales of physical items deals with the same issues. Fortunately, there are businesses that can handle this for you.

If you want to do it yourself, do the following:

1. **If you are handling shipping yourself, find a storefront vendor.** There's no end of businesses that handle transactions for you while

you handle the shipping. Solutions include Toto Merch (totomerch.com), Amazon Webstore (webstore.amazon.com), Yahoo! stores (smallbusiness .yahoo.com/ecommerce), or ProStores (prostores.com).

2. **If you want others to handle your shipping, use a fulfillment vendor.** Vendors that are geared toward musicians include Nimbit (nimbit .com) and Topspin (topspinmedia.com), which will handle inventory, shipping, and orders for you. For a business-focused solution, you can use Amazon Services (amazonservices.com/fulfillment) to handle fulfillment, stock your merchandise, take the orders, ship the items, and handle payment.

3. **Add the stores to your own site.** Once you have a vendor, make sure to promote it on your Web site and Web presences, like the other options.

HOW TO HANDLE ONLINE TICKET SALES

Even if you are playing smaller venues, you can still sell tickets and make money off of the ticket sales. The biggest issue you'll run into is how to take the sales online, and this, fortunately, can be handled by a few useful services.

To offer online ticket sales, do the following:

1. **Choose a vendor.** Try Nimbit (nimbit.com) or Songkick (songkick .com). Both handle ticket sales, with varying options and fees.

2. **Promote the ticket sales on your sites.** Wherever you have a song calendar, you should have a link to the ticket sales. The vendors that handle this have helpful tools to promote ticket sales.

HOW TO MAKE MONEY SELLING OTHER PEOPLE'S MERCHANDISE OR PROMOTING THEIR BRAND

Some companies will pay you to promote their brand and help them sell their merchandise. This is called a sponsorship deal. While it may seem that getting sponsored is out of your reach, a great deal of sponsorships come from smaller businesses. For example, the indie musician Franken-dread, who plays island and reggae music, talked to some beach-clothing manufacturers and got them to sponsor him. They supplied his band with their beach apparel and a small advertising fee in exchange for wearing the clothes and touting them to their audiences while onstage. If you can think of connections that make sense for your brand, you might be able to make the same kind of deals. For more information on getting sponsorship deals, see IndieGuide.com/Sales.

To get sponsorships, do the following:

1. **Start with local businesses and reach out.** If you can prove that you will be advertising and giving local businesses exposure, you might be able to get some real advertising revenue for your shows or Web site ads.

2. **Try online services to connect to sponsors.** Sites like Sonicbids (sonicbids.com) connect musicians to sponsors by creating live opportunities, promotional opportunities, and other connections that are worth investigating. Companies are trying to reach new audiences and are increasingly turning to musicians to do it.

3. **Find brands that suit your band.** Think like Frankendread and see if you can find sponsors that match your look and feel.

LEARNING MORE

Go to IndieGuide.com/Sales for a clickable version of every link, Web site, and service mentioned in this chapter, as well as free extra materials to help you handle music sales of all kinds.

CHAPTER 7

THE STRATEGIC GOAL: to plan, book, and promote your live shows and make the best of your performances to emotionally connect and engage with the audience so you can get fans, sell more music, and boost merchandise sales

REFERENCE PAGE: IndieGuide.com/Gigs

REFERENCE PAGE: IndieGuide.com/Gigs

	What	Description
CHECKLIST	Booker	A specified contact to book your band—either a band member or a booking agency so one person is responsible for getting gigs, and so customers know who to contact.
	Band Bio	A bio specific to booking, which emphasizes style of music, live music experience, and your draw for booking press kits.
	Music Samples	Live samples are best to demonstrate the style of your music to bookers.
	Press Clippings	Clippings that emphasize your live show to show your experience to bookers.
	Live Music Video	Any videos that show your band in action to give bookers a feel for what your show is like.
	Testimonials	Testimonials from customers (if you are booking for weddings, parties, etc.) to help sell bookings.
	Band Photo	Official band photo for the venue's press materials. Should be a 8" x 10" 300 DPI JPEG.
	Set Lists	Provide lists of songs you play, especially if you are a cover band so bookers know what kinds of songs you play, and so customers can choose which songs they want played.
	Booking and Stage Info	Live requirements, stage chart, instrumentation, booking/pricing info for booking customers and sound guys.
	Show Calendar	Calendar that shows your booking dates for fans to know where to hear you play, and for bookers to get an idea of how active you are.
	Scheduling Calendar	A calendar for the booker so that they know dead dates that the band can't make, as well as booking dates that you need to make.
	Booking Targets	A target list of where you will focus booking efforts: bars, live music venues, house concerts, conventions and festivals, weddings, college tours, etc. so you can make a booking plan.
	Video Camera/ Audiorecorder	A way to record gigs so that you can improve your stage performances.
	Posters	Show posters for gig promotion.
	Merch Store	Albums, merchandise, mailing lists, change, credit card systems, and Christmas lights (or something to grab their attention) for the merch store.

YOUR GIGS

"Talent won't get you the gig, but it will let you keep the ones you get."

—GEORGE HRAB, INDIE MUSICIAN AND PODCASTER

WE ASKED both Jim DeRogatis, former music editor for the *Chicago Sun-Times* and cohost of NPR's *Sound Opinions,* and Todd Martens, a music writer who has written for *Billboard* magazine and the *Los Angeles Times,* how they find out about new bands. Their answer: live shows. At some point a musician or band gathers enough of a local following to fill the larger or more noteworthy venues. After all, those venues don't take chances. When these music editors couple the "buzz" they hear on the Web and through their personal connections with seeing the band's name at a good venue, they check them out.

Getting to those venues takes time, but it's no secret: you need to put on great shows. Shows that connect emotionally with your audience. Shows that create big moments. Shows that leave the audience hungry for more. How to do that is part of what we'll discuss in this chapter, but we can boil it down to one sentence: you are there for the audience, not the other way around. We've seen plenty of musicians go onstage thinking that the audience is there for them. It's not. A gig is more than just music; it's a show. Many musicians forget that music is entertainment. The audience is there to be entertained and socialize and you're there to make sure you connect with each and every one of them and leave a lasting impact so they become fans.

Gigs are also one of the most stable and consistent sources of income for musicians. As Panos Panay, founder and CEO of Sonicbids (sonic-bids.com) says, "No social media prowess will ever replace the innate connection between a musician and a live audience. The live music experience will never be a commodity." Unlike recorded music, which can be copied easily, each show you perform is a unique event.

In this chapter, we'll cover all aspects of playing live, from practicing to publicity to pulling it off to packing up afterward.

PREPARING TO PLAY LIVE

HOW TO MAKE A BOOKING KIT FOR YOUR BAND

Unless you're booking at a tiny venue, any serious booker will want to see your booking materials. They will want to know where else you've played, what kind of music you play, your draw, and whether you are reliable. (Nearly every venue has had musicians flake on them, and they put a high value on reliability.)

Dealing with bookers is one of the few times as an indie musician that you might need physical materials and a CD to hand them. But whether you have a physical press kit or an online one, you will need to prepare all of these materials. The goal of a booking press kit is different than your regular press kit, which has a goal of trying to convince an audience of journalists to write about or cover your band in a story. Your booking press kit needs to be aimed at convincing an audience of bookers at venues to book your band.

A booking kit should have the following:

1. **Your Band Bio.** See chapter 4, "Your Brand," for information on how to create a band bio. You will include this one-page document here.

2. **A CD or Music Samples.** Include a CD of your latest album (or links to music samples online). And if you use a CD, keep *all* of your contact information on the CD itself, in case it gets separated from the rest of the kit.

3. **A Cover Page (for Physical Press Kits).** Include your contact information, your Web site address, and some basic details about booking. Note that you should have contact information and your Web site address on every page of your press kit.

4. **Press Clippings.** Nothing sells a band to a venue better than a press-clippings page, or a page of review quotes if you're fortunate enough to have

them. Sometimes, it helps to have a list of prior show dates to convince a new venue that you're an experienced band.

5.   **An 8" × 10" Band Photo.** The 8" × 10" band photo is the size most often used by venues, so you should have one available on your Web site.

6.   **A Live DVD or Video.** Possibly the most effective part of your press kit would be a DVD of your band in action, especially if you're trying to book a wedding or corporate show. Video will prove better than anything else that your band can perform.

7.   **Testimonials.** Providing testimonials about the show that you put on and the crowd that you bring can propel someone who is on the verge of booking you to make the commitment. Include them if you can.

8.   **Set Lists.** Provide songs you play, especially if you are a cover band.

9.   **Live Requirements, Stage Chart, and Instrumentation.** Provide all the information a venue needs to know about what you require to play live.

10.   **Booking and Pricing Info.** For event booking, don't forget to add your pricing, however it's okay to say "contact us for pricing info." For regular show bookings where you may get a percentage of the door or ticket sales, pricing information is not needed and can be negotiated upfront.

Note that you can use services like Sonicbids (sonicbids.com), Reverb-Nation (reverbnation.com), or myPPK (myppk.com) to host an electronic press kit, or else set aside a part of your Web site explicitly for booking with this information available.

HOW TO GET YOUR FANS TO TELL YOU WHERE TO TOUR SO YOU SAVE TIME AND MONEY

In the past, the way to build your fan base was to tour in concentric circles (or on a whim) based on where you were located. If you were lucky, or promoted yourself well, people would show up to listen to you in an area or city that you'd never visited, perhaps just to check out a new band. But since the Internet lets you win fans worldwide, no matter where you—or your fans—are located, musicians now face a unique problem: all of that hard work you did for online promotion doesn't help you fill a specific venue with an audience.

THE INDIE BAND SURVIVAL GUIDE

Services like Eventful (eventful.com) have changed this. Eventful is a Web service that tracks events across the world and makes it easy for people to find and share the events they are most interested in—whether by subject (music, sports, performing arts, comedy, politics, etc.) or by location. As Jordan Glazier, CEO of Eventful, explains it, "Eventful is a global platform for local event discovery. As an artist you don't need to post your show in ten different calendars and social networking sites. You can use Eventful as a one-stop shop." This alone makes it more likely that music lovers will find the kind of shows that they are looking for in their area.

But Eventful offers another tool that can help musicians fill their venues: a free service called Eventful Demand. This service allows fans to request that you perform in their area. Using this service, your online campaigns can now not only build a global fan base, they can let you plan a tour *where your fans already want you to play*.

Here are the steps to get this free service:

1. **Register at Eventful and create an account.** Once you have your account, you'll have access to the Performer Dashboard and the Eventful Demand widget. The Performer Dashboard allows you to

   o find out who is demanding that you play in their area, and where they're located;

   o track your Demand campaigns and how they're progressing;

   o communicate directly with your fans on a city-by-city basis or within a 250-mile radius of wherever you're demanded (that way, you can send a message to all of the fans in the same region as your shows); and

   o automatically send an e-mail from Eventful to your fans whenever you schedule an event in their area.

   Note that if you've never registered at Eventful but have a MySpace page, thanks to an integration arrangement between the two sites, you may already have Eventful Demand data waiting for you. You'll be able to "claim this performer"—and any requests on the Demand widget you may have gotten—once you sign up.

2. **Get the Eventful Demand widget.** Create an Eventful Demand widget for your account and copy the embed code. Embed it at your Web site

and Web presences. Your fans can then click on the widget and request that you play in their area.

3. **Tell your fans what the Eventful Demand widget is all about and how it helps you.** Do the following:

o Write a blog post and e-mail your mailing list asking recipients to use the widget to request that you play in their town. Explain that this will help you plan upcoming tours. Explain how the Eventful Demand service works, since some fans might not know, and remind them that registration at Eventful is free.

o Encourage your fans to promote your campaign using your Demand widget on their own Web sites and social networks. If you have a street team, make this one of its missions to help get the word out.

o Get people who come to your shows to sign up and demand you so you can get the demographic information and message them through Eventful's service in the future.

4. **Monitor your Performance Dashboard to see your numbers.** You'll be able to see who's demanding you and where (along with demographic information) at the Performance Dashboard. Keep in mind that Eventful Demand numbers often *undercount* the number of people that may come to your shows. Not everyone who would like to see you play in their town will have signed up on Eventful. So there can be a gap between the Demand numbers and the number of people that show up. As Jonathan Coulton said, "I've found that if there were 40 people who demanded me at Eventful, that meant about 80 people would come to the show that night." This happens for a number of reasons. For one, fans don't normally come alone—they bring their friends or their significant others. But also, if you effectively manage your publicity campaign for a show, there will be people that show up through other means such as newspapers, blogs, radio interviews, your mailing list, and word of mouth.

There are venues that will use your Eventful Demand numbers as a better way of judging a band's draw, instead of relying on the band's word and the (supposed) size of its mailing list. Therefore, if you have significant Eventful Demand numbers in a particular city or area, add them to your booking kit.

HOW TO BOOK YOUR BAND YOURSELF

Booking gigs is another of those art forms that could fill a book by itself. We can't cover everything here, but as in the rest of this guide we will give you an overview and all the essentials.

If you decide to book your own gigs, use the following steps:

1. **Designate a booker.** We suggest designating a single person in the band to handle bookings. If you use an agency, you should still have just one contact for venues to use. You don't want any embarrassing collisions when multiple gigs are booked for the same date at different locations. Nor do you want any confusion among the venue bookers over whom they should talk to.

   The person doing booking should be a "people person." Booking is about relationships. It's about having a beer with the people who book bands at the bars, and also about having a thick skin to deal with rejection. Your booker should be persistent. It also helps if your booker researches the bands that are most similar to your own that book in your area.

2. **Use scheduling tools.** Bookers struggle with scheduling more than any other obstacle. Most bands need every single member to be available to put on a gig. We recommend creating an online band calendar marked with all the dates that band members *can't* make, and of course any dates that have been booked. Google and Yahoo! both offer shareable online calendars for this purpose, although there are lots of options. We prefer the Web-based ones, though, because they allow the band members to add dates to the calendar as they learn of activities or dead dates wherever they are, and this lets the booker check the calendar from any Internet connection.

3. **Set a price and get paid.** When setting prices, consider how much you *need* to do the show, rather than how much you're *worth*. This will give you a solid basis for your price quote. You'll also have a better idea of how far you can bend on the prices that you set.

   To do this, take stock of all of the expenses for doing the show, especially if you have to travel. Also factor in your time, and the lost opportunity to do other shows or projects during those dates. Once you determine this number, you'll feel more confident when it comes time to negotiate.

   Make sure that you are clear on any cuts of your CD and merchandise sales that the venue demands. The larger venues will ask for as much as 20 percent of your take. If there's a contract, read it carefully. Some venues, such as colleges, won't let you sell merchandise at all. All of these factors need to be figured into your costs.

Carla Ulbrich (carlau.com), a successful touring folksinger and comical songwriter, warns that musicians often think they're making more money than they actually are because they get paid in cash and don't consider taxes. If you've got a fat wad of cash in your wallet from the CD and T-shirt sales, it can feel as if you've hit the jackpot, even though some of it has to be shared with your silent partner—the government—in the form of income tax.

4. **Work with fans to help you book gigs.** Some bands have had luck letting their fans help them book gigs. The advantages are that your fans know the venues in their local area and can actually do the legwork for you. By the time you get contacted by the venue booker, a lot of the difficult initial steps have been handled, and you can just deal with the details. For example, fans were always demanding that indie artist Jonathan Coulton tour in their hometowns. When he realized he had to travel halfway across the country to Seattle at the last minute for a personal matter, he blogged that he'd have one night free and could play a show if something was set up. Fans in Seattle—who didn't want to pass up a rare opportunity to see Coulton live—immediately took up the challenge and, within twenty-four hours, had arranged a respectable venue. All Coulton had to do was contact the place to cement the details. Twenty-four hours later, he was onstage playing to a packed house.

The Brobdingnagian Bards have gone a step further and requested that their fans make the arrangements for them. This worked out so well that they eventually put together a list of steps for their fans to take to help book them. Of course, another advantage of fan booking is that fans don't usually ask for a booking cut. They just want you to play in their area and are happy to get you to come to their town.

HOW TO GET A BOOKING AGENCY

If your band gets really busy, it's often a good idea to use a booking agency, which has established connections with bookers and venues. If they are a reputable company, they will audition you first to make sure you have a quality group. Venues will put more trust in bookers that are picky about which bands they represent.

1. **Find an agency you feel comfortable working with.** Agencies are usually local to your area, so use your favorite search engine to find one

nearby. Separately, you could also ask venues which agencies they work with.

2. **Choose an exclusive or nonexclusive agreement.** In an exclusive booking arrangement, all of your bookings go through the agency. The booker will be listed as your main contact, and anyone looking to book your band will have to call the booker. And your booker will get a cut of every gig you get, whether the booker found it or not. In a nonexclusive agreement, you can still find bookings through others. Usually, a booker will book their exclusive clients for gigs before their nonexclusives.

3. **Have a clear, signed agreement with an out clause.** You want your agreement with the booker to be clear, and with an agreed way to terminate the relationship if it doesn't work. This is especially important with an exclusive agreement.

4. **Choose a single booking contact within the band.** Booking agencies don't want to deal with multiple people in a band. They prefer to deal with the band manager. If you're managing yourselves, designate a single contact to deal with them.

BOOKING GIGS

HOW TO GET YOUR FIRST GIG

Most venues hate taking a chance on new bands, so first shows are some of the most difficult ones to get. It's the famous old saying "How do I get an audience if no one will give me a gig?"

One way to ensure you draw a large crowd for your debut show is to throw a big party afterward. Invite all of your friends and fans in advance and use it as a hook when you market your show to build excitement. By making a celebration out of your first show, you'll be able to pack the house and impress the venue, making it easier to get your next gig.

Try one of these techniques to get your first gig:

1. **Ask smaller local venues how they book new bands.** You might have to do some legwork to get that first show. Ask around at local venues to see how they handle new bands. Some require you to perform at an open mic. Others will give you an off night, a Sunday or Monday, to prove yourself. Some will ask you to pay to play the first time—which you should only do if you feel that this is the only way to get your first show in your area.

2. **Open for an established band.** One of the easiest ways to get that first show is to open for an established band. As we explained earlier, it's a good idea to build relationships with other bands in your area because they can leverage you into venues where you haven't played before. But be ready to play for the exposure and the experience—in other words, for free—rather than for a cut of the door.

3. **Offer to sub if they need a band on short notice.** Sometimes, being there if they have a cancellation will get you that first gig, since they will want to have someone fill in.

HOW TO KEEP THE GIG MACHINE RUNNING

Once you're an established player, it might still be difficult to book new venues. In Chicago, where we operate, until you become well-known, getting into one venue doesn't help you get into any others. You need to prove yourself to each one.

Here's how to keep yourself booked:

1. **Make a list of target venues that you'd like to play at.** Your favorite search engine, or sites like Indie on the Move (www.indieonthemove.com), can help you make a list of venues.

2. **Have your previous show calendar handy and keep any ads or press mentions of your gigs as proof you've played out.** We collect newspapers or mentions on the Web that could prove that we played a show at a specific venue on a specific date. That way we could share these clippings with other venues we were targeting to prove that we had a successful history of playing out around town at their competitors' venues.

3. **Personal relationships matter the most.** Your most important tools in booking venues are personal relationships and persistence. Every venue has an in-house booker, so the key is to know who it is, to present your materials, and then to follow up. It takes a special knack to know the difference between being persistent and being annoying. Make sure your band's booker possesses that knack before setting him or her loose on the venues. Most bands that we've interviewed agree that persistence gets them their shows, but you don't want any restraining orders either.

4.   **Form a band cartel.** Form a cartel of bands that you can work with, and alternate opening for each other. Often, venues want an entire night of entertainment. A group of bands can work together to provide this.

5.   **Get a substitute if there's absolutely no way to play the show.** Once you do book a gig, *never* cancel. Ever! Venues will often ban you if you cancel, especially if it's on short notice. Our drummer once canceled on us a few weeks before a gig, and we ended up playing anyway. We called it the Beatnik Turtle "acoustic night." Although it was a difficult gig, the bar was grateful, and we kept the relationship. We've played there many times since. Another option is to find another band to play in your place. It's always useful to have subs available.

HOW TO USE ONLINE TOOLS AND SERVICES TO GET GIGS

Playing live is a huge part of a musician's life, so it shouldn't be surprising that online tools now help to connect performers with venues. Try the following:

1.   **Use message boards that connect musicians.** Many message boards help musicians get each other shows, even in different cities. It can be as simple as posting that you'll be on tour in that area, and asking for suggested venues to call. Some bands will offer to let you open for them.

   Naturally, you should also watch these boards to see if there's anyone you can help book in your own city. Some of the message boards we recommend are Just Plain Folks (jpfolks.com) and the Velvet Rope (velvetrope.com).

2.   **Use online booking agencies.** Naturally, the Web has sites that help people book bands online. We're going to cover just two examples of this, both with a different focus.

   • Sonicbids (sonicbids.com) allows you to create an online press kit so that you can connect with talent buyers and venues, book shows, and perform other show-management tasks. Bands can then use the site to apply for open slots at venues and to host their online press kits for the general public. Some festivals and venues use it as their exclusive way to handle submissions. Note that Sonicbids has a monthly fee, plus fees each time you apply for an opportunity.

- GigMasters (gigmasters.com) aims itself more directly at people booking events like weddings, parties, and corporate events. If you are on a social committee of an organization and just want to "book an act," GigMasters can find you a band based on style, size, or any other needs. GigMasters also has a monthly fee.

HOW TO BOOK AT A HOUSE CONCERT

Thanks to the Internet, house concerts—small shows hosted at people's residences—have continued to grow in popularity. Although these types of concerts are better known in the folk-music community, where the intimate setting is appropriate, some bands have added these small shows to supplement a standard tour.

There are some legal issues associated with house concerts due to zoning laws, so keep in mind that sometimes shows get shut down. For more information about house concerts, we recommend the book *Host Your Own Concerts,* by Joe Taylor Jr., or go to IndieGuide.com/Gigs for more resources.

Do the following to book house concerts:

1. **Book gigs using your fans, or visit Web sites that help you book house concerts.** There's a surprising number of resources about house concerts, but a few to start with are HouseConcerts.com (houseconcerts .com), Concerts in Your Home (concertsinyourhome.com), and Slowbizz (slowbizz.com). Head to IndieGuide.com/Gigs for more house concert resources.

2. **Ask your hosts to guarantee a minimum payment (or play for a flat fee).** What you get paid shouldn't have to depend on your host's ability to bring in people, so negotiate this upfront.

3. **Make sure you have the right equipment to put on your own show.** Of course, houses don't have PA systems, so you'll have to come up with your own amplification if you need it.

HOW TO BOOK CONVENTIONS AND FESTIVALS

Playing conventions and festivals can be good money and introduce you to new audiences. Follow the steps below to get yourself booked:

1. **Research and target the festivals or conventions you want to book.** Many bands make the mistake of focusing only on *music* festivals or conventions such as South by Southwest (sxsw.com), the National Association of Music Merchants (namm.org), and the College Media Journal (cmj .com). This is a mistake since there is so much competition for play slots, and some of these music conferences charge the band to play because of the opportunity of playing for "music industry" folks.

Remember that every type of festival or convention can have music. For example, Carla Ulbrich makes a good living playing conventions, especially medical conventions, because some of her music is based on her experiences as a patient. But your music doesn't even have to be related to the convention in order to provide musical entertainment and get a paid gig.

You can find festivals and conventions using your favorite search engine, or try Festivals.com (festivals.com).

2. **Get to know the music committees.** Getting into festivals and conventions is mostly a "who you know" activity. Find out who the committee members are and research them online.

On top of this, it can sometimes take multiple years of work to get in. But once you do, and you're proven, getting back in can be made much simpler. If at all possible, you will want to use a warm handoff—getting your application in from someone that already knows the committee—rather than sending it cold.

3. **Follow the submission guidelines carefully.** There are usually so many acts that apply that a bad application can wreck your chances of getting a slot. Many festivals and conventions use tools like Sonicbids (sonicbids .com) to simplify the process.

HOW TO BOOK WEDDINGS

Many bands play weddings to supplement their income. It's an area with its own pitfalls, but those who can successfully navigate it can secure a dependable source of gigs. George Hrab buttresses his indie music income with steady work playing with a wedding band, the Philadelphia Funk Authority (phillyfunk.com).

One of Chicago's top wedding bands is the High Society Orchestra (highsocietyorch.com), run by Allan Heiman, who has been in the booking business for decades (in fact, he used to manage Curtis Mayfield back in the day). Heiman started his wedding band with a splash. He rented out a hotel ballroom and catered an evening for wedding planners, hotel-venue managers, and others in the wedding industry. That one event, along with an advertising campaign in bridal magazines and other publications, got him fifty-two bookings that first year. The point isn't that you need to spend a lot of money to start a wedding band, although that helps. Instead, remember that you need to win over the wedding planners and the hotel-venue managers. These are the people who can refer new business to you.

The High Society Orchestra gets all their gigs through word of mouth. They don't bother advertising anymore. In fact, they're completely booked for years ahead. Each wedding at which they perform gets them multiple new bookings from people in attendance. This is a key lesson: the better your wedding show, the more likely your band will be hired for additional bookings by other guests.

Here's some advice on how to book weddings:

1. **Impress wedding planners, hotels, and others in the industry.**
Anyone that is trying to put on a wedding has the exact same needs: flowers, music, venue, catering, etc. Anyone in the wedding business may get asked if they know bands that play weddings. The more people you know in the business who can give you referrals, the better your business will be. If possible, provide those who send gigs your way a "referral fee" so you encourage them to keep throwing opportunities your way.

2. **Prepare flawless marketing materials.** The professional expectations for a wedding are very different from those at regular venues. Your marketing materials need to be flawless, your band's presentation has to be polished, and your dealings with customers need to be managed with extreme care.

3. **When it comes to putting on a great wedding show, use these techniques.** Heiman suggests the following to put on a great wedding show:

   o **The emcee is key:** the emcee should interact with the audience throughout the evening.

   o **Focus on talent:** many of High Society's musicians are members of organizations like the Chicago Symphony Orchestra or the Lyric Opera. Your wedding band should feature the best musicians you can find.

o **The set list is critical:** Heiman is constantly tweaking his set lists to provide an enjoyable variety of both recent and older songs for his audience.

o **Don't lose momentum between songs:** the music should always be going unless the band takes a full break. High energy is key.

o **Stick to tried-and-true favorites:** dancing songs, medleys, and sing-alongs are always sure bets with wedding audiences. Get people up on their feet and involved.

4. **Have marketing materials and cards at the wedding.** Each wedding is an opportunity to get new customers. If you do a great job, you can get more bookings out of each one.

5. **Thank everyone when done, including the staff.** When you finish a wedding, definitely thank everyone. George Hrab always thanks the maître d' and the caterers. Some have told him that, in years of working in the business, they've never had any other wedding bands thank them. They were grateful, and you never know when one of them might direct new business to you in the future.

6. **Ask for testimonials.** Have a happy customer? Ask them for testimonials. They are one of the most important parts of your marketing materials.

HOW TO BOOK COLLEGE TOURS

College tours are a perpetual source of live-music booking. Colleges have their own world of student organizations and campus activity groups that you need to learn to navigate. But it can be worth it: college audiences are always hungry for new music. Each college town also provides opportunities to play in local venues as well as the actual college venues. For in-depth information on this topic, try *How to Tap into the Lucrative College Music Market* (www.bob-baker.com/buzz/college-booking.html), by Bob Baker.

Here are the basics of this in-depth topic:

1. **Join campus activity organizations like NACA and APCA.** The National Association of Campus Activities (naca.org) and the Association for the Promotion of Campus Activities (apca.com) are organizations that help colleges find entertainment for their campus events. It costs money to join these groups, but the costs are usually recouped within about three gigs.

2. **Play live at college entertainment conventions.** NACA and APCA hold conventions all over the country every year where the activity committees from hundreds of colleges go to find and book acts. NACA's national convention takes place every February, and they also have six smaller regional conventions. Four of them are in the fall and two are in the spring. If you attend a regional conference, aim for one in the fall because by the spring campus activity planning is winding down for the school year. APCA's national conference is also in February and they have regional conferences in November.

3. **Talk to activity committees at the conventions.** Most of the time the representatives from the event planning committees at these conventions will be students. Talk to them and make yourself memorable. Leave them with a CD and some contact information.

4. **When you get booked at a college, send your press kit to other venues in that town.** Venues near colleges are always looking for bands to bring in student crowds. You might be able to book extra gigs, and if you have to travel this will make your trip more worthwhile. Don't forget the contacts you've been working with at the college may have connections at these local venues. So, be sure to ask if they suggest other places to play in town.

THREE OTHER OPPORTUNITIES FOR GIGS WORTH LOOKING INTO
Try the following if you're looking for more ideas:

1. **Charity Events.** Charity events deliver a lot of benefits to bands that play them. Usually, all proceeds are donated to the charity, but the events have their own press releases, which often get mentioned by the media. The resulting articles invariably list the participating bands. You can also do a press release of your own about the show and the cause that you're supporting. Those press releases can get more attention than your typical release because of the human-interest element and the fact that the charities are known by the media.

Playing a charity event is a great way to piggyback, as well as network with other bands and even other community artists—sometimes charity events are more than just music shows. It's a good value for fans, too, because they can sample a variety of bands for the price of admission.

2. **Corporate Shows, Bar and Bat Mitzvahs, and Other Special Events.** The High Society Orchestra also does corporate shows, bar and bat mitzvahs, and other gigs. But these are much more sporadic and difficult to get. Still, the secret to any of these other types of shows is again in the presentation of your materials, and in knowing who handles hiring the bands.

For corporate shows, the bookers can often be employees on a company events committee or someone in the human resources department. Because these positions often rotate, it's hard to keep getting steady shows at each firm.

For other types of shows, your booking information on your Web site and the personal contacts that you make will be the best way to keep a steady stream of opportunities coming in.

3. **Street Performances.** The Brobdingnagian Bards started out playing in a park four days a week, for free. Eventually, after a year of playing, they had a hundred people showing up regularly to hear them. This group formed their initial fan network. When the Bards recorded their first album and played their first paid gigs, they already had an audience.

It's not always necessary to play formal shows—parks, streets, and other public areas are perfectly good alternative "venues." But keep in mind that most cities impose restrictions on public performances of this type, and you may need a permit.

THE LIVE SHOW

Musicians often argue the issue of "staying true to the music" versus "pandering to the audience." This might make an interesting debate over beers, but it's not useful when it comes to putting on a show. In the end, you're there to entertain the audience. Of course, you need to follow your aesthetic tastes—which might include a dark, brooding look or a screaming spandex serenade—but don't forget: *you are there for them.*

Having the attitude that your audience is "lucky to hear you" will *not* result in a good show. David Bloom, one of Chicago's jazz gurus, captured it best: "Don't reduce music to the size of your ego. It's a lot bigger than you. It was here before you, and it'll be here long after you're gone. Music is something to look up to." If you look up to music, the audience will look up to you. But if you look down at the audience, they won't be there next time you play.

If you want to win fans, it doesn't matter the size of the audience you play to. Every show counts. As Brian Austin Whitney, the founder of the music community Just Plain Folks, says, "Don't worry about playing to twenty people; play like you're playing to twenty thousand. If you make the best music you can and play the best you can play, you will grow your audience."

FIVE THINGS YOU NEED TO DO TO PUT TOGETHER
A KILLER LIVE SHOW

Think back and try to relive one of the most memorable live shows you've attended. Why exactly do you remember it? Did you feel involved? connected? energized? Were you transported to another place? In other words, did you feel something—not just hear it?

In the best shows, the band and the audience connect.

Tom Jackson (tomjacksonproductions.com), a musician and one of the leading live music producers of tours, showcases, and shows, has spent decades figuring out what makes audiences connect to musicians and what keeps fans coming back for more. He's boiled it down to three reasons: audiences come to be captured and engaged, to experience moments, and to experience a change in their lives. While this might sound lofty, there's no question that music can do this for people. What Jackson does for a living is teach musicians how to *create* this connection in their own shows.

A live music producer acts somewhat like a sports coach does with his athletes—teaching the skills, testing out the "plays," and getting the individual parts to work together as a team. It's not about developing your musical chops (which you should do on your own time); it's about developing your show for the stage. This may mean having the lead singer walk to the side of the stage at a certain point, having the lead guitarist come forward when it's his time to solo, and rearranging the song in ways that you wouldn't have done in the recording, but work well live to get an audience involved. These are the same techniques used by performers like U2 and Prince to pull off such spectacular shows.

As Jackson says, "Just because you learned how to play music doesn't mean you automatically know how to perform in front of an audience." If you want to win fans, your live performances must be more than just taking your recorded music and playing it really well on stage. According to Jackson, a live show is 15 percent technical, 30 percent emotional, and 55 percent visual. Most musicians spend their time practicing the technical part, but neglect the other 85 percent. Since the visual part of a show is the most important, think about your own set. Even though it's likely that each of your songs *sound* different, be honest: do they *look* different on stage? As Jackson says, "Audiences get bored and disconnect when all of your songs look the same."

Here's a small sample of the advice that Jackson gives to help build that connection with the audience:

1. **The performance should visually match the song.** You can't control the audience's eyes, but you can control what you do onstage. Give the audience *visual* cues that match moments in the song. When one musician has a solo, he or she should be forward and the others should step back "out of the picture." If a song builds, bring musicians forward as they add their parts. The audience's view of the stage changes dramatically depending on where your band members stand, so always let the audience know where they should focus their attention.

2. **What's good for a recording isn't necessarily good for the stage.** Abandon the idea of reproducing your radio-friendly, three-minute-long track at the stage door. In a live show, three minutes goes by so fast that most audience members don't even know what happened. They didn't pick up on that cool riff. They didn't notice that harmony vocal. Jackson will often work with musicians to find the highlights of songs and then retool those parts for stage performance. Techniques that he uses include extending intros and outros to songs, repeating the cool licks or hooks that sound great on the recording but go by too quickly on stage, extending a bridge or solo, or breaking down a part and vamping on its underlying rhythms.

3. **Less is more.** Most bands try to pack a set with as many songs as they can. After all, they're musicians and want to play. But the point is to make the songs you do play special and memorable for the audience. Applying the techniques above lengthens the songs you do play, and this means you'll play fewer songs in a set.

4. **Learn how to move onstage.** If you study the top musical performers, you quickly realize that movement is just as important a part of a performance as playing the notes. This is not just for the U2s of the world. And to the extent that you can bring it into your performances, your shows can become electrifying. The biggest moments of your music are not likely to come out with you standing behind your microphone for the full forty-five-minute set.

Instead, they should match the visual part of the performance. This isn't dance choreography, and these are not mysterious skills. In fact, Jackson suggests that there are four different ways to get around onstage: walking, running, skipping (think AC/DC), and walking with purpose (walking like you own the stage). Each can be used to match the song. Now, you can easily do each of these things around your living room, but what about when you're in front of an audience playing your guitar and singing? Football players practice footwork, and musicians should practice the fundamentals of movement *while playing* so that they can marry it to the music.

5. **Plan and rehearse.** Just as you practice your instrument and the songs you play, you must spend time practicing your live performance and planning your set. As Jackson notes, all those live shows of your favorite big-name bands looking like they're making it all up as they go along are really planned. Your practices should reflect this. Jackson recommends that you first learn the music on your own; next, practice as a group in a circle to learn the songs; and finally, practice as if onstage. This includes practicing the produced song—moves and all.

This is an area that sets apart the great shows from the amateurs. The best place to get information on how to make a live show sizzle are Jackson's book, *Live Music Method: All Roads Lead To The Stage*, and his videos (tomjacksonproductions.com).

THE NUMBER ONE THING YOU CAN DO TO IMPROVE
YOUR LIVE SHOW

If you're heading out the door to a party, chances are you'll check the mirror to see how you look, straighten out your hair and clothes. If you're practicing for a show, it makes sense to record your performance to accomplish the same thing. Athletes use "game tapes" to review their performance, so should musicians.

Your game tape doesn't have to be a high-quality recording to be useful. For actual performances, ask someone you trust to watch the equipment and hit record when the show begins so you don't have to worry about it. By studying recordings of your band in rehearsal and at gigs, you'll learn a lot of surprising things, and some fixes will be as simple as straightening your hair before a party.

HOW TO DO A SOLID SOUND CHECK

Sound guys (and, yes, we call them sound guys even if they're women) can never make a bad band sound good. But they can definitely make a good band sound bad. The quality of how you sound to an audience is the most important part of the show that you can't directly control. If you don't have your own sound guy, make friends with whoever is running the board. And, most important, *do not skip the sound check*.

In our experience, sound guys tend to be an unusual breed, and it's always interesting to get to know them. One of them that worked the boards for our band would get drunk, hit on our female friends, and do a lousy job with the sound to boot. Another did great work, but posted a note facing the stage: "Do not play 'American Woman'." Naturally, we announced that we were going to play it in the middle of the set. He made this hilarious hand-waving motion as if he were trying to get a plane to stop landing on a runway that was mined to explode. Of course, our audience missed the entire joke and just wondered why we wanted to play *that* song.

Here's how to make the most of a sound check:

1. **Get to the venue early.** We know. This never happens. But make it happen if you can.

2. **Provide your microphone chart and instrumentation, so the sound guy can see where things go.** This will make the setup go so much quicker. For examples of stage plots, see IndieGuide.com/Gigs.

3. **Designate one band member or representative to work with the sound guy.** Have one person answer the sound guy's questions and tag along with him or her throughout the check to make sure things get resolved quickly and correctly. Every band has some oddities with its microphone setup, so it pays to have someone there to make sure that the sound is right.

4. **Be particular about the sound, especially monitors.** If you need more volume or a different mix, take care of this now. It's impossible to change the monitors besides yelling "Turn it up" or "Turn it down" during the actual show.

5. **Let each vocalist try his or her mic.** If there are a lot of harmonies, make sure that each vocalist can hear the others during the check.

6. **Have the member with the best ears stand in the room to double-check the sound.** This is exactly where you can catch the mistakes of a bad sound guy.

7. **Tell the sound guy about any instrument changes to expect.** Give your set list to the sound guy and highlight any special parts. For example, one member of Beatnik Turtle plays sax, sings, then plays flute. He often gets one mic for saxes and one for flute *and* vocals. When he switches between flute and vocals on that mic, he needs different levels.

8. **Buy the sound guy a beer or give him a tip.** Make friends with your sound guy. Offer free CDs or other band merchandise. This gives him or her an incentive to make you sound good. Also, the sound guy is usually connected to other venues in your area, and that connection might just get you more shows. Sound guys can put you in touch with other musicians and otherwise expand your skill and opportunity networks.

FIVE THINGS YOU SHOULD DO AT EVERY SHOW
Consider doing these things at every show:

1. **Announce your name.** Always remember at every show that there are some people in the audience that do not know who you are. Ideally, bring a sign or banner onstage.

2. **Build your list.** Make sure that you bring your mailing list and ask people to sign up. To maximize sign-ups, have a giveaway (but don't give away anything that you are selling at the merch counter or you could hurt sales). Make some entry slips with spaces for audience members to put in their contact info. Then do a drawing from the stage later in the show. They are more likely to give their contact information if there's a chance of winning something. Also, if you use Eventful to help you build your tours and demographic information, get audience members to demand you and become part of your Eventful following so you can message them when you have future shows.

3. **Sell merchandise.** While onstage, remember one thing above all: *Don't forget to announce that you have music and merch available for sale!* Don't just announce once that you have music for sale. Do this a few times during your show. Some people just need a reminder, that extra push to get them to make the purchase. And remember that some people might have just walked in the door.

4. **Make a call to action.** Announce your next shows and upcoming projects to draw people in. If you have a poster for your next show, place it around the venue.

5. **Thank the sound guy and anyone else who helped you during the show.** Recognize others and cross-promote. This can make a difference in the future.

PROMOTING YOUR SHOW

HOW TO MAKE POSTERS TO PUBLICIZE YOUR SHOW

You've seen them at every venue: posters for every band with an upcoming performance. When you have a show coming up yourselves, you should join them and get a poster up at least a few weeks ahead of time.

Here's how to make posters:

1. **Brand every poster with your logo, your color scheme, and your fonts, and make sure that your band name, Web site address, and the *correct* date and time of your performance can clearly be read.** You may want to get your posters professionally printed ahead of time, in bulk, with a blank space in the middle so that you can write in the show information for each gig.

2. **Put QR codes on your posters with your Web address, and make a page with a sample of the music.** Posters alone don't give an idea of what the band sounds like, and it's a pain to try to type in a Web address. But nearly every smartphone has the capability to read QR codes, which are little square boxes with an embedded Web address that phones can read. They are increasingly common on every type of poster. Head to sites like MyQR (myqr.co) or ZXing Project (zxing.appspot.com/generator) to make a QR code that will send your fans to a Web address, so you can put it in the poster art.

3. **Consider using a text-message site with sound samples for the poster.** Another idea besides QR codes is to use sites like Myxer (myxer .com), which can provide you with a phone number and code to send people music and ringtones. For instance, you can send people messages like: TEXT BEATNIK TO 69937 FOR FREE SONG SAMPLES FROM BEATNIK TURTLE (note: standard carrier charges apply!).

4. **Consider hanging posters in these locations:**

o **The Venue.** Place them in front of the venue, as well as throughout. And don't forget the bathrooms—those posters actually get looked at.

o **Music Stores.** At each store, give the employees free CDs and offer to leave one for the shop itself so they can play it on their PA system. These employees are your best advocates. If they allow it, sell your CDs on consignment at the stores, too.

o **Local Shops.** Music stores and coffee shops are usually good about supporting local music. It's easy to figure out if they're friendly, because you'll see posters for other shows in the window or on the walls. Also, offer any of the workers or the shop itself free CDs. Again, they may recommend your band if they like your music.

o **Colleges.** Any schools near the venue are a good target. Local colleges are great places to get new fans.

Be careful about putting posters in your neighborhood, since local laws may prohibit you from putting posters on public walls. Consult local regulations before you go nuts with that tape.

NINE PLACES TO PROMOTE EACH SHOW

Use this as a checklist to make sure that you've promoted your shows through every venue available to you. You need to plug the shows multiple times, long before the show, so your fans can plan to go, and multiple times closer to the shows so that you remind people.

1. **Your Show Calendar.** This lets your fans plan to come out when you're playing, and if you've set it up right, will filter to all of your Web presences. If you've set up your calendar through a service like Eventful, you can also use their messaging service to contact fans in the area of your show who've requested that you play there. Additionally, you can promote your show to the top of the list by upgrading your event listing at Eventful's site and their weekly newsletters for a fee.

2. **Radio Stations.** See chapter 13, "Get Heard," for how to get played and mentioned on local radio stations before your shows.

3. **Social Networks.** When you announce the show on social networks, it has a good chance of getting reposted to each of your fan's friends or followers. It's even more effective if you can do this with a digital poster or image.

4. **Your Mailing List.** Naturally, if you have a mailing list, you'll want to announce the show.

5. **The Media.** Only try to engage the media if you have more of a story than "indie band plays show." But if there's an event of some sort, such as an album release, charity tie-in, or other interesting angle, engage them. Use the techniques in chapter 12, "Get Publicized," to perform a media campaign. Especially try to get coverage in new media, which is more accessible to indie musicians.

6. **Displays and Giveaways.** Yvonne Doll of The Locals (localsrock.com) came up with a clever idea that ended up drawing a lot of new audience members to her shows: put a little display up at the bar venue that you're going to play at and stock it with free discs of your music. Make sure each one is labeled with the show information—either on the disc or as an insert—to help market the show.

We also have a technique that has worked well for us, which arose as a result of a happy accident at our CD manufacturer for our second CD, *Santa Doesn't Like You*. We got an extra thousand CDs (discs only) for the cost of shipping due to a production error. We packaged the discs in thin cases with a photocopied cover and little brochures about an upcoming concert. Then we went to record stores all over Chicago and offered to let them sell the discs. Before they could finish saying the word *consignment*, we added that they could sell the discs for a dollar and keep it. There isn't a local store in any town that will turn away free money. The little display was usually placed right next to the cash register—a pure impulse buy. Few people could resist spending an extra buck to get another disc. We didn't give the discs away for free for two reasons. First, it gave the store a reason to push them and place the display by the cash register. Second, people don't value things that are free. That show was one of the best attended we've had. And even years later, we've had people write us that they listened to the disc for years. If you find yourself with extra CDs, we highly recommend this technique.

7. **Flyers.** Flyers that you can hand out or leave at local stores and venues can work to bring people in. But they are most effective when you give them a

value, such as a discount or free drink of some kind. That gives people the incentive to take it and to actually show up. If you can work out a drink deal with the venue, that can work best, but if you have to, give away something at the venue or offer money off the door or ticket cost.

8.   **Street Promoters.**   If you can have friends or a street team personally hand out flyers to passersby right before the gig to bring them in, it's a surprisingly effective way to get people to your shows (especially if your friends or street team are attractive!). One last trick we picked up from some Las Vegas escort promoters handing out leaflets along the strip. It's a strangely effective technique that helps get people's attention. Just snap the stack of flyers twice quickly against your hand so it makes a *taptap* sound and hold it out to be picked up. The sound forces passersby to pay attention to you, and they'll take the flyer from you instinctively. Try it; it works.

9.   **Your Web Site After the Show.**   Your goal, once you get them to show, is to bring audience members back for another show. Get them to show up at your Web site after the show to keep that connection with your band. Here's another idea to consider that came from our friend Yvonne Doll (localsrock .com). Her band has a cute little doll named Danger Boy, and they take pictures of their fans with the doll for the band Web site. They even have little cards to give out with the Web address explaining that the pictures will appear there. This connects fans with the Web site *after their shows,* ensuring that they bring other people to see their picture at the site as well as visit it themselves.

SELLING AT SHOWS

HOW TO SELL MERCH AT SHOWS

Your shows are when it's most likely a fan will buy something from you. For one thing, there are no shipping costs. Also, you've just played live in front of them, and people like to support bands they've seen in person. Be aware that the larger venues will take a cut of your merchandise sales, sometimes as much as 20 percent.

1.   **Get someone to run your store.**   Always get someone to run the store for you. It's a fairly easy job, but it can be difficult to convince someone to do it. We once teamed up with other local bands and did an exchange program,

where we ran the stores at each other's shows. (And we promoted the other bands' shows as well.) You should do everything you can to get people to help out the band in this way. Offer your friends incentives such as free CDs and T-shirts, free shows, or anything else that would entice them to help you. The alternative is to sell from the stage.

2.   **Make the table presentable and dress it up.** We suggest putting up a sign, getting a tablecloth, putting up some Christmas lights, and then displaying your CDs and merch so it's visible. Presentation matters.

3.   **Offer payment options.** First of all, make sure that you have enough singles and fives for change. You don't want to miss a sale just because you don't have enough. Second, people will often spend all of their cash on beer. Fortunately, it's now possible for independent bands to handle credit card transactions. Try the following:

o   **CD Baby's credit card program:** for a little money, CD Baby (cdbaby.com) will give you a credit card swiper and some receipts. They take a small cut of every sale for handling the credit card transaction, but on the other hand these sales are tracked by Nielsen SoundScan.

o   **Mobile device credit card sales:** if you have a smartphone or mobile device, you have the ability to take credit card transactions. These services usually take a cut, but it can really improve your sales. Try Square (squareup.com), Intuit GoPayment (payments.intuit.com/products/basic-payment-solutions/mobile-credit-card-processing.jsp), or Authorize.Net (www.authorize.net/solutions/merchantsolutions/merchantservices/mobileapp).

4.   **Give away swag.** Give away stickers or other inexpensive items so that fans get a little something for their purchase. You should also have your flyers available to hand to anyone who buys something.

5.   **Encourage mailing list sign-ups.** Have your mailing list at your store so you can get and encourage sign-ups. And, if you use Eventful, get them to sign up and demand you as well so you can get demographic information and message them in the future about your shows.

LIVE BROADCASTS

HOW TO PUT ON AN INTERNET CONCERT

Want to go on a worldwide tour without leaving your town? All you need is a webcam, a decent microphone, a fast Internet connection, and, of course, a computer. Internet broadcasting sites make it possible to put on shows no matter where in the world your audience is. This technology represents a wonderful opportunity to play for thousands of people all over the world.

Treat a broadcast concert just as seriously as any other gig. Plan for Web broadcasts exactly as you would any show, with the same level of attention to publicity. It's possible that you'll get even more people watching you on-line than at a local venue. Especially since most Internet broadcast services archive what you record for later viewing.

Here's how to put on your own Internet concert:

1. **Create an account at one of the live streaming sites.** Ustream (ustream.tv), Livestream (livestream.com), or JustinTV (justin.tv). Ustream, in particular, lets you even host a live event using nothing but your smartphone. Alternatively, you can use video chat applications such as Google+ Hangouts (plus.google.com/hangouts) or Skype (skype.com).

2. **Create a setup with good lighting and good sound.** Although you could set up a microphone in the corner of the room to capture the sound, it's better to set up your performance like any other gig—with multiple microphones plugged into a sound board or an analog-to-digital audiorecording interface plugged into a computer. Since lighting matters as well, try to illuminate the room so it looks good on camera. If possible, use 3-point lighting. You should work with this until you're happy with the result. For links to lighting and sound resources, see IndieGuide.com/Gigs.

3. **If you want to get fancy, get a switcher for multiple camera angles.** A switcher box lets you handle multiple video input sources. Applications like Vidblaster (vidblaster.com) and Wirecast (www.telestream .net/wire-cast/overview.htm) let you have multiple cameras, so it's not just one static shot. See IndieGuide.com/Gigs for more options. This is a complex area that has many hardware and software solutions available.

4. **Promote the show like any other gig.** Use all of the promotion techniques we talk about in this chapter to promote the show as well as those

in chapter 11, "Your Marketing Strategy" and chapter 12, "Get Publicized." Also, since services like Ustream and Livestream have embeddable video players, you should add one to your Web site so it's easy for your fans to watch your show.

5. **Have someone handle the chat.** One of the best parts of using these video-streaming services is that you can interact with your fans. They will be able to chat with each other, and you. Since the band will be performing, you should have someone handling the comments. See chapter 14, "Get Seen," for more information about video.

Keep in mind you may do all of this on stage at a local venue. If you do, make sure the venue has the equipment and capability to stream the show. Tapping into the sound board will result in higher sound quality while using their lighting and stage may make for better visuals. Lastly, make sure the venue gives you permission to broadcast a video feed from their venue.

LEARNING MORE

Go to IndieGuide.com/Gigs for a clickable version of every link, Web site, and service mentioned in this chapter, as well as free extra materials to help you put together your shows. We also recommend reading *How to Be Your Own Booking Agent: The Musician's and Performing Artist's Guide to Successful Touring*, by Jeri Goldstein.

PART THREE
GET ON THE WEB

CHAPTER 8

THE STRATEGIC GOAL: to plan and organize your global Web presence so you can (1) share media and content once and have it spread across the social Web automatically, (2) know when people are talking about you and where, and (3) stay as connected and engaged as you want to be, so you can promote and sell your music worldwide with minimal effort

REFERENCE PAGE: IndieGuide.com/WebStrategy

CHECKLIST: This is a strategy chapter—the chapter is the checklist.

YOUR WEB STRATEGY

"Creating global awareness is part art, part science, part technology, and all strategy."

—REGGI HOPKINS, EXECUTIVE DIRECTOR OF THE MUSIC INDUSTRY
WORKSHOP AND THE CENTER FOR MUSIC TECHNOLOGY

IMAGINE THE following: you've just released a new album, posted a blog entry about it, and headed to rehearsal. Shortly after, your Twitter account automatically tweets a link to your announcement. Just like Twitter, your Last.fm, ReverbNation, and Facebook pages automatically post the announcement as well. You continue with your rehearsal, and, when you take a break, you notice an e-mail on your phone from your social-networking-alerting tool notifying you that someone retweeted your announcement and another person posted a comment about your new album. You also receive an email from Google Alerts with a link to an MP3 blog that reviewed your album. You sent it to them weeks ago, giving them a chance to check it out before release, and, even though they never told you that they had decided to review it, your alert found it. You click the link, read the review on your phone, and share the good news with your fans and followers through your HootSuite app. HootSuite automatically takes your message and posts it to all your social networks, Web presences, and the mobile app for your band so your fans can get a link to the review. Your five-minute break is over and you head back to rehearsal to share the good news with the band.

This is the Web, social, and mobile world you'll be able to put together for yourself in this and the next two chapters. One of Facebook's successes was how it made it easy to share the moments in your life at the click of a button. Your whole band's Web existence can be like this, too—across all of your Web sites. The goal of this chapter is to present a strategy that will allow you to decide what kind of Web presence you want to create for you and your music, and then to put it together in a way that makes it easy to share on all of your Web presences with minimal effort.

This chapter outlines everything you need to build a complete Web presence for your band and music. *You don't need to do all of it.* You can choose what parts you want to create and maintain. And you should definitely start small but grow it over time. Although the Web is always changing—and you *will* see some sites get labeled "the next best thing" while others disappear and take your data with it—this strategy will let you keep up with the changes and keep it simple to let your fans find you no matter where they hang out.

WHY YOU NEED TO DO THIS

WHAT MUSICIANS NEED TO UNDERSTAND ABOUT THE "MARKETING FUNNEL"

We're musicians. We make music. Why should we have to worry about the Web, or any of this stuff? How can having a Twitter account really help us? And why give away free downloads of your music? How can that turn into more music sales?

These are all legitimate questions that any musician should ask. And, the truth is, if you get so lost promoting your music that you lose sight of *making* it, there's no point.

But, of course, there are great reasons to spend time building a solid Web presence: it's the easiest and cheapest way you have today to communicate with other people and expose them to your music, get them to support you, and promote yourself to others. In short, it's the mechanism to build a global fan base.

Your goal should be to not only get yourself and your music "out there," but to convert people from casual visitors who may never return to your site or presences into fans, customers, and promoters who can't wait for your next album or show. Convert just enough people and you've built a fan base. This process is called the Marketing Funnel. The short version is simple. You want to:

- **Turn casual visitors into fans:** people who subscribe to your feeds and will hear from you whenever you communicate through your Web presences.

- **Turn fans into customers and promoters:** people who not only support you by buying your albums and merchandise or coming to your shows, but also actively spread the word about you and your music to others.

Once you realize the name of this game is to convert as many people out there from casual visitors into fans, customers, and promoters, you can understand why having a unified Web strategy is at the heart of your marketing strategy and making money with music. You need as broad of a presence as possible in order to hook as many visitors as you can, because only a small number will become fans. The more Web, social, and mobile presences that you can put you and your music on, the wider your funnel will be. And you need to make it very easy for fans to buy your music and spread the word so they become customers and promoters. If your marketing efforts aren't aimed at getting people down this funnel—to get casual visitors to take notice of your music and to get fans to buy or promote you to others—you're not marketing, you're just talking.

What this means, more than anything, is that when you establish a presence anywhere on the Web, or even when you meet someone in person offline, if your Web strategy and marketing message are not geared toward turning visitors into fans, customers, and promoters, you will be missing out on opportunities to grow your fan base. From a Web-strategy perspective, once you've captured the attention of visitors, you need tools to make it easy for you to get them to take an action, whether that be to subscribe to your feed, follow you on Twitter, join your e-mail list, buy a song or album, come to a show, or promote you to their social networks.

This chapter and the next two will tell you exactly how to create a unified Web, social, and mobile presence. But you should keep the Marketing Funnel in mind since it not only gives you the reason why you're doing this, but gives you a way to judge how successful you've been going forward so that, as needed, you can adjust your strategy.

THE SIX-POINT WEB STRATEGY

HOW TO ORGANIZE YOUR WEB SITE, WEB PRESENCES, AND SOCIAL NETWORKS: A SIX-POINT PLAN

The six-point plan below is a simple way to think about all of your Web presences and to organize your Web strategy. You should have Web sites and services in each of the categories below to make it easy for you to share music, photos, videos, and text and to stay on top of what people are saying about you, no matter where they're saying it.

1. **Content Hosts.** Content hosts are the places where you will post blog entries, photos, videos, music, or any other content. The goal is to choose one for each type of content, and then, no matter what you want to share, you will only have to post it once. The autoposting tools will pick up the content generated from content hosts and automatically share it with all your presences. Note that some content hosts are also outposts, and vice versa.

2. **Outposts.** Outposts are places on the Web where anyone can find you or your band. They include Web sites (including your own), social networks, stores, mobile presences for your music, music hosts, and even your Xbox LIVE account. With some simple steps, most outposts have a way to pull from your automated feeds so they always have the latest news and stay alive and fresh.

3. **Autoposting Tools.** Autoposting tools pick up feeds and automatically post them to your outposts. With tools like HootSuite (hootsuite .com) or Ping (ping.fm) you will post just once and spread the same data everywhere.

4. **Conversion Tools.** No matter where your audience finds you, the goal is to turn them from casual visitors into fans and bring them into your circle. The term "conversion" comes from Web-marketing terminology, and it means converting a visitor into a customer. Conversion tools entice visitors to join your mailing list, purchase a track, or talk about you on their social networks, and they build on relationships so you can stay in touch.

5. **Alert and Notification Tools.** Whether someone tweets about you, writes about you in a blog, or mentions you in a story written for an online

magazine, you want to know about it. And with alert and notification tools like Google Alerts (www.google.com/alerts) and SocialOomph (socialoomph.com) you will get an e-mail every time that happens.

6. **Metrics Tools.** How many people listened to your tracks across all the music Web sites, like Last.fm, Myspace, and ReverbNation? How many new followers, fans, and Facebook follows did you get last week? Rather than going to each site and counting them yourself, metrics tools will do the hard work for you and bring the data back to you. This makes it easy for you to see how effectively your campaigns have been going. Sites like Next Big Sound (nextbigsound.com) can bring it all together and show you what you have.

These six categories will help you as we cover the types of Web presences you should have. We will tell you which of these six categories they appear in.

HOW TO DETERMINE WHERE YOU NEED TO SIGN UP: A WEB-STRATEGY CHECKLIST

Here are all the Web presences you should consider signing up for. While we go into detail about what all these tools do and provide concrete steps on how to create and use them, it's easy to lose sight of what you need to do across *all* of them. Use the table below as a checklist. You can also go to IndieGuide.com/WebStrategy for more tools, information, and links.

Type	What	Description
Outpost	Domain Registrar	Domain registrars let you register your website domain name. They include Namecheap (namecheap.com), Go Daddy (GoDaddy.com), or Dotster (Dotster.com). For example, we own beatnikturtle.com and TheSongOfThe Day.com, which we have registered at Namecheap.

Continued...

Type	What	Description
Outpost	Web Host	Web hosts are services that host your Web site itself. Many domain registrars provide this, too, but it's not required to use theirs, even though they go out of their way to make it seem that way. Sites like HostBaby (hostbaby.com), Reverb-Nation (reverbnation.com), and FourFour (fourfour.com) provide hosting, although there are numerous choices (see IndieGuide.com/Web for more).
Outpost	Web Platform or CMS	Many Web hosts will also provide a content management system, or CMS, for you. But we also have used generic Web hosting and solutions like Word-Press (wordpress.org), Joomla (joomla .org), and Drupal (drupal.org), which have systems that can make it easy for you to manage your Web site and content, with a lot of flexibility.
Content Host, Outpost	Blog	Although some musicians skip this, everyone should have a blog. It's the easiest way to post your news in one place and share it to all of the Web presences. Your Web site may have one that you can use built in, but there are advantages to using blog hosts like Blogger (blogger.com), Tumblr (tumblr .com), or WordPress (wordpress.com).
Content Host, Outpost	Photo and Image Hosts	Keep your photos and images in one place so that you can easily make albums and share them on all of your presences. All the major photo hosts make it easy to post new photos and then autopost your photos to your other Web presences. Some examples include sites like Picasa (picasa.com), Flickr (flickr.com), and Photobucket (photobucket.com).

Type	What	Description
Content Host, Outpost	Video Host	While YouTube (youtube.com) dominates this space, and every musician that has any video should have a presence there, you may want to consider other high-end video hosts like Vimeo (vimeo.com), which has advanced video options. See the section on video hosting for details.
Content Host, Outpost	Audio Host	Audio sharing, while it seems simple—after all, video is easily embeddable everywhere—has turned out to be harder to find because of music rights. You will want to consider having your music in places that aren't easily shareable just to have another place for fans to find your music. For embeddable players, see the section on this topic or try sites like ReverbNation (reverbnation .com), Bandcamp (bandcamp.com), or SoundCloud (soundcloud.com).
Outpost	Social Music Discovery Sites	Sites like Last.fm (last.fm), Spotify (spotify.com), and Turntable (turntable.fm) have a social element to music listening and are places where you can maintain a presence.
Outpost	Social Networks	You should be part of as many social networks as you feel that you can keep up with, including Twitter, Facebook (including a fan page), and Myspace.
Content Host, Outpost	Live Media Presence Sites	You can interact with your fans live using sites like Ustream (ustream.tv) and Livestream (livestream.com) to basically have your own live TV show. And services like Google Hangouts (google .com/tools/dlpage/res/talkvideo /hangouts) and Skype (skype.com) allow you to have two-way video chats. Taking it a step further, sites like Second Life (secondlife.com) allow you to have a presence in a virtual world.

Continued...

Type	What	Description
Outpost	Location Sharing Sites	While you may want your location to remain private, some musicians may want to broadcast where they are using social sites like Foursquare (foursquare.com). This is especially useful when you are on tour.
Outpost	Mobile Presences	You can have your fans carry you around with them on their phones and mobile devices using services like Myxer (myxer.com), Mobile Roadie (mobileroadie.com), or ReverbNation (reverbnation.com).
Content Host, Outpost	Gig Calendar	You can keep gig calendars in many different ways on your Web presences, but it's best to do it through services that allow you to easily share it to your Web presences and have your fans request you play in their cities. Use tools like Eventful (eventful.com) or JamBase (jambase.com) as we discuss in the chapter.
Conversion Tool	Music Store	As we talk about in chapter 6, "Your Albums, Merchandise, and Sales," you will want embeddable stores for music. No matter whether you sell digital, physical, or on-demand products you can easily drop in widgets, apps, or plug-ins to sell your merch directly to your fans from all of your Web presences.
Conversion Tool	Merch Store	Similar to selling music through a music store (above), there are embeddable stores for merchandise.
Conversion Tool	Donations	If you take donations, have the widget available so that you can post it directly to your Web presences and take donations no matter where you go. Sites like PayPal (paypal.com) or Kickstarter (kickstarter.com) can allow you to do this.

Type	What	Description
Conversion Tool	Mailing List	If you have a mailing list, you will want to embed a widget to capture e-mail addresses in all of your Web presences. Sites like ReverbNation, HostBaby (hostbaby.com), and Band Letter (bandletter.com) allow you to create widgets and embed them into Web presences.
Conversion Tool	Contact Tools	Use contact tools to embed e-mail or contact forms in your Web presences to make yourself easy to reach.
Conversion Tool	One-Click Sharing	When you work with your Web presences, especially your Web site and blog, you may want easy ways to let fans show what they think of them or share them with their friends. Tools like the Like button on Facebook (facebook .com), the +1 button from Google (google.com/+1/button), and autoposting tools like ShareThis (sharethis.com) or Shareaholic (shareaholic.com) can help make it easy for your fans.
Autoposting Tool	Autoposting Solutions	Once you create your content hosts, listed earlier, use tools like HootSuite (hootsuite.com) or Ping (ping.fm) to automatically post the information to all of your outposts. (And note that in some cases, you can autopost without a tool.)
Alerts and Notifications	Google Alerts	Set up Google Alerts (google.com/alerts) to get e-mails when your artist name, your album or project names, and the names of your band members appear anywhere on the Web. You should also watch bands with music that is similar to yours to get ideas about where to get mentioned yourself. This tool can watch blogs, social media, and nearly everywhere on the Web that you get talked about.

Continued...

Type	What	Description
Alerts and Notifications	Social Media Alerts	Tools like SocialOomph (socialoomph.com) allow you to get e-mails when someone tweets your band name or mentions your Twitter ID. This allows you to be very responsive with very little effort.
Metrics Tool	Web Analytics	Tools like Google Analytics (google.com/analytics) allow you to hook metrics into your Web sites and even your blog and Web presences to find out where your visitors came from, what they clicked on, and how long they stayed.
Metrics Tool	Band Statistics Tools	Sites like Next Big Sound (nextbigsound.com) and ReverbNation (reverbnation.com) grab stats from multiple presences and combine them into a single dashboard to tell you how you've been doing.
Metrics Tool	Social Statistics Tools	If you have a Facebook fan page (facebook.com), you will get weekly stats as to how it's doing. This also includes tools that track sites like Twitter, using tools like Twitter Counter (twittercounter.com) and Klout (klout.com).
Helpful Hint	Log-in and Password Solutions	Keeping track of all of the sites, log-ins, and passwords is a challenge. Use tools like Google Docs (docs.google.com), where you can make a spreadsheet that is protected to keep track of it all, or, for a more secure solution, use password tools like Password Gorilla (fpx.de/fp/Software/Gorilla).

WHAT EVERY MUSICIAN SHOULD KNOW ABOUT USER AGREEMENTS AND PRIVACY POLICIES

Most every Web site where you create an account will have a user agreement. When you signed up for these sites as an individual, you probably didn't bother reading them. Unfortunately, with your band and its music at stake, you need to start paying attention to these, since some may require you to give up certain rights.

You must make sure that these agreements don't overreach and hamper any plans you have for your music, videos, or other content you upload. For example, the user agreements for music sites can be especially aggressive about copyrights, sometimes dictating that you give them the right to sell your music on compilation albums or to use it in other ways you might find objectionable. We routinely find Web sites that have bad user agreements and decide not to use them.

Also, if you're sharing on the Web, you should be aware of your own privacy rights, as well as the band's. Photos you share often have GPS location data embedded as metadata—and so, while you're thinking you're sharing just the photo, you may also be sharing your location.

To avoid these kinds of problems, read the agreement of every Web site and make sure that you can live with it. If you are uncertain about the meanings behind any agreements, you should consult with your attorney.

HOW TO SET UP YOUR OWN PRIVACY POLICY
FOR YOUR WEB SITE AND MAILING LIST

If people are going to be sharing their information with you, which they may do on your Web site, on your mailing list, or by giving information to any one of your Web presences or conversion tools, then they'll want to know their private information is safe with you. With identity theft and spam on the rise, it's not hard to understand why. To set people at ease, you should post a policy for how you plan to handle the personal information you collect from them and adhere to it.

We suggest that you keep it simple and set a policy that all personal information you collect from others will only be used to keep the band in contact with those who sign up. Promise you won't sell or otherwise give any information to any third parties for other purposes. The idea, after all, is to build trust with the fans that are willing to give you their information so you can contact them.

You should create a page at your Web site where you announce your policy. It doesn't have to be in legalese. Plain English will do. You should link to this page from all pages related to your mailing list.

If you'd like a sample privacy policy, go to IndieGuide.com/WebStrategy for one that you can use or modify for your own needs.

HOW TO AUTOMATICALLY SIGN UP FOR DOZENS OF WEB PRESENCES AND KEEP THEM UP-TO-DATE

If you've done even a small amount of research, you've noticed that there's a multitude of places to post a profile and try to get your music out there. While you can post on them by hand, one by one, if you want it done for you, pay services can handle submitting your music to many sites and keeping the profiles synchronized.

To use a pay service, do the following:

1. **Choose a service.** Services like ArtistData (artistdata.com) will open profiles for you at many different sites using the same data and then keep them synchronized.

2. **Prepare your bio, pictures, music, and avatar.** Although these sites will submit you to many places on the Web, you still need to prepare your profile information, as discussed in chapter 4, "Your Brand."

3. **Keep the user agreements in mind.** Just because a service is submitting profiles on your behalf doesn't mean that you get out of the user agreements. Make sure that you are comfortable with the user agreements on the places that are posting music.

4. **Visit the sites afterward.** Even while using services like this, keep track of every site that you're on and log on often. You may be able to configure them to pick up your blog automatically or have more services. Also, keep a list of everywhere that you're mentioned in case you decide to stop using these services.

LEARNING MORE

Go to IndieGuide.com/WebStrategy for a clickable version of every link, Web site, and service mentioned in this chapter, as well as free extra materials to help you build your brand.

CHAPTER 9   YOUR WEB,

THE STRATEGIC GOAL: to set up your global Web, social, and mobile presences so you can (1) share media and content once and have it spread across the social Web automatically, (2) know when people are talking about you and where, and (3) stay as connected and engaged as you want to be with minimal effort so you can grow your fan base, build engagement, and make it easy for your fans to share and promote you and your music worldwide with their social networks

REFERENCE PAGE: IndieGuide.com/Social

CHECKLIST: Refer to chapter 8, "Your Web Strategy."

SOCIAL, AND MOBILE PRESENCES

"The fundamental desire for an artist to connect with an audience has always existed and will always exist. Technology just amplifies this."

—PANOS PANAY, FOUNDER AND CEO OF SONICBIDS

AS WE discussed in chapter 8, "Your Web Strategy," the goal for your band is to share parts of your musical life just once and have them automatically appear everywhere that you have a presence. To reach this goal, you need to set up your Web presences in the first place and then weave them together so they are coordinated. When you snap a photo, post a song, upload a video, or write an occasional blog entry, you want all of your outposts to get the latest news and let computers do the hard work.

In other words, you want to "set it and forget it." This chapter covers how to "set it." It covers all of the tools you need for each of the six categories.

Here's a summary of the types of services that you will find here:

1. **Content Hosts.** Your home bases for photos, audio, news (text), videos, and more.

2. **Outposts.** Web, social, and mobile presences where fans can find you.

3. **Autoposting Tools.** Tools that pick up new posts from your content hosts and effortlessly update of all of your outposts.

4. **Conversion Tools.** Widgets and services that will get your customers to take an action, such as buying music, signing up for your mailing list, or share a song with their friends.

5. **Alert and Notification Tools.** Tools that send automated alerts whenever you are talked about on the Web, within blogs, or on social networks.

6. **Metrics Tools.** Provide statistics so you can keep track of how well your sales are doing, how often you are getting played, and how many fans and subscribers you have across all of your presences, allowing you to measure how effective your marketing and publicity strategies are doing.

For each of these categories, we will cover what each presence or service is and why it's important, how to set it up, how to handle autoposting to and from it, how to use it effectively, how to get notified when people use it, and how to get statistics from it.

In this chapter, as in chapter 6, "Your Albums, Merchandise, and Sales," you will see some presences or services mentioned repeatedly, since some of them can do many things. While at times, piecemeal solutions are best, know that there are more comprehensive and complete solutions that may be worth looking into such as ReverbNation (reverbnation.com), Bandcamp (bandcamp.com), or Topspin (topspinmedia.com).

Finally, the easiest way to use this chapter is to use the table from chapter 8, "Your Web Strategy," so you can make a plan, fill in each slot, and then use the specific steps below to get the most out of each type of service.

AUTOPOSTING TOOLS

HOW TO SET UP ALL OF YOUR PRESENCES SO YOU CAN
"POST ONCE AND SEND EVERYWHERE"

What autoposting is and why to use it

Autoposting tools allow you to post each type of content—like photos, videos, or news stories—just once and send the data to your outposts. For example, when you post a new video, the autoposting tools will automatically tweet "New Video: Cube Farm http://bit.ly/u16ntI." Or when you post a new blog entry, you want the blog text to appear on your Facebook fan page. Autoposting tools are how everything that your band shares can appear on all of your outposts with no effort on your part.

Note that autoposting tools are used for many content types, but when it comes to sharing your blog, you may be able to hook it up directly to outposts. For example, if you want to hook up your blog to Last.fm, you'll just use the feed from your blog directly. (Don't worry: we'll explain how at IndieGuide.com/Social).

How to set up autoposting

To set up autoposting tools, use the following steps:

1. **Choose your autoposting tools.** Sign up for a site like HootSuite (hootsuite.com) or Ping (ping.fm) to automatically post the information to all of your outposts. Try them out, since their basic functionality is free. Autoposting tools don't necessarily talk to the same networks, so it's possible you might have to use multiple autoposters to ensure good coverage.

2. **Configure the tool you've selected to send your posts out automatically.** Follow the instructions in each tool to automatically pick up new posts and send them out. As you add more content hosts and outposts, make sure to add them to the autoposting tool.

How to get metrics from autoposting tools

Most autoposting tools have great metrics built in—there's no need to get external tools to get metrics out of them. Explore the tools and see what they provide!

CONTENT HOSTS AND OUTPOSTS

HOW TO SET UP AND USE A BLOG (AND WHY EVERY MUSICIAN SHOULD HAVE ONE)

What a blog is and why to use it

Blogs have changed the nature of how people communicate and interact with each other and have even changed the nature of journalism itself. Originally coined from the terms "Web" and "log," early blogs were essentially online diaries. Blogs soon evolved into a communication form to rival the popularity and quality of print media.

Every band should have a blog. Blogs are the perfect place to share news, stories, and info. They can accommodate updates from many different band members. They're easy to use: in fact, most blogs make it as easy as writing e-mail. And the most important part is that they are easy to share. Using RSS or Atom feeds from your blog (which every major blog provider has), your latest news can be posted to every outpost, social network, or Web site where you have a presence. If you don't have a blog, you'll have to find some other way to post your latest info to all of your Web presences and social networks.

How to set up a blog

To set up a blog, use the following steps:

1. **Choose a blog host.** If you already have a Web site, it's possible that you have a blog built in. Otherwise, it may be a good idea for you to use a blog host such as Blogger (blogger.com), Tumblr (tumblr.com), or WordPress (wordpress.com)—or, see IndieGuide.com/Social for links to more blog providers. Once you settle on a host, fill out the profile and see if you can make an about page for a longer bio. Most blogs also have a links page, so that you can link to all of your Web presences, including your Web page.

2. **Set up band members and promoters as users so that they can write articles.** Each of your band members can contribute, and you can set them up shortly after making your blog.

3. **Embed your blog into your Web site.** Blogs are the first thing you see on most Web sites, showing the latest info and news about the band. Different blog hosts will give you different options of embedding your blog into your Web site, for example as a snippet of HTML code or as an RSS or Atom feed.

How to autopost to blogs

While it's not too common to autopost to a blog, if you need your blog to mirror posts from other sources, it's fairly easy:

1. **Decide which autoposting technique to use.** Go to your blog host and check the options for posting. Your autoposting tool may also be able to handle it. The most common methods to look for are e-mail, RSS, or Atom feeds. The site Posterous (posterous.com) is particularly good at picking up autoposting.

2. **Set up and test the autoposter.** Before depending on it, try it out. Be ready to delete the test posts.

How to autopost from blogs

Autoposting from a blog is the most important feature and is relatively simple to do. But you need to do one technical step: get the feed URL. It will be used over and over again to hook up your Web presences. Here's how to do it:

1. **Determine the feed URL for your blog.** Depending on your browser, you can find out the feed URL for your blog by clicking on the little RSS icon (which is usually orange with what looks like a radio wave) or a FEED icon and copying the URL out of the address bar. Knowing your feed URL is critical, so if you need help doing this, go to IndieGuide .com/Social for tools that will help you pull your feed URL.

2. **Consider using a feed tool.** If you're a little more technically savvy, try using tools like FeedBurner (feedburner.google.com) to help you manage the feed. It will keep track of how many people are subscribing to it, as well as give you more flexibility: your feed URL won't change, even if you move your blog to different hosts or tools.

How to use blogs effectively

Because you will be using autoposting tools to send the latest news about your band to social networks, Web presences, and your Web site, you will want to use the blog to post news, show info, embed videos, share major announcements, and post links to any articles, blogs, or reviewers that write about you.

Also, you should use your blog to highlight and link to other people with blogs of their own. Why? Because when you do this and tell them about it, they are inclined to link to your blog, which can bring you new readers.

How to get alerted and notified when people read
the blog and comment on it

Most blog hosts will have configurations to alert you when people comment on your blog posts, usually giving the option of sending you an e-mail when they do. Unless you have a very active blog, turn this on. You'll be able to keep up with your fans' posts with very little effort on your part.

How to get metrics from blogs

Many of the blog providers have built-in metrics that let you see how many visitors you have, what articles they read, how long they spend, and what links on other Web sites visitors click on to find your blog. Explore your provider's features to see what they do. And some blogs will easily let you build in metrics tools like Google Analytics (google.com/analytics), which you should use to give you even more advanced metrics features to track the people who use your blog.

Finally, if you can use FeedBurner for your feed, you can get an idea of how many subscribers you have to your feeds.

HOW TO HOST YOUR PHOTOS AND IMAGES ON THE WEB

What photo hosts are and why to use them

Photos are a surprisingly important part of a band's existence. Similar to the rest of the Web presences we talk about here, you'll want to host and share your photos from just one place, to make it easy for you to manage and share them. Nearly all of the larger providers of photo hosting allow you to use feeds, autoposting tools, embedded albums, and social applications to easily share images with social networks. Keep in mind when choosing a photo-hosting site that many begin charging money for additional storage space or advanced features.

How to set up a photo host

To set up a photo-hosting site, do the following:

1. **Choose a photo host.** Photo hosts are often initially free and vary widely in terms of what services they provide. It's worth it to play with a few of them before you settle on one. Try out Picasa (picasa.com), Flickr (flickr.com), Photobucket (photobucket.com), or Instagram (instagr.am). For more options, go to IndieGuide.com/Social since there are dozens of services that provide this. Make sure to read the agreements on any photo host that you use, since they may affect the rights that you have to pictures you post. Once you settle on a host, fill out the profile with your bio, avatar, and links to your Web page.

2. **Set up band members as users so that they can post pictures.** It's possible for each of your band members to contribute, and you can set them up as users as well.

3. **Embed your photo host into your Web site and social presences.** Most music Web sites have a photo or image section, and nearly every photo host makes it easy to embed to your site. Also, see if the host has social sharing tools, like Facebook apps.

4. **Verify the rights settings.** Many of the photo hosts will let you set the license rights of the photos that you post, which you may want to be aware of before you post them. Some of these rights are Creative Commons licenses (creativecommons.org), which are perpetual rights that let people share the photos at will as long as they give you attribution, some granting commercial or noncommercial rights. Make sure you are comfortable with the rights that you are granting.

How to autopost to a photo host

Explore your photo host for the methods that it allows for the autoposting of photos. Methods can include sending e-mails with photo attachments to it or using mobile applications that automatically post photos, or the host can give you uploading tools that make it easy to organize your pictures.

How to autopost from a photo host

Autoposting from most of the major photo hosts—for example, posting to Twitter when you upload new photos—is usually built in to tools like Hoot-Suite (hootsuite.com). Photo hosts also provide RSS or Atom feeds that you can use in order to pick up the pictures and send them elsewhere. And most of the largest providers make it easy to share your photos on Facebook and other social networks using Facebook apps.

How to use photo hosts effectively

Consider using these techniques when using photo hosts:

- Take pictures of every band event and show. Also, make sure to take a lot of pictures while recording your music or even preparing for any events. Each of these can provide great behind-the-scenes photos for your band to use.

- Don't post every single photo that you take. The reason you will want to take a lot of pictures is so that you can post the best ones.

- Crop and color-correct the best pictures; don't just post them raw.

- Make albums so that it's easier for people to find particular photos, and separate one folder just for publicity shots.

HOW TO HOST YOUR MUSIC ON THE WEB

What music hosts are and why to use them

As soon as you have music ready to go, you will likely want to share it with people on the Web in music players, on Web sites, and on your social presences. Similar to photos and videos, you will want to post your music just once and let a tool autopost it to the rest of your Web presences.

Unlike photos and videos, many of the places that allow you to post your music do not make it possible for you to easily share it. There are a few that allow this, many of which charge fees for the service (because they often have to pay licensing fees to music companies).

It's worth your time to research the services that provide music hosting, since many of them provide other services like handling music sales and providing widgets to let your fans more easily share your music with friends. In fact, since a large amount of Web browsing now happens on mobile devices, you will want to make sure that your site handles this as well.

Finally, many music-hosting sites have questionable user agreements that give them rights to your music—sometimes perpetual or licensing rights. These are often buried in the agreements. Even phrases like, "you will always own your music," don't mean that the agreement is safe from bad clauses. Read them carefully before you use them. Our band skips bad ones all the time.

How to set up a music host

1. **Choose a music host.** Similar to sites that host other types of media, the basic level of many of the music-hosting sites is free, but advanced features and extra storage will cost you. Each one also has very different capabilities. Compare ReverbNation (reverbnation.com), Bandcamp (bandcamp.com), SoundCloud (soundcloud.com), and Topspin (topspinmedia.com), or, if you want more options, go to IndieGuide .com/Social since there are dozens of services that provide these features.

    Features that you will want to compare between services include the following:

o   Selling tracks directly from the player (or providing a link to where listeners can buy).

o   Embeddable widgets that you can post elsewhere on the Web.

o   Downloadable tracks from the player and the optional ability to ask them to provide an e-mail address.

o   Integration with social media, such as Facebook applications.

o   Players that work in mobile devices.

o   E-mail widgets, to make it easy to e-mail tracks out to people.

o   Good metrics so you can get an idea about who is playing your music and when.

Of course, fill out the profile with your bio, avatar, and links to your Web page.

2.   **Set up band members as users so that they can post music.** If you have more than one person who is posting the music, configure the site to let others post to these sites.

3.   **Embed your music into your Web site and social presences.** Music-hosting sites have widgets and methods to share music to Web sites, Web presences, and social sites. Also, check if the music host has social sharing tools such as Facebook apps.

How to autopost from music hosts

Many of the sharing sites have methods to automatically tweet or post when there's new music, or they hook into the more popular autoposting tools. Some also have RSS or Atom feeds that can be used for autoposting.

How to use music hosting effectively

By the time you've gotten a visitor to hit play on one of your music players, you've got a chance at turning a casual visitor into a fan. The best music players will allow your fans to do more than listen: they will make it easy to buy the song (or download it if you're giving it away) and share it, or they will capture a visitor's e-mail address for your newsletter. Each song you put out can help with this.

Use the features in your music host to get visitors to connect with you, and capture as much information about your fans as possible.

Do the following to use a music host effectively:

1.   **Post a lot of tracks, especially extras.** The more tracks you post, the more there is for your fans to explore. Also, you will want to add alternate takes and other versions of songs that you release. Note that even if you like sharing as many tracks as possible, you may want to hold some back as giveaways for joining your mailing list or other actions you'd like to reward.

Most music sharing sites allow you to choose which tracks are available for download (although, once it's online, it can always be downloaded even if it's not as easy). For those that you decide to give away, make sure you've filled in all of the ID3 tags on MP3s (and see chapter 2, "Your Music," on how to fill in these tags).

2.   **Post links to buy your music alongside the tracks.** You want to make it easy for fans listening to your songs to immediately buy them. The players that embed buy links are the most effective at capturing impulse sales.

How to get alerted and notified when people listen to and comment on your music

Each hosting site will have methods to notify you if someone makes a comment on your music or uses your songs. Make sure to explore these options and turn on the automatic notifications so you can be responsive to your fans without having to keep an eye on the site.

How to get metrics from music hosts

Nearly all music-hosting sites have useful metrics, including the number of plays and other stats related to the fans themselves. Also, depending on the site, they may report their song plays to Next Big Sound (nextbigsound .com).

how to host your videos on the web

If you create videos, they can be a major part of your Web presence. Video sites make it so easy to upload and share video that the days when musicians were to be heard but not seen are long gone. And, just like the other media-hosting sites, you will want to post your videos in just one place and share them on the rest of your Web presences.

Video is better at getting a visitor's attention, but it has some shortcomings. For one thing, video has a lower replay value. People are more willing to watch a video they've never seen than to listen to a song they've never heard, but if they like the song, they will listen to it over and over. Videos are lucky if they get watched more than once by the same user. The goal is to use the video not just to introduce people to the song in the video but also to get people to buy the music or visit your Web site so they'll discover what else you offer. It's critical to brand your video and link back to your site so that they can find out more about you. This is especially true since you can never be sure where your video is embedded on the Web.

We talk about making and encoding videos in chapter 14, "Get Seen." In this section, we'll talk about how to use video hosting services as a place to host your videos and embed them into your Web site and other presences.

How to set up a video host

1. **Choose a video host.** Two video hosts you can use are YouTube (youtube.com) and Vimeo (vimeo.com). Go to IndieGuide.com/Social for a full list of video hosts. No matter what you use, you should have a YouTube account in addition to any other ones you may want to use. The channel-subscription features of YouTube can make it compelling for fans to follow you. Don't forget to fill out the profile with your bio, avatar, and links to your Web page.

2. **Set up accounts so that more than one band member can post.** If you have more than one person who is posting the music, configure the site to let others post videos (or have a shared user and password).

3. **Embed your videos into your Web site and social presences.** It's a good idea to create a page on your Web site that contains many of your videos.

How to autopost from video hosts

Nearly all video hosts allow easy autoposting based on feeds or other players. It's especially simple to use autoposting tools to post to Twitter when you add a new video, and many of the video sites, including YouTube, can post to your social presences without external tools.

How to use video hosting effectively

Do the following to use your video hosts effectively:

1. **Use quality sound and video encoding.** Go to chapter 14, "Get Seen," for detailed information on how to encode the highest-quality sound and video.

2. **Use compelling titles that tease people into watching the videos.** You are not stuck just posting the name of the song as the title for your video. Think about the videos that you click on: more of them have over-the-top titles than you might think.

3. **Don't just go with the default image from the middle of the video: choose an appealing frame to use as the video's image to make it more likely that people will click it.** A lot of musicians make the mistake of not choosing which frame to use as the default image for the video. Your best choice is to use a frame that's sexy, sensational, or otherwise eye-catching.

4. **Post buy links with the videos.** If you post a music video and the song is for sale, post a link to where the song is for sale as the very first comment for the video so you can capture impulse buys.

5. **Add a video coda to the end of the video so it's not the same as the versions that are for sale.** Add a little extra video at the end so that the video audio—which is easy to rip into an MP3—is not the same as the song that people can purchase.

6. **Consider making a video blog.** If you want to do a video blog, you can use your YouTube channel for hosting it. There are two ways to do it: use a separate channel, or just make a separate playlist with your video blog. If you do this, keep a regular and consistent release schedule, and make sure all the information you want to share is inside the videos. For a good example of this, see what Nice Peter, co-creator of the incredibly popular Epic Rap Battles of History (youtube.com/user/erb), does on his second channel Nice Peter Too (youtube.com/user/nicepetertoo), where he shares personal stories and answers letters.

How to get alerted and notified when people watch and comment on your videos

Each video site, especially YouTube, makes it easy to get e-mails when people post comments to your videos. You will want to activate this so that you can actively respond to fans.

How to get metrics from video hosts

Video sites often have stats worth exploring. YouTube has a stats feature that can also give you demographic information about your viewers. Most video sites also report their song plays to Next Big Sound (nextbigsound.com).

HOW TO SET UP YOUR OWN PODCAST

What podcasting is and why to use it

Podcasts are like a radio show that people can subscribe to. Although every band should have a blog, starting a podcast is optional. A podcast can be quite a time commitment. Then again, it can give you a regular audience and a platform to share regular content with fans. George Hrab has gotten a lot of regular fans with his *Geologic* podcast (geologicpodcast.com). His large subscriber base is excited when he releases new albums, and he has a great platform to announce anything that he's doing in music.

How to set up a podcast

Do the following to set up your podcast:

1. **Do the research.** Podcasting is a big topic, and if you are going to make one, it's worth learning how to do it well. We suggest reading the excellent guide *Podcasting for Dummies*, by Tee Morris and Evo Terra.

2. **Choose a podcast host.** You can podcast from music-sharing sites like SoundCloud (soundcloud.com) and WordPress (wordpress.org) or from plug-ins like PodPress (podpress.org), or you can explore hosted solutions like Libsyn (libsyn.com) or Podbean (podbean.com). Once you do, fill out the profile with your bio and avatar.

3. **Submit the podcast to iTunes and other podcasting directories.** By far, iTunes is the most active podcast directory. You will want to get an iTunes account and then submit your podcast once you have some episodes released. (They will actually review the podcast to make sure

THE INDIE BAND SURVIVAL GUIDE

that it's acceptable to them.) See their podcast page for info (www.apple.com
/itunes/podcasts/specs.html). Also consider submitting to Podcast Alley
(podcastalley.com) and Podcast Pickle (www.podcastpickle.com).

How to autopost from podcasts

Podcasts, by definition, have RSS or Atom feeds. It's easy to use autoposting
tools to send new entries to all of your other sites using the feed.

How to use podcasts effectively

Here are some points of advice specifically about music podcasts that aren't
well covered in podcast books:

1. **Precreate episodes.** If you want to keep people subscribed and
   interested in your podcast, create a group of episodes ahead of time so that
   you don't get behind. The most important factor with podcasts is to have
   regular releases. And it's best to just do them all at once, in just a few sessions
   in the studio, so it doesn't interfere with your music.

2. **Use high-music-quality encodes.** Music podcasters, such as
   yourself, can't afford to have poor encoding for your podcast. Bad sound
   quality can reflect on the music. This occurs often because even musicians
   will use MP3 files of their music instead of the raw WAV files when they
   make a podcast. This ends up encoding the music *twice*. Always use WAV
   files for your music before you encode the podcast into MP3.

3. **Boost the talking tracks if you have any.** If you do any talking in
   your podcast, perform compression, EQ, and boost the volume the same way
   you would to release a music track. If you want a quick way to make the
   talking parts pop, use the Levelator (www.conversationsnetwork.org/
   levelator) on the WAV files of the tracks, *before you encode them into an
   MP3*. And do not use Levelator on your music WAV files.

How to get metrics from podcasts

Almost every podcast host will have stats that you can explore about your
podcast, including the number of downloads. Explore the host. Also, since
the feed itself is an RSS feed, if you are more technically savvy you can use
FeedBurner (feedburner.com) for your feed, so you can see how many subscribers you have.

SOCIAL SITES

HOW TO USE TWITTER AS A MUSICIAN

What Twitter is and why to use it

Twitter at its heart is simple: it's a site where you can post updates, as long as they are 140 letters or fewer. It's also become nearly mandatory for every artist to have a Twitter account. The good news is that nearly everything you do online can automatically post to Twitter. Even better, it's easy to get automatically notified when people talk about you or to you. This means that you can be active on Twitter while doing what you normally do as a musician, with no extra effort beyond setting it up. And you can answer anyone that talks directly to you without needing to constantly check into it.

Here are a few reasons why you will want to use Twitter as a musician:

- You can easily hook it up and have it tweet automatically when you do anything online, such as posting a video, blog, song, or picture.

- It allows you to give people updates that are too short for blog or news entries.

- Marketing research states that it takes 7–10 mentions of a name to get people to recognize a brand. After reading 7–10 tweets, they will start remembering you.

- Fans now expect musicians to have Twitter accounts.

Here are a few terms and facts that will help you navigate Twitter if you haven't used it:

- **Tweet:** a single post on Twitter.

- **Tweeting:** the act of posting on Twitter.

- **The @ (at) sign:** this is the best way to mention someone else on Twitter. It makes it easy to notify them that you mentioned them (and it's simple to find out when someone directs an @ post to you). For example, our band is @beatnikturtle and this book is @indieguide (go ahead and shout out to us, we love it and do answer posts).

- **The # hashtag sign:** adding this to a word (for example #indiemusic) will tell people that you're talking about a particular topic. Twitter will easily let you see all posts marked with a particular hashtag and group them together.

- **A direct message (DM):** a direct message is like a little e-mail inside Twitter. They are still just 140 characters long, but only the recipient can read it.

- **Retweet:** reposting another person's tweet. Twitter makes this easy, allowing you to retweet by just pressing a button on the post.

- **Follow Friday:** on Fridays, you will see tweets with the hashtag #ff where people make recommendations of other Twitter accounts to follow. You know that you've gotten some traction when people recommend your Twitter account.

How to set up an account on Twitter

1. **Sign up on Twitter.** Twitter's sign-up is right on the front page. You should also verify your account immediately by clicking on the link that gets sent to your e-mail, which will give you extra capabilities in your account. Also, after setting it up, follow anyone that you are interested in, especially if you're new to Twitter and want to get a feel for it.

2. **Fill out the profile.** Fill out the short profile with your band's tagline, post your avatar, and include a link to your Web page.

3. **Start posting.** You'll need to warm up your account with a few posts in order to start getting followers yourself and prove that you're not a spam account. You may want to just make some posts for a few days before you do the next step.

4. **Start getting new followers by finding accounts of bands similar to yours and following their followers.** Getting new followers is simple. Just find bands or artists that have music similar to yours, and follow their followers. Make sure to avoid the spam accounts that are clearly just there to promote something. If you're the tagline on your account and there are some good posts in your account already, some of them will start following you back.

5. **Put your Twitter links on your Web sites and Web presences.** Most Web presences now have a place to enter your Twitter account so it can

display your feed; you should also link to Twitter from your Web site so people can follow you if they want to.

How to autopost to Twitter

Nearly everything you do online can autopost to Twitter, which makes it a perfect place to keep a feed of everything that you're up to.

Use the following steps to autopost to Twitter:

1. **Autopost to Twitter from RSS or Atom feeds (such as blogs or podcasts).** Use autoposting tools like HootSuite (hootsuite.com) or Ping (ping.fm) to autopost new tweets when there are updates from any feed. Simply put in the address of a blog or other source, and these tools will be able to post new entries to Twitter.

2. **Autopost pictures and videos from your mobile devices.** Autoposting sites for Twitter allows you to automatically post pictures and videos by just e-mailing them to an account. Try services like Twitpic (twitpic.com) or yfrog (yfrog.com). Also, many of the photo-hosting sites like Flickr (flickr.com) or Photobucket (photobucket.com) allow you to do the same thing. For a fancy twist, try Instagram (instagr.am), which has preset filters allowing you to edit the photos on your mobile device.

   If you are going to be active on Twitter, and you have a phone that can take pictures, it's a good idea to snap photos often, and post them to your Twitter feed, because it's a way to bring your fans a more immediate experience about your band. We especially recommend taking pictures when you are doing music-related activities that fans don't normally get to see, such as being inside the recording studio or backstage before a show.

How to autopost from Twitter

Twitter itself has RSS and Atom feeds that can be easily picked up to use for autoposting. Also, many other tools and sites that can use the Twitter feed will just need your Twitter account password so that they can pick up the latest status.

How to use Twitter effectively

Being successful on Twitter is simply about being active and sharing. Fans that enjoy your music already have a reason to follow you, but the goal is to gain new followers by sharing things that that new fans might enjoy. Here are ideas:

1. **After setting up autoposting tools, share often.** Pictures and videos are easy to take and automatically tweet (see the autoposting section on page 223 for sites that do this for you). If you have a mobile device, do it often, since it gives your followers a glimpse into your life as a musician.

2. **Use the @ sign to get people involved and retweet often.** Since people will know when you post an @ message, mention people by name if you are active on Twitter. Many major musicians and media companies have teams of social media staff that just keep track of who is talking about them, and they'll follow back so fans feel like they have a personal relationship with the musician. They also appreciate when you retweet their posts.

3. **Follow people that can help your career, and ask questions to see who can help you.** For example, we once wanted to get in touch with the music planning committee for a convention at which we wanted to perform. We knew that some of the people who followed our posts were associated with that convention, so we posted our query on Twitter. Within minutes, they put us directly in touch.

4. **Interact with your fans.** You can do more than just send tweets back and forth with your fans. For example, reading our friends' posts, it occurred to us that a lot of the more witty tweets might make great inspiration for songs. We soon started writing a few "TwitterSongs," all appropriately shorter than 140 seconds, and posting them to our Web site TheSong OfTheDay.com. We wrote a song called "I Am My Mom and Dad's Tech Support," based on a lament by one of our friends. And "Leftover Leftovers," after a post about cleaning a fridge.

Naturally, when we posted "TwitterSongs," we'd tweet about it and include a link to the file as well as a shout out to whomever wrote the original tweet. Many times the posters who'd inspired the songs would blog about them on their own sites. The next thing we knew, we'd get more followers, with people hoping their own tweets would inspire the next Twitter song.

5. **Ask fans to tweet about you.** Simply asking fans to tweet about you, or your music, is a surprisingly good way to get some exposure.

6.   **Use @ mentions and try for retweets.** People tend to retweet anything that promotes or mentions their own names. If you tweet @ someone and provide a link to, say, a video or song that is related, they may pass it on to their own Twitter audience.

7.   **Read up on Twitter promotion.** There are always new ideas on using Twitter to promote since it's such an active social site. If you want to research this more, go to IndieGuide.com/Social for links to the latest blogs and books about promoting yourself on Twitter.

How to get alerted when people mention you, talk about you, or follow you on Twitter

Twitter has so many users and it's such a great place to find out what people are talking about that you will want to know when people are talking to you. Fortunately, it's easy to get notified if your Twitter name or band name are mentioned. Use these tools to automate all of the aspects of your Twitter account:

1.   **Use tools to automatically follow people who follow you, and send them a welcome message when they do.** Tools such as SocialOomph (socialoomph.com) will automatically follow people who follow you and will allow you to send a direct message to any who do. You might want to think about giving them a link to a free song on your Web site in the welcome message.

2.   **Set up an alert on keywords so that you get e-mailed when you are talked about.** Sites like SocialOomph (socialoomph.com) and Twilert (twilert.com) can watch for any words that get mentioned on Twitter. We suggest getting e-mail alerts when the following comes up: @ mentions of your account, your band name, the names of your albums (only if they're unique; we'd skip this if your album is called *Love*), your Web site name, and the names of your band members. This will make you responsive to fans, reviewers, or even casual mentions.

How to get metrics from Twitter

Twitter allows Web sites and programmers to pull data from it very easily, so there are many sites that let you analyze your Twitter presence. Try using tools like Twitter Counter (twittercounter.com) and Klout (klout.com) to see how effective your Twitter presence is.

HOW TO USE FACEBOOK AS A MUSICIAN

What Facebook is and why to use it

Facebook is a social networking site that allows its users to connect to friends. If the users of Facebook made up a country, it would be the third biggest in the world with a population twice the size of the United States. This is not just a site with a lot of users, it's a site that makes it trivially easy for each user to share links, pictures, videos, and sounds with all of their friends. It's a word-of-mouth multiplier.

Similar to the rest of the Web presences in this chapter, while you certainly should be involved in Facebook, you will not want to spend time on Facebook that you should be spending working on music. Fortunately, you can set up your account so that it picks up everything you do automatically. When you post a picture to your photo host, it should show up on Facebook. And when you post an update to your blog, it should update your fan page.

You will want to use Facebook in two ways. First of all, you'll want to have a fan page so your fans can interact with you and your music on Facebook, including being able to buy music and merchandise. Second, you will want to make it easy for your fans to share things that they enjoy about your music (your albums, videos, and anything else you have) so that their friends will hear about it. We'll talk about how to do both of these here.

How to set up a Facebook fan page

1. **Set up a personal Facebook account for yourself.** If you do not have a Facebook (facebook.com) account yet, create one. Every other step that you need to do requires this. If you are just creating a new account now, search for your friends (or use the feature provided by Facebook that allows you to scan e-mails) and connect with them. This is the first group of people that will help you get the word out.

2. **Create a Facebook fan page for your band.** Go to the bottom of any Facebook page, and find the link Create a Page. Then choose Artist, Band, or Public Figure. Choose Musician/Band from the list, and enter the name.

3. **Fill in the profile fully.** The profile will help people find your booking agent, your Web sites, know what style of music you play, and read your bio.

4. **Invite all of your band members and friends to become fans, to get your fan page started.**

How to autopost to Facebook

It is critical to autopost to your fan page, and especially to hook your fan page up to your blog, so that your latest status updates mirror your blog (or possibly Twitter). Here's how:

1. **Use notes or tools to autopost blog entries.** Install and use the Facebook app Notes (facebook.com/notes) or NetworkedBlogs (facebook.com/networkedblogs) to import an RSS feed from your blog.

2. **If photo-, video-, and audio-content hosts provide Facebook applications, use them to add content to your fan page.** Note that for each content host, most of the applications are focused on sending content to regular accounts, and you will want to make sure that the content reaches the fan page rather that your personal account.

How to autopost from Facebook

Go to your fan page and find the link that says Get Notes via RSS. This is the RSS feed for your fan-page notes and can be picked up by autoposting applications.

How to use Facebook to promote your music effectively

There are many disparate items that you will want to pull together to make the Facebook-fan-page experience promote your music. Go through each of these steps separately to weave together a solid Facebook presence for your band. Note that some of the applications, such as ReverbNation (reverb nation.com), Nimbit (nimbit.com), Bandcamp (bandcamp.com), and Top-spin (topspinmedia.com) have a host of features that cut across many of the solutions you might need. Because this area is complicated, changes quickly, and has more than a handful of links that could solve the problem, visit IndieGuide.com/Social if you would like more information and solutions to these problems.

1. **Interact with your fans on Facebook.** The most important part of using Facebook is to interact so that your band is appearing on your fans'

walls. The reason you do this isn't just to reach out to fans but to reach the friends of your fans.

2. **Let your fans listen to music from the fan page.** Apps such as ReverbNation (reverbnation.com) and BandPage (bandpage.com) let you stream music directly from the page. Visit IndieGuide.com/Social for a full list of options for streaming music to fans on Facebook.

3. **Sell music from Facebook.** Music stores such as Bandcamp (bandcamp.com), Nimbit (nimbit.com), ReverbNation (reverbnation.com), BandPage (bandpage.com), Topspin (topspinmedia.com), and CD Baby (cdbaby.com) integrate into your band fan page and allow you to directly drive music sales from Facebook. This space is quickly changing and has many options, so visit IndieGuide.com/Social for a full list of services for selling music on Facebook.

4. **Boost your mailing list from Facebook.** Research the provider you use for your mailing list and see if they have a Facebook application that integrates into your fan page. If you use ReverbNation (reverbnation.com) the MyBand app can capture e-mails and even lets you offer exclusive downloads in return for sign-ups.

5. **Share your show calendar.** You can try out applications like Eventful (eventful.com) and ReverbNation (reverbnation.com) to share your show calendar on your Facebook fan page. The Eventful application has the added benefit of allowing fans to "demand" that you play in their town, which might give you ideas for where you should tour.

6. **Sell merchandise from Facebook.** Applications such as Nimbit (nimbit.com), Topspin (topspinmedia.com), District Lines (districtlines .com), and many of the merch-on-demand sites all have stores that can be integrated into Facebook for sales from your fan page.

7. **Promote your page.** Besides just asking your friends and fans to talk about your fan page with their friends, Facebook makes it simple to buy an ad campaign to promote your fan page. This is only as good as the words you use to promote your page. If you'd like some help with this, ReverbNation (reverbnation.com) has a Promote It service that comes up with a rotating ad campaign for you.

*How to get alerted and notified when people interact
with your Facebook fan page*

If you use any of the applications listed in the above section, make sure to research them to see what kinds of notifications they provide. Further, Facebook itself can send you e-mails when people interact with your fan page. In the settings section, choose to send notifications to you when people post or comment on the page so that you will be automatically notified.

How to get metrics from Facebook

Facebook does a good job of providing metrics and even demographic information on the Insights page in your fan page, and also offers to mail you weekly statuses on your Facebook fan pages. Also, for each post you make, it will tell you how many people you reached and who talked about it afterward. Further, all of the applications you use may have metrics that may be worth exploring.

HOW TO USE GOOGLE+ AS A MUSICIAN
What Google+ is and why to use it

Google+ allows you to share posts, photos, and videos and connect with people. But it has a few key differences from all of the other social networks:

- Google+ entries that are public are indexed by the Google search engine and get a good ranking. This means your posts have two lives: one within Google+ and another on the broader Internet—something that does not happen to posts on Facebook.

- Google+ uses circles to target your posts to particular groups. These circles can let you tailor and aim messages at audiences. This makes your posts more relevant and effective.

Since Google+ accounts are free, this is another social outpost you don't want to miss, especially because it's indexed so well by Google.

How to set up Google+

1. **Create a Google+ account for yourself.** You must have a personal account to create one for your band.

2.   **Create a page.** Use Create a Page, and under Category, choose Arts, Entertainment, or Sports.

    For the page name, enter your band name, add your Web site, and choose Music Band as the type.

3.   **Enter your tagline, avatar, bio, and info, just like on any other site.** Fill in the profile fully. All of this helps you because it's searchable and a potential landing page for your fans.

How to autopost to and from Google+

Because Google+ is changing quickly, go to IndieGuide.com/Social for tools for autoposting to and from Google fan pages.

How to use Google+ effectively

Google+ is one of the newer social networks, and there are always new ideas to explore. Visit IndieGuide.com/Social for links to the latest tools.

1.   **Organize people into circles.** Circles are one of the key advantages of Google+. You might want to organize the people you know into specific groups, such as by location, so you can target messages to them.

2.   **Use hangouts.** Hangouts are meant to be quick, informal ways to video chat with people on Google+. As a musician, you can use it to hold performances and interact with fans in an entirely new way. We talk about this in chapter 7, "Your Gigs," and chapter 14, "Get Seen."

3.   **Use Google+ to link back to your Web pages, and encourage your fans to link to you from their posts.** The links in Google+ are counted highly in the search engine rankings. Links from Google+ can make a real difference in where your Web sites will come up in searches.

For more detailed information on how to use Google+ effectively as a musician, head to IndieGuide.com/Social.

HOW TO USE LAST.FM AS A MUSICIAN
What Last.fm is and why to use it

Many people are familiar with Last.fm as a player that lets you try new music, but at its heart it is a social network based on music. Last.fm has a little application called a Scrobbler that hooks into your music player. This will keep track of what you're listening to and automatically make a feed of the songs, which you can pull into other social networks. As Richard Jones, one of the founders of Last.fm, explained, the idea for "scrobbling" grew out of his frustration for the standard ways to find new music. "I wanted to figure out a way to discover artists I'd like without having to do all the work of culling through music magazines, music Web sites, and doing all that research."

While Richard Jones approached the problem from a *fan* point of view, the implications that scrobbling has for those of us *making* music are profound. Scrobbling can help answer the question: what other music do my fans listen to? Knowing this can help you market to the right people (see chapter 11, "Your Marketing Strategy," for how to target the right audience).

As long as you set up your ID3 tags before distributing your music (see chapter 2, "Your Music," if you want to know how), you will see any Last.fm users that are listening to your music, anywhere in the world. You can reach out to them and friend them, giving you a way to find and reach out to fans that you didn't even know that you had. You will also get an idea of which songs your fans listen to.

How to set up Last.fm

1. **Create a free account on Last.fm.** Your account name can be whatever you want since it is your personal account. You will be using this to create an artist profile, so the name does not matter.

2. **Make sure that all of your song files are properly ID3 tagged.** Last.fm pulls the ID3 tag information off of your MP3s so that it knows the song title and artist name. See chapter 2, "Your Music," for instructions on how to tag your songs correctly.

3. **Search for your band in the music search bar.** If your band's name comes up, that means someone has added you to Last.fm's song database already or it's been added through a digital aggregator that sells your music (CD Baby, TuneCore) and you must claim the artist page as yours.

4. **Download the Last.fm Scrobbler program.** The Scrobbler scans the music you play on the media-player programs on your computer and adds them to your Last.fm profile. You will be using it to listen to your own music.

THE INDIE BAND SURVIVAL GUIDE

5. **Play one of your songs in a media player while the Scrobbler is open.** This will add the song to Last.fm's database or, if it has already been played in the past, bring up current information about the song. You can add and edit a description and tags for the song, too.

6. **Register as an artist or a label.** Go to your Last.fm profile and scroll to the bottom, then click the link that asks if you are an artist or label, and register as one of the two since either one will allow you to claim your songs. Registering as an artist or label allows you to manage your presence on Last.fm.

7. **Perform a search for your band name and then click the link Claim This Artist.** Since you have played one of your songs, your band name should appear now in a search. Claim the artist page as yours.

8. **Select the option to claim royalties.** When your songs are played you are entitled to royalties, so click the box that lets you claim royalties. Remember now that you must only upload songs that are yours—for which you hold the copyright. You will then be asked to add your contact information.

9. **Upload all of your albums and songs.** You can upload your music directly to Last.fm and its streaming radio services (last.fm/uploadmusic). There is no limit to the number of songs or albums you can put on your page, but they must be MP3 files. Add album art to each album if possible. Select the options for how listeners can use your music. You can allow previews, full-length plays, and free downloads. It's your call on how available you want your music to be.

10. **Add and edit the information on your profile.** Now you are the manager of your artist page. Add a band photo or avatar and a band biography. If someone has already added information on your band and it is incorrect, you can click a link on the right-hand side of the page to submit a correction.

How to autopost to Last.fm

1. **Log in to Last.fm.** Note that you'll need to log into the account that "owns" the band. This will give you access to a dashboard so you can edit your band information.

2.   **Have your blog RSS or Atom feed handy and paste it in to the news feature of your band page.** On your band profile within your dashboard, you will see a link to add your latest news; click this and it will ask you for the address of your blog feed; paste this feed in and it will automatically grab the latest posts.

How to use Last.fm effectively

Last.fm is a great place to interact with actual listeners. You'll want to convert them to fans and friend them.

1.   **Friend people that listen to your music.** Our band has a Last.fm account, where we listen to our own music, as well as other music in our collection. We always friend new listeners since this gives us the ability to send messages to them and connect as well as learn more about who they are, what else they listen to, and where they live.

2.   **Sign up to Blaster.fm.** Blaster.fm is a convenient social tool that gives you a way to more easily interact and have online discussions with your Last. fm friends. You can also see what your friends are listening to, suggest tracks to listen to, and more. Signing up with the tool is free.

3.   **Set up the buy links to go to your music stores.** Under the Manage tab you will find Buy Links, which allows you to link to your online music store so listeners can buy your songs easily.

4.   **Participate on Last.fm groups and forums.** You can join Last.fm groups, where fans discuss their favorite music, to connect with even more people and share your songs. If there is one for your own band or your style of music, it's a perfect place to interact with fans.

How to get metrics from Last.fm

First of all, Last.fm has a Statistics page to let you learn more about your listeners. Find out who your top listeners are and where they are located. This can help you plan future tours, see what is most popular, and create personal dialogues with your fans. Check out the tags that your fans use and add applicable ones to your songs and profile.

HOW TO SET UP AND USE LOCATION-SHARING SERVICES
What location sharing is and why to use it

Location sharing sites allow you to post where you are physically located and share that information with followers. Although there are Web sites that have this capability, this is easiest to do with mobile devices that have GPS built in, making it easy to "check in" and show people where you are. The site Foursquare (foursquare.com) has over ten million users.

It's certainly not for everybody, as some people would rather remain private, but if you feel comfortable, try using it when you're on tour. It's an easy way to let people know where on the road you are. You can even just check in at more official locations, leaving hotels that you stay in secret, so that you can have some private moments when you need them, but still share your public appearances.

How to set up location sharing

1. **Choose a location-tracking service.** Services like Foursquare (foursquare.com), Google+ (plus.google.com), and Facebook (facebook.com) all have location-sharing services, but all have different capabilities. They are all free, so it's easy to experiment. Foursquare has the most features out of all of these.

2. **Set up your profile, your avatar, and tagline. Mention this on your Web presences.** Set up your profile for your band and invite people to follow you. Also provide links to your profile on your Web presences.

3. **Share as often as you want.** Each check-in can become part of your story, a way of automatically blogging about where you go. You can add comments and pictures to posts, so this can enhance the experience. If you use location sharing and Twitter, you may want to use these posts to take pictures and share your location in multiple ways.

How to autopost from a location sharing service

Autoposting from tools like Foursquare to Facebook or Twitter is built in, and well worth doing to show where you've been.

How to get metrics from a location sharing service

Besides the sites themselves which often visualize where people are or have been on maps, sites like 4sqmap (4sqmap.com) can analyze Foursquare and give a visual representation of your locations.

HOW TO GET ON WIKIPEDIA (AND HOW NOT TO)

What Wikipedia is and why to use it

Wikipedia is a massive, collaborative encyclopedia that anyone can edit. Surprisingly, even though anyone can change it, the site has developed a large and dedicated community of editors who make it their business to uphold standards of quality and consistency.

Wikipedia covers far more topics than any traditional encyclopedia could. One such area is popular culture, including entries on many bands. Since Wikipedia entries tend to get high page ranks in search engines, these entries are valuable. Wikipedia entries are a decent contributor to traffic for your own Web site.

Some things musicians might not realize about Wikipedia:

- It's an encyclopedia, not a promotional tool. The Wikipedia community frowns on autobiographical entries and especially on blatant self-promotion.

- The Wikipedia community will question any entry that seems insignificant or doesn't live up to its encyclopedic standards: fact-based, no opinions, plenty of citations. Many entries about indie bands are routinely removed if they fail these tests.

- If a Wikipedia entry is created about your band, you don't own it. In fact, your own input about your entry, either in edits you make or on the discussion page that accompanies your entry, will tend to work *against* you. We advise you to avoid taking part, or to at least avoid advertising that you're with the band.

- More and more Web, social, and mobile presences are reposting Wikipedia content, making it even more important as a presence. This means what your article says about you and your music may populate many different sites and services you may not even be aware of. For example, Facebook creates fan groups based on entries and Spotify uses it to populate the bios of many musicians on its service. If you do have a Wikipedia entry and the information is wrong or incomplete, that information may give fans the wrong impression and harm your brand.

How to set up a Wikipedia article

As mentioned above, Wikipedia discourages autobiographical entries. While you can write your own, if the community finds out, they may remove it. Any entries written about you should be factual.

1. **Build your credentials.** You should wait until you have a proven following and established history that can be verified by cited sources such as magazines, blogs, and other third party authorities before creating your own entry. Wikipedia depends on outside sources for verifying its material, so press and media coverage of your band will help a great deal in giving your page legitimacy.

2. **Have a fan or someone outside the band write the entries, if possible.** This follows the rules of Wikipedia most closely. Otherwise, if you write it yourself, keep in mind that it could be used against you.

3. **Find other Wikipedia entries that may be related, and link to and from those entries.** Our entry is linked to podcasters and other pages that have related material, and this gives the page extra legitimacy and weight so that it can be more firmly established.

HOW TO USE VIRTUAL-WORLD SITES LIKE SECOND LIFE TO PROMOTE YOUR MUSIC

What Second Life is and why to use it

Second Life (secondlife.com) is a virtual three-dimensional world, similar to games like World of Warcraft—but without the game. Second Life users, or "residents" as they are called, are represented as three-dimensional animated avatars that can be completely customized. It takes time and technical artistry to create a realistic avatar, but thanks to Linden Lab's decision to give users the right to sell their creations, many residents are happy to sell their creations to you for the right price.

Second Life mirrors real life. There is no game, per se. Rather, living your virtual life is about interaction, creation, and sightseeing. It's both business and entertainment. As a result, it should come as no surprise that there's a place here for music and musicians. Musicians have created avatars of themselves, set up stores to sell their music, and promoted themselves within this world by putting up virtual posters on virtual walls of virtual buildings. Events such as virtual CD releases and signings are frequent.

Don't spend time in Second Life unless you truly enjoy it and want virtual interactions with fans (as well as some very strange residents). It also takes a fair amount of time to establish a user in this world, and there are far better payoffs for spending time on PR, marketing, and other promotion. Then again, this is a unique way to grow your audience.

How to set up Second Life

Before you use Second Life to promote your music, you will want to explore the world as a user first. Head to the site and create an account. Account names on Second Life have first and last names, like a real person. And then make an avatar that you can live with as you explore the site. There are no special steps for this, since there are no music accounts in particular.

How to use Second Life effectively

1. **Consider getting land of your own.** You can buy or rent a space, just like in real life, for fans to hang out at. Once you own land, you can stream music, including your own.

2. **Get to know music-venue owners.** In Second Life, there are music venues just like in real life, and they are happy to play and feature music if they like you.

3. **Make friends and interact.** Similar to every other type of social network, Second Life makes it easy to send messages to friends, which can help you build a network and allow you to announce things like new albums, shows, and events.

4. **Put on shows.** Second Life has a very useful Web page that tells you how to put on virtual gigs at wiki.secondlife.com/wiki/Live_Performances. Make sure to use the events feature to announce the gig so that other residents can find the shows.

HOW TO CREATE A MOBILE PRESENCE FOR YOUR BAND
What mobile presences are and why to have one

Phones and mobile devices are becoming the primary way that people connect on the Internet. Besides browsing the Web, many mobile users are interacting using apps.

First of all, you can create a mobile presence for your band by making sure that your Web site and the other key Web presences you keep all look good on phones and tablets. But that's just the beginning. There's no need to stop there. You can even create apps that allow you to share music, videos, calendars, and information on mobile devices.

Another advantage to having a presence in the mobile space is that it may provide another way to reach fans when you have a message to send. If you have an app, for example, you can send notifications when you have new shows, album releases, or news. Or, if you work with providers that capture phone numbers of people that want to receive texts, you can send text messages.

For now, having a mobile presence should be lower on your list of priorities. But if your band is larger, and you are touring regularly, you may want to consider it, since an app is the perfect thing to include on posters as a way for fans to check out your music.

How to set up a mobile presence

Keep in mind that you may already have a mobile presence through your Web site or blog. You will want to check to see if your Web site or blog is mobile friendly. However, if you want to or need to create a dedicated mobile presence, then follow the steps below.

1. **Choose a mobile app provider.** You have two choices: first, you can create a mobile friendly Web site, and second, you can create mobile apps that people can install on their smartphones. One provider that can easily create a free mobile site for you is Myxer (myxer.com). By setting up a MobileArtist account you will create a mobile friendly Web site and a mailing list for text messages.

    If you'd like to create an installable app for smartphones, services like Mobile Roadie (mobileroadie.com), ReverbNation (reverbnation.com), and MobBase (mobbase.com) will do so for a fee. Note that if you are already using ReverbNation for your mailing list and show calendar, it will automatically use that data to power your mobile app. The mobile space is rapidly changing, so head to IndieGuide.com/Social, where we track the latest options.

2. **Hook up all of your feeds.** Each mobile-app provider will have a way to connect your blog, mailing list, photo stream, show calendar, videos, and social feeds so that your mobile app or site stays fresh.

3. **Promote your mobile presence on your other sites.** Remind fans to sign up or download your mobile app. Services like Mxyer provide widgets that can promote your mobile site via the Web, as well as the content you provide.

How to get metrics from mobile presences

Most mobile providers offer a lot of metrics and statistics. Check your service to see what metrics they provide and the way in which they provide them.

CONVERSION TOOLS

THE SIX CONVERSION TOOLS YOU SHOULD INCLUDE IN AS MANY
WEB PRESENCES AS POSSIBLE

The reason you work so hard to get visitors to show up at your Web presences and Web site is to convince them to do something. You want them to join your mailing list, buy songs, make a donation, or contact you to make a booking. The technical term that Web marketers use to describe this is "conversion"—for instance, converting a visitor to a fan.

Another set of technical terms you will want to be familiar with are widgets, apps, and plug-ins. Each of these are methods to connect your Web presences to conversion tools—for example, putting your music store on your Facebook fan page uses apps from a music-store provider. Once you choose which stores to use and which presences to sign up for, you will want to see if they offer apps, plug-ins, or widgets. Fortunately, there's usually help available on each presence that tells you how you can do this.

The key is to think about your Web presences from a marketing standpoint: no matter where you put a presence, keep in mind which conversions you want to get out of your visitors, and make it easy for those conversions to happen. Otherwise, you've wasted all of your hard work.

Go through each presence that you have and see what you can do to help your fans make any or all of these six types of conversions:

1. **Buy something.** Get your fans to buy music, merch, or tickets to shows by incorporating online music stores. Go to your stores and find out the methods that they use to incorporate themselves into each presence. Note that, at the least, you can and should always provide links so fans know where they can buy music and merch.

2. **Join the mailing list, follow you on your social networks, or friend you.** Get your fans to make a connection to you so that you can send them messages in the future such as announcing new albums,

shows, or news. Provide links and buttons if your social networks provide them.

3. **Donate to your band.** Get your fans to donate money to you. Most donation tools have widgets or buttons that can be easily added.

4. **Contact you.** Anytime you take customer contacts for booking, licensing, or business, you want to make sure that it's simple for them to contact you. Note that you can go beyond just giving phone numbers and actually embed contact applications into your Web presences. You should also make sure to put detailed contact information in your e-mail signature, including phone numbers. You never know when an e-mail can turn into a sale. To make contacting you easier, try the following:

- Services like Google Voice (google.com/voice), which has proprietary widgets (support.google.com/voice/bin/answer.py?hl=en&answer=115128), and Skype (skype.com), which has buttons for easy access (www.skype.com/intl/en-us/tell-a-friend/get-a-skype-button).

- Contact-us forms that make it easier for people to write e-mails. There are a large variety of web forms available, and if you'd like a list, head to IndieGuide.com/Social.

5. **Come to your show.** If you play shows, one of the conversions will be to boost your draw. You need to make it as easy as possible.

6. **Talk about you.** If you can get your fans to talk about your music or news to their followers, you've just increased your reach. You can make it easy for them to do this by using Tweet This buttons, Like buttons from Facebook, +1 buttons from Google+, or all-in-one solutions such as ShareThis (sharethis.com) or Shareaholic (shareaholic.com).

HOW TO SET UP A WAY TO TAKE DONATIONS FROM FANS AND PROMOTE IT SO YOU GET MONEY
What donation tools are and why to use them

It's increasingly easy for any musician to sign up for financial services and make it simple to allow for fans to offer support by donating money. Here's how to integrate this into your Web presences.

How to set up donation tools

1. **Sign up for a donation site.** Sites like PayPal (paypal.com), Kickstarter (kickstarter.com), and Go Fund Me (gofundme.com) allow you to take donations online, although all of them work in different ways. See IndieGuide.com/Social for more services that allow you to take donations.

2. **Use buttons, widgets, or apps from the donation site and embed them in your Web presences.** Make it as easy as possible for fans to make donations, and make this feature as prominent as you can.

3. **Tell your fans to donate, and consider giving each donor a thank-you gift.** PBS and NPR fund-raising drives teach us is that if you are going to try to get donations, you should very clearly and persistently ask for money and give thank-you gifts to entice donations.

HOW TO SET UP AND USE A MAILING LIST

What mailing lists are and why to use them

Mailing lists are simply tools that allow you to send e-mails to all of your fans at once. It's still the best way of reaching any fans from whom you have collected e-mail addresses. It's also a different form of communication than just posting a message on Twitter or Facebook, since it goes directly to your fans and does not require that your fans drop by your blog or check out your latest status on Facebook.

Mailing list services are usually an expense for musicians. There's so much spam on the Internet that you need to use an established provider to be able to send legitimate bulk e-mails. Also, people are quick to unsubscribe if the newsletters aren't interesting and informative. In spite of these pitfalls, a good newsletter can make good use of the e-mails that you collect at shows and at your Web presences.

Consider this list of features that you will want to look for in an e-mail provider:

- Subscription widgets, apps, or plug-ins that make it easy for you to embed these tools in all of your Web presences

- Automated subscribe/unsubscribe features

• Tracking metrics, such as how many people open the e-mail and what links your fans click on

• Templated e-mails that allow you to embed pictures and HTML in the e-mail

• The ability to give a digital download, such as free songs, videos, or pictures as a reward for subscribing

How to set up a mailing list

1.   **Choose a provider.** Consider the features that you will want to look for in an e-mail provider:

 o   Subscription widgets, apps, or plug-ins that make it easy for you to embed these tools in all of your Web presences.

 o   Automated subscribe/unsubscribe features.

 o   Tracking metrics, such as how many people open the e-mail and what links your fans click on.

 o   Templated e-mails that allow you to embed pictures and HTML in the e-mail.

 o   The ability to give a digital download, such as a free song, videos, or pictures as a reward for subscribing.

 Solutions include ReverbNation (reverbnation.com), Band Letter (bandletter.com), or HostBaby (hostbaby.com); or go to IndieGuide .com/Social for a large number of options for newsletters.

2.   **Integrate the widgets, apps, or plug-ins into your Web presences.** If you decide to get an e-mail list, you should plug it as much as possible wherever you have Web presences.

How to autopost from mailing lists

The best newsletter providers will give you a feed for posting newsletters to other places. Explore and see if these features are available to you. Also, you should always let fans browse older ones.

How to use mailing lists effectively

Follow these steps to get the most out of your newsletters.

1. **Give fans a reward for signing up and for staying signed up.**
When recording your music, you should set aside exclusive content for your subscribers to give them a reason to sign up and stay connected. Also, your mailing list should have a thank-you message that gets sent automatically. Include a welcome message.

2. **Your newsletter needs to be about your fans, not you.** People read news because it's of interest to them, but many bands think a newsletter is a place to talk about themselves. Naturally, you will want to let them know where you are playing and your new releases, but to the extent that you can make your newsletter help them—such as who else in your style of music is playing in their town or other events of interest—the more likely they will want to read your newsletter.

3. **Don't write too often—no more than twice a month.** Spamming your fans is a sure way to lose subscribers.

4. **Call them to action.** Never forget the intent of your e-mail list. Besides keeping your fans informed, it's purpose is to deliver a marketing message to them. Although your content shouldn't be just about marketing, in the end it needs to drive sales, draw crowds, or spawn discussion of your band. When you do deliver your marketing message in the content, be very direct: "Click here and buy the album." "Come to the show on Saturday at Martyrs'."

How to get metrics from mailing lists

All of the best newsletter programs will have methods to find out how many subscribers you have, how many fans open the newsletters, and even which links they click on.

HOW TO SET UP A SHOW CALENDAR FOR YOUR FANS
What it is and why to use show calendars

You will want to post your show information in just one place and have it update all of your Web presences, making it as easy as possible to let your fans know when and where you are playing. Fortunately, there are many services that will let you post the information and pull a feed from it so that it can be shared. Further, many of the best services have widgets, apps, and plug-ins that make it simple to share.

These tools can go beyond a simple calendar. For example, Eventful (eventful.com) allows your fans to "demand" that you play shows in their town, which will let you know where you should tour. Eventful then lets you contact them when you have any show dates in their town.

How to set up a show calendar

1. **Choose a provider.** Although there are many sites that track shows from musicians, the ones that make it easy to export include Eventful (eventful.com), as well as ReverbNation (reverbnation.com), Bands in Town (bandsintown.com), and Jambase (jambase.com). Many of these services vary in size and reach. For instance, using Eventful to keep track of your shows gives you a reach of over one hundred million through visitors to Eventful's site who browse events, readers of their weekly e-mail newsletters advising of events in their area, and hundreds of data-licensing partnerships. These partnerships include services that use Eventful data to power their own calendars such as television and radio Web sites, closed-circuit television channels at stores like Wal-Mart, digital signage at coffeehouses and other shops, and mobile partners. To compare services, head to IndieGuide.com/Social.

2. **Use the widgets, apps, and plug-ins.** Once you have chosen a provider, use the widgets, apps, and plug-ins to allow you to display this on all of your Web presences while updating the information in just one place.

How to autopost to a show calendar

Many of the show calendar providers will allow you to hook in your Twitter or blog feed to the artist page, to give you another place to display your latest news and information.

How to autopost from it

Many of the tools have RSS or Atom feeds. Also, many have APIs that allow people to pull in the data and easily share it. For example, Reverb-Nation can pull data from Eventful, Bands in Town, and Jambase so that it always has the latest show data.

How to use show calendars effectively

1. **Put in show dates as early as possible, so fans can get notified and make plans.** Sometimes, it seems that bands think that fans can drop everything and show up at a moment's notice. The show calendar lets them plan ahead.

2. **If you can, sell tickets ahead of time.** Most show calendars can include buy links so that your fans can buy tickets directly from your Web site.

ALERT AND NOTIFICATION TOOLS

HOW TO TRACK WHO'S TALKING ABOUT YOUR BAND

While many people search for their own names and band names, it's necessary to do this on a regular basis to find out who is talking about you.

You can do this by reminding yourself to search your name every week, or you can have the search engine automatically e-mail you when it finds new Web pages and blogs that talk about you. This takes just a few minutes and is a very powerful way to keep up with anyone who mentions you. Don't skip this section: it's free, simple to do, and is a very powerful feature for anyone who is in the media.

If you use it you will:

- Find out about articles and reviews of your band that you may not know about

- Catch message-board posts that talk about you

- See blog entries that mention your music

- Be able to find new fans and new opportunities for your music, publicity, and marketing

To track mentions of your band and find out the rank of your Web site, you will need to do the following:

1. **Go to Google Alerts (google.com/alerts) and set up an account.** If you have a gmail account, you can just use the same log-in.

2. **Learn the advanced search features.**

o **Quotes:** adding a search in quotes, like "Beatnik Turtle" will only find pages that have the entire phrase "Beatnik Turtle" rather than pages with just the word "beatnik" or "turtle."

o **OR and AND:** You will likely use OR searches for misspellings or alternative spellings of your name. We use " 'Beatnik Turtle' OR 'Beatnick Turtle'" as a search term. The other term, AND, means that *each* term needs to be in the result.

o **- and +:** Searches with a + (plus sign) are required terms. "+'Beatnik Turtle'+Chicago" will require the word "Chicago" be found on any pages that mention our band name. Use this if your band name is unique not worldwide but in a particular city. Searches with a − (minus sign) exclude results. "+'Beatnik Turtle'−turtlenecks" will find our band name except in pages that talk about turtlenecks.

3. **Add search terms.** We suggest adding the following search terms:

    o Your band name and all misspellings of your band name

    o Your Web site address

    o The names of your band members (use the + and - search techniques to narrow it down)

    o The names of your albums, projects, and songs with unique names

    o The names of bands with music similar to yours (Why? Because any Web sites or blogs that cover them should be interested in you, too.)

    o The name of your music genre along with your town

LEARNING MORE

Go to IndieGuide.com/Social for a clickable version of every link, Web site, and service mentioned in this chapter, as well as free extra materials to help you put together your Web, social, and mobile presences.

CHAPTER 10

THE STRATEGIC GOAL: to set up your Web site to meet the needs of your worldwide audience and to promote, inform, distribute, and sell your music, merchandise, and shows

REFERENCE PAGE: IndieGuide.com/Website

CHECKLIST: Refer to chapter 8, "Your Web Strategy."

YOUR WEB SITE

*"The hub of your operations has got to be your own
personal website—something you own and control."*

—BOB BAKER, AUTHOR, TEACHER, AND MUSIC-MARKETING GURU

NO MATTER where people find out about you, if they are interested in you, the first thing that they will do is search the Web. The question is, What link is at the top of the results? You need a home base: a place of your own for your band and music. Your Web site is the best place to do it. It is the best promoter, salesperson, agent, publicist, distributor, disc jockey, and news reporter you can have.

Although some musicians skip creating a Web site, once you get established, you will find that Facebook fan pages don't do a great job of speaking to bookers, and your music store doesn't do a good job pitching licensing options for your music. You need a place that is entirely under your control to be able to maximize your sales, licensing, booking, and show draw.

And while some people consider Web design confusing, it can be boiled down to one simple concept: understand who the audiences are (fans, journalists, licensors, etc.), what they are looking for (music, info, licensing terms), and what you want them to do (buy music, write about the band, license music). This will let you outline what goes on your site to give your audiences what they want and will let you design the best way to convince your audiences to take action—getting you more sales, press coverage, and so on. And the goal is to make it simple for them. As Jed Carlson, COO of

ReverbNation says, "the confused mind always says 'no.'" We'll cover how to organize your site to make it easy for your audiences below.

And, finally, if you've followed the advice in chapter 8, "Your Web Strategy," by the time you think about putting up your Web site, you should have a place for all of your content: your photos, videos, blog, and more. All you need to do is embed these in your Web site and your site can stay active and alive.

PREPARING

HOW TO GET YOUR OWN DOMAIN NAME

Your domain name is the shortest, most powerful marketing message you have. By putting just a single phrase on your merchandise, your press kits, or your albums, people can hear and buy your music, watch your videos, subscribe to your mailing list, find out where you are playing, or write an article about you.

Here's how to register a domain name of your own:

1. **Choose a domain registrar.** While some Web-hosting companies will be happy to register a name for you, do it yourself instead. Some will register your domain in *their* name, which means you may have a legal battle on your hands if you need to move to a different Web host.

   Try sites like NameCheap (namecheap.com), Dynadot (dynadot.com), or Go Daddy (godaddy.com); or go to IndieGuide.com/Web for many more options.

2. **Search for the domain you want and choose one if it's not taken.** See chapter 4, "Your Brand," for information on how to choose a name that's trademarkable and completely yours.

3. **Register and pay for the domain only; don't pay for extra services.** Most domain registrars will try to get you to pay for Web hosting, or other extras that sound important or necessary. You don't need them. Just get the basic domain. Also, keep in mind that all of these options often accept coupons, so don't click the buy button before searching for coupon codes.

4. **Configure your domain for your Web host.** Your Web host will tell you how to do this. (See the next section.)

THREE OPTIONS FOR CHOOSING A WEB HOST FOR MUSICIANS

Depending on how technically savvy you are, you will want to choose one of these three options to host your Web site. Your best choices will use a content management system (CMS), which allows you to set up the design of your Web site and type the words that appear on the site in an editor that looks like a word processor. This separates out the more technical aspects of creating a Web site from the text and information.

Note that if you've signed up for content hosts as discussed in chapter 9, "Your Web, Social, and Mobile Presences," and have chosen your music and merchandise distributor as covered in chaper 6, "Your Albums, Merchandise, and Sales," then all you need to do is insert the widgets, apps, and plug-ins from your content hosts and stores into your Web site, and it will be a living, breathing site, and you won't have to do a great deal of further work. When you add new pictures, they will automatically appear, your blog entries will give the latest news, and your show calendar will have the latest info.

Consider the following options:

1. **Simplest option: use a site-builder Web site.** Many Web hosts will now allow you to just make some simple design selections and plug in all of your information to make a standard site. Hosts that will do this for you include ReverbNation (reverbnation.com), HostBaby (hostbaby.com), and FourFour (fourfour.com), although there are many options in this category that you can find on IndieGuide.com/Web.

2. **Advanced option: use a CMS host.** Using installable CMSs like WordPress (wordpress.org), Drupal (drupal.org), or Joomla (joomla.org) gives you a very configurable site with lots of options for plug-ins and customizability. It's also possible to find Web-hosting companies that will install these CMSs for you. WordPress, in particular, has a lot of plug-ins useful for musicians, such as GigPress (gigpress.com) or WordTour (www.wordtour.com).

    Another alternative is to use a free blog host like Blogger (blogger.com) and point your domain at it.

3. **For the tech wizards: build your own site from scratch.** We generally don't recommend this unless you have very special requirements

and have tech gurus at hand. Using tools like Dreamweaver, and raw tools like PHP, Perl, and DBMSs, you can design and build your own site. We did this for our TheSongOfTheDay.com Web site and built a CMS so that we could upload music, make our own word-of-the-day-style calendar design, have an automated podcast RSS feed, and set the order of the songs through an automated system based on a database. But don't attempt this unless you have the tech skills and a lot of time.

PLANNING YOUR SITE

THE SEVEN AUDIENCES YOU SHOULD DESIGN
YOUR WEB SITE TO HANDLE

Most band Web sites we surveyed were either designed around the assumption that only fans visit or, worse, were designed as ego-trip billboards that focus only on the people in the band. Instead, you need to determine who your audiences are and design it for *them* and meet their needs.

In fact, before you sit down to plan your site, you need to understand this key point: your Web site is primarily a marketing tool (even if you're just giving music away, you still need to convince your fans to download the music). You need to aim your Web site at getting your fans to *do something*: download music, talk about your music on their social networks, buy music or merch, come to see your show, license your music, or book your band. These actions are all called conversions, which is a Web-marketing term. The goal is to convert a visitor into a fan, customer, or gig host.

Here are the seven audiences you will likely find on your Web site:

1. Music fans

2. Live music fans

3. Bookers and talent buyers

4. The press and journalists

5. People that want to license your music

6. Sound people

7. Random visitors

Each has a different expectation, and you want each of them to take a different action. See the table "Your Audiences, What They Want, and What You Want Them to Do" to put this all together. Once you view your Web site in this way, you can structure the site around their needs and your goals and put the conversion tools in the right places (conversion tools are discussed in chapter 9, "Your Web, Social, and Mobile Presences").

WHAT MUSICIANS NEED TO KNOW ABOUT DESIGNING MUSIC WEB SITES

Before you can design your Web site, you need to think from each audience's viewpoint since that will affect the type of content you provide, where it's located, and your navigation structure. After all, you don't want audiences finding themselves in the wrong section of the Web site, lost and with no idea what to do next. Fortunately, audiences of band Web sites aren't too complicated to unravel. But remember, catering to each of the audience profiles is only half the story. The other half is steering them where you want them to go. Use the table below to accomplish this.

TABLE: YOUR AUDIENCES, WHAT THEY WANT, AND WHAT YOU WANT THEM TO DO

Audience	Expectations	Conversions	Site Features
All fans	Knowing who and what you are, buying your albums and merchandise, listening to your music, viewing photos and videos, discovering your latest projects, participating in the fan community	Joining the mailing list, subscribing to the blogs, participating in the forum, buying the albums and merchandise, telling friends about the band	News, blog, forums, about the band, music, photos, videos, store, calendar, mailing list

Continued...

Audience	Expectations	Conversions	Site Features
Live music fans	Finding tour dates and upcoming shows; an address, directions, map, and phone number for the venue; the time of the performance and the acts going up before and after and determining the cover charge and any drink minimum	Coming to the show, bringing friends, promoting the event, discussing the event in the forum	Show information, gig calendar, news, blog, forums, mailing list
Bookers and talent buyers	Knowing the band's music style, location, and performance history; contacting the band; reading fan and venue testimonials; downloading pictures so they can put up ads, flyers, bios, and other text and images	Hiring the band	Testimonials, booking information, calendar, music, photos, contact link
The press and journalists	Downloading the press kit and press releases, contacting the band for interviews, finding images and image credit info for the article, reading testimonials	Writing articles about the band, reviewing the latest album, featuring the latest project, contacting the band	Press information, news, music, photos, contact link
Sound people	Determining the style of music and instrumentation, preparing for any special sound needs, viewing stage-plot and microphone layout	Contacting the band, making the band sound right onstage	Stage plots, instrumentation, sound/performance information, music, contact link

Audience	Expectations	Conversions	Site Features
People that want to license your music	Listening to songs, requesting high-quality versions, determining licensing requirements, finding noncommercial-use requirements, determining pod-safe status	Contacting the band to license songs	Contact link
Random visitors and Web surfers	Finding instant gratification	Listening to music, watching videos, buying albums and merchandise, joining the mailing list, subscribing to blogs	Music, photos, videos, about the band, store, news, blog, forums

THE TWENTY DIFFERENT PAGES YOU CAN PUT ON
YOUR WEB SITE

Use the table below to decide what pages you want to have available on your Web site. You should only put up pages that you need for your own band.

Note that not every page needs to be on your major navigation area. Many of the pages on your site may be in a set of links at the bottom of the Web site.

TABLE: THE TWENTY DIFFERENT PAGES YOU CAN PUT ON YOUR WEB SITE

Content	Description
About the band	Basic information about your band: name, style of music, similar bands, members and bios, instrumentation, hometown, and band history
News	Latest news on your band. Place the latest story on the front page with older stories cycling to a separate news page. If possible, offer an RSS feed. Can also just be the blog.

Continued...

Content	Description
Blog	Offer one or more band blogs with more personal perspectives on the band
Show calendar	Upcoming shows as well as a catalog of past shows you've played
Music	All the music you've made available to the public as well as samples of those available for purchase. Ideally, provide an embedded player to listen immediately.
Store	All albums and merchandise available for sale with photos and descriptions of each, or links to the appropriate vendors such as CD Baby, iTunes, Spreadshirt, etc.
Album information	Information on each of your albums, including lyrics, liner notes, and possibly guitar tablature or full sheet music
Photos	Albums of photos of your band, recent performances, and other events
Videos	Music videos or videos of the band performing
Information for the press	The band bio; press releases, press-ready photos, logos, and other images; contact info including the band press representative's e-mail and phone number; and press clippings
Information for bookers	Band contact info, including the band representative's e-mail and phone number; booking information; stage and microphone plot; and press-ready photos and images
Testimonials	Quotes from fans, bookers, venues, and satisfied customers from corporate events, festivals, weddings, and parties
Stage and performance information for sound people	Stage and microphone plot, band instrumentation, and any other information a sound person might need
Forums	A place for fans to meet up, arrange shared rides to your performances, coordinate grassroots promotion, and so on

Content	Description
Mailing-list information	Information about your mailing list and an easy sign-up process
Contact Us	Usually a Web contact form, but can be as simple as a band member's e-mail address
Site map	A map of the entire site to help people find what they want
Legal information	Any legal information such as the copyright or Creative Commons license, privacy-policy statement (for your mailing list), and so on
Links	Links to external sites such as the Web sites of individual band members, other bands, favorite venues, and so on

BUILDING YOUR WEB SITE

THE EIGHT ELEMENTS YOU CAN PUT ON YOUR FRONT PAGE

You can't assume that the average visitor to your Web site knows who you are or, in fact, even knows that it is a Web site for music. You need to design your site to make that clear. In fact, as Bob Baker (bob-baker.com), author, teacher, and music-marketing guru, says, "What do you want your fans to *feel* when they go to your website?" As you design your Web site, keep asking yourself this, and keep playing with it until you're happy with what visitors see when they first get there.

That said, Web sites are now multimedia experiences, with video, audio, and pictures weaving together a story. There's no one right way to do this; you need to put something together that meets the needs of your fans and your music. What we can provide are ideas for common elements that bands like to put on their front page:

- Your blog, for the latest news

- Your music player

- A video player

- Your logo and tagline

- Pictures from your photo album

- A way to join your mailing list

- A gig calendar

- Your Twitter feed

Each of these pieces can be segmented in different parts of your Web page, which can give an at-a-glance way to look at the latest information about you. If you use the techniques from "Your Web Strategy" (ch. 8), you can pull in the latest videos, pictures, and blog entries, which keeps the front of your Web site fresh.

YOUR MOST IMPORTANT PAGE: YOUR CONTACT-US PAGE

No matter what content you put up, you have to have a contact-us page. Almost all of our best opportunities have come through the site this way. Gigs, music-licensing opportunities, press articles, interviews, and songwriting commissions have all come to our attention via the Web form and e-mail address on this page. We can't imagine what we would have missed out on if we hadn't made it easy for people to contact us. You may include a phone number, too, if you're comfortable releasing it. For instance, when ABC Family/Disney wanted to license one of our songs for a commercial, they left multiple voice-mail messages with all of the numbers we had posted in addition to e-mailing because they were under a deadline.

You should have the Contact-Us link at the top or bottom of each page and built into your template so that any new pages feature it automatically. If you use a Web-contact form rather than a direct e-mail address, verify that it works properly. We've had more than one Web-contact form fail on us. It's hard enough creating opportunities for yourself; you don't want to block the ones that come knocking. We've configured our Web form to send all submissions to multiple members of the band.

To do this, see chapter 9, "Your Web, Social, and Mobile Presences," for ways to include contact information on your Web site (under the heading "The Six Conversion Tools You Should Include in as Many Web Presences as Possible").

THE FIVE THINGS JOURNALISTS WILL LOOK FOR ON YOUR WEB SITE SO THEY CAN WRITE ABOUT YOU

Your Web site should have one page dedicated to the press. Essentially, it should be your online press kit. This gives bloggers, journalists, and other people in the media a page where they can get information they need. We suggest having the following available on your site:

- Press photos

- Bio (with links to a PDF and Word or other editable file)

- Press clippings and quotes

- Contact info

- Fact sheet (to make it easy for them to write articles when doing research)

If you use a service such as Sonicbids (sonicbids.com), then you should include a link to it on the page and send them there. We talk about the details of an online press kit in chapter 12, "Get Publicized."

THE SEVEN THINGS BOOKERS WILL LOOK FOR ON YOUR WEB SITE

Another of your pages should be dedicated to bookers and talent buyers. Essentially, it should be your online booking kit. This allows bookers and talent agents to get what they need, such as the following:

- Who to contact for bookings

- Style and genre of music you play

- The number of sets you can play, and what kind of events

- Whether you play cover songs (and if you do, which ones)

- Stage plot

- Instruments and other sound requirements

- Press photo(s)

If you use a service such as Sonicbids (sonicbids.com), then you should include this information on the page and send them there. We talk about the details of an online press kit in chapter 7, "Your Gigs."

Your site has a huge advantage in that you can frame all of your content in any way you want. You can write what you want about your own music, and you can share things in a way that can promote your band. Once you have a Web host, you can use the tools on your site to build in your music, videos, pictures, and blog. Just follow the provider's instructions to do this.

But the idea is to do this just once and to not have to update this in multiple places. We suggest using all of the work you did in the previous chapter, "Your Web, Social, and Mobile Presences," to pull in your content hosts (like music, pictures, videos, and blogs), conversion tools (like contact pages, stores, and mailing lists), and outposts (such as social media). As we describe in each section of the previous chapter, you will have ways to autopost this same information to your Web site or to use widgets, apps, or plug-ins to mirror the same information. This takes a bit of time to get working, but once it does, updating your content hosts will update your Web site as well as everywhere else you have a presence.

1. **Decide on what media you'd like to incorporate in your Web site.** Use the checklist in chapter 8, "Your Web Strategy," for descriptions of each type of media you can include. See the previous chapters for details about each step if you'd like additional guidance.

2. **Frame each of the widgets and plug-ins with your own information to personalize your site.** Your Web site needs to be more than a bunch of widgets on a page. You can incorporate music players, videos, and pictures from your content hosts throughout your site.

3. **Use your own ads to promote your own work.** Once you have your content, you can still use parts of the design of your site to promote your albums, merchandise, mailing lists, or any of the other conversions that you want to make happen. We tend to put ads on the right side, plugging our latest album or other actions that we'd like our fans to take.

THE NUMBER ONE THING TO DO WHEN YOU THINK
YOU'RE FINISHED: TEST YOUR SITE

Designing your site to speak to the various audiences is difficult. You need to test it—from each of the seven audiences' perspectives. Pretend you're a booker, a journalist, a fan, and so on, and see if you can find the information they would each be looking for quickly and easily. Browse your site as one of these audiences and purposefully put yourself in the wrong place on your site. Can you easily find your way back to the information they need?

After you've test-driven your site, get your friends and family to try it out. Stand over their shoulders as they click around. Don't lead them or answer any questions they have, because you won't be standing over the shoulder of any visitors to your site. Can they find your music easily, or do they get lost? Do they learn what your band is up to, or are they distracted by other things? Are they confused and frustrated? If your friends and family are, you can bet others will be as well. And others won't have the patience to keep clicking to find what they need. Take this feedback and make the necessary changes. Then test again, until you get it right.

TRACKING YOUR WEB SITE
HOW TO TRACK METRICS ON YOUR WEB SITE

Some Web hosts will give you tools so that you can see how many visitors you are getting, the search terms that people used to find your page, and even what URLs they came from to get to your Web site (which is particularly valuable to you because you can find out where fans are finding out about your Web page).

If they don't provide any tools, consider tracking your visitors in the following ways:

1. **Use Google Analytics.** Google Analytics (www.google.com /analytics) is free and relatively simple to use. Many Web-host providers make it simple for you to sign up and put in the little code that Google gives you for tracking your Web statistics.

2. **If you are more advanced, try more detailed tools.** Two additional tools you may want to try include TraceWatch (tracewatch.com) and AWStats (awstats.sourceforge.net). Our band uses both of these at the same time, since they give different views of the same data.

ENSURING YOUR WEB SITE COMES UP IN WEB SEARCHES

If you are serious about making your Web site work well with search engines—to make it more likely to come up on certain keywords than other sites—you will want to get into a field called search-engine optimization (SEO). You can draw in new fans and new business if you can optimize your site for search engines. If you are going to get involved in this, research SEO as a topic, since it is a constantly evolving field.

This is a topic that changes more quickly than any other: it's like a war out there. But for some bands, it's worth the time. Here's how to do it:

1. **Get a lot of sites to link to you.** By far, this is the easiest and best way to succeed in SEO, since each link to your pages is a "vote" for your site. If you do nothing else, getting a lot of links inbound to your site will raise its stature.

2. **Grade your Web page at Marketing Grader.** Once you've finished your page, the best place to start is Marketing Grader (marketing.grader.com). This will point out the issues with your design from a search-engine perspective and give you direct tips on what to start working on. We use this against all of our sites and try to get the highest grade possible. This has measurably raised our rankings.

LEARNING MORE

Go to IndieGuide.com/Web for a clickable version of every link, Web site, and service mentioned in this chapter, as well as free extra materials to help you build your Web site.

PART FOUR

GET NOTICED, HEARD, AND SEEN

CHAPTER 11

THE STRATEGIC GOAL: to discover who your audience is and where they are so you can create a targeted message to entice them to listen, buy, and promote your music, merchandise, and shows to others

REFERENCE: IndieGuide.com/Marketing

CHECKLIST: This is a strategy chapter—the chapter is the checklist.

YOUR MARKETING STRATEGY

"When you fail to plan, you plan to fail."

—ANONYMOUS

IN TODAY's world, the means of making and recording music is in any musician's hands. And, with the Internet, you can find nearly any piece of recorded music ever made anywhere in the world and download it within moments.

So the question is: How do you market yourself when you are literally competing against every musician in the world?

The answer starts with your music. Even if you had a one-million-dollar marketing budget, if the end product sucks, you will have a hard time selling it. But even if the music is perfect, there's another element that needs to be right. As Jed Carlson at ReverbNation (reverbnation.com) says, "Marketing can't fix a broken brand." If your marketing succeeds in bringing in new people, and they show up on your Web sites or music stores and see a crappy Web design, a muddled logo, or a bio with misspellings, you will likely turn off any customers or members of the press and waste your hard work. Basically, everything that we cover in chapter 2, "Your Music," chapter 4, "Your Brand," and chapter 8, "Your Web Strategy," counts here. If you have not taken the steps outlined in those chapters, don't worry about marketing until you have.

We covered the "marketing funnel" in chapter 8, "Your Web Strategy," which answers why you want to have a presence in as many places as possible: the wider the funnel, the more fans that you can catch. "You have to realize that you'll only monetize a fraction of a percent of the people that hear your stuff. If, for the sake of argument one person out of a hundred buys your music it becomes very much about the numbers. It becomes about casting an incredibly wide net," says Gavin Mikhail, an indie musician making a living from his music (gavinmikhail.com). The goal, then, is to turn visitors into fans, fans into customers, and customers into promoters. But that doesn't answer how you get people into the funnel in the first place. That's what this chapter covers.

Jim DeRogatis, the former music editor for the *Chicago Sun-Times* and cohost of National Public Radio's *Sound Opinions*, said, "There's this perception that there's some mystery button that gets pushed, and buzz starts. It's this magic, elusive thing that every group is trying to get. But buzz just means that people are excited about the band and are talking about it."

This initial publicity and chatter about a band is rarely organic. It needs a push to get it started. If you see a new artist appear and seem to be talked about everywhere at once in every media outlet, that's nearly always because someone is throwing money at armies of marketers, publicists, and radio stations. But music can and often does grow through fans picking up on great acts through a longer-term campaign, managed by independent artists on almost no budget.

Although marketing isn't like making music, it does use a lot of the same kind of creativity to make it work. So you already have the skills you need. Marketing is not just compiling lists and following steps mechanically. It can and should be fun and creative, too.

MARKETING STRATEGIES

MARKETING IN THREE STEPS

The purpose of marketing is simple: to get sales. But those sales are not just about dollars. In fact, audiences pay you in two ways: attention and money. You have to get the first before getting the second. Keep this in mind as you make your marketing plans, since you need to remember that your fans feel that there's a cost to hitting Play on your music or video.

At its heart, marketing can be broken down into three steps:

- Knowing who your audience is, and where they spend their time and attention

- Putting a message in front of them that they notice (and that is tuned to them)

- Getting your audience to act on the message

Keep in mind that most everything that you do depends on the first step. The next two fall into place once you know who you are aiming your marketing at. And the interesting thing about the audience question is how many musicians start with the idea that their audience is everyone. Really? Everyone? Four-year-olds? Seventy-five-year-old grandmothers? College students? Business people? Although you probably want everyone to buy your music, you need to narrow your focus, or else you will be trying to market in nursery schools, bars, and assisted-living facilities.

Here's the key: the more narrowly you define your audience, the easier it is to market to them.

As Bob Baker (bob-baker.com), author, teacher, and music-marketing guru, says: "If you want to punch through a wall, you would use an awl, not a board. The sharper your message, the better chance you have of punching through."

A narrowly defined audience makes marketing possible, especially when competing against every musician in the world. For example, even though Facebook grew to be an international phenomenon, a social network usable "by everyone," it was limited to Harvard University at first. And this gave the early users a reason to join. It was exclusive. It was part of their identity—and the most effective marketing has more to do with the identity of your customers than anything else. In fact, music is even more a part of an identity than nearly any other product that customers buy. Just think about the times when you show someone your music collection: you are really saying something about yourself.

Once you know the audience and where they spend their time and focus their attention—and we'll have techniques and services we talk about later on that will help you find out who your audience is and where they hang out—you can put your message in their language, presented where they are already hanging out, targeted directly at them.

And, finally, always remember that marketing messages have a purpose. They should be aimed at making the sale.

WHAT MUSICIANS NEED TO UNDERSTAND ABOUT
HOW FANS PICK UP NEW MUSIC

Once you think about your audience in terms of marketing, you should understand how fans pick up new music.

First of all, as Felice Ecker, cofounder of the media, marketing, and management firm Girlie Action (girlieaction.com), explains, there are two types of music fans. One type, the "buzzmakers," will seek out new music and want to talk about it. They rarely buy new music, instead seeking out free downloads. Fortunately, they like to show off that they found something new. It's the hungry fans that you are giving your music away to, in order to influence them to talk about it. The buzzmakers are watched by the press and media who want to help break "the next big thing."

The second type of music fan, the "mainstream consumers," eventually learn about you thanks to magazines, the press, public or commercial radio, TV, and (now that it's so easy to use Facebook to communicate) friends. These mainstream consumers don't necessarily visit your Web site or dive into your brand to learn more about you; instead, they simply go to iTunes or other digital stores and buy your music there, because they don't want to go to the trouble to find it anywhere else. This is where your sales are coming from. It's the buzzmakers that you're aiming at first.

Now that you know this, the next thing is to take a page out of Marketing 101, called the "product diffusion curve." Don't worry, there's no math. These are just fancy names to put on the categories of customers based on when they pick up a new product after it's introduced. Here's the list, along with a table of how to market to each.

The group	What they want	How to market to them
Innovators	The innovators are hungry for the newest, freshest stuff out there, and in fact they like trying things just because they are new. They want to be first, and they don't worry about the fact that something is buggy and not proven. These are the first 2.5% to pick up a new product.	In this part of the campaign, you will emphasize how new and fresh your band is—and this is one of the times when being new and unknown is an advantage. Innovators love being thought of as being "in the know," so encourage them to talk about it.

The group	What they want	How to market to them
Early adopters	The early adopters wait for the innovators to go through the huge amount of the newest stuff to find what's worth having. They still like to get things before anyone else. This is the next 13.5% of buyers.	Quote any reviews or momentum that you get from the innovators, to show it's proven music but still fresh.
Early majority	These fans want recommendations, and to know that music has been out there and is solid. This is 34% of customers.	Use reviews, recommendations, ratings, and quotes to show that your music is out there and proven.
Late majority	The late majority will only pick up products after they're mainstream. This is about 34% of fans.	Same as above, but at this point, you should have even more proof that people love your music.
Laggards	Laggards will only pick up a new product when there's basically no other choice—which doesn't really happen with music. This is about 16% of buyers.	Honestly, it's not even worth marketing music to these guys. They will basically just listen to the music they already own, and if they pick yours up, it's because "everyone is talking about it" and they can't avoid it anymore.

Source: QuickMBA (www.quickmba.com/marketing/product/diffusion)

Note that Ecker's "buzzmakers" are the innovators and early adopters. The mainstream audience starts with the early majority and beyond.

THE TOP EIGHT QUESTIONS YOU SHOULD BE ABLE TO ANSWER ABOUT YOUR AUDIENCE

The more narrowly you define your fans, the more effective your marketing message will be. Your marketing plan can almost write itself if you understand your audience clearly. Answer the following questions about your audience. (Note: if you are just starting out, and are not sure who your fans are, assume that they are probably people that are just like yourself. Answer these questions as if you were the audience. You will improve your answers as you gain your fan base.)

- How old are they?

- What mix of male/female are they?

- Do they live in a particular area or areas?

- What other bands do they listen to?

- What do they usually do for a living, or where do they go to school?

- Do they have a name they already call themselves or a group they already identify with (e.g., Juggalos, geeks, free thinkers, soccer fans, bikers, bronies, etc.)?

- For each name they go by or group that they identify with, where do they hang out online (message/discussion boards, Facebook groups, Web sites, YouTube channels, etc.)?

- What TV shows, movies, or other media do they like?

Don't stop with these. Just add more questions if you have ideas that will help you make your marketing plan.

HOW TO FIND OUT WHO YOUR FANS ARE, WHAT THEY LISTEN TO, AND WHERE THEY LIVE

In this world of social media, as people are volunteering all kinds of information about themselves, it turns out there are actually quite a few resources within your reach to give you information about your fans. Some fee-based, but others are free.

1. **Use Facebook stats.** If you already have a Facebook fan page, you already have some great, free demographic information. Go to the insights link, and take a look at what it provides. You will get the ages and sexes of fans, how many talk about you and how many make comments on your fan page, and a lot of other useful information. If you end up friending your Facebook fans, you can then see other information about them and gain a lot of additional insights.

2. **Try Twitter stats.** Most Twitter users put in their location. So it's easy to use applications like Tweepsmap (tweepsmap.com) to show you the location of your Twitter followers merged with maps you can glance at. This can help your marketing, as well as touring.

3. **Look up your listeners on Last.fm.** As we talked about in chapter 9, "Your Web, Social, and Mobile Presences," Last.fm has locations, sexes, and listening habits of people who are listening to your music. Last.fm is also absolutely the best place to find out what other bands your fans really listen to.

4. **Use ReverbNation stats.** ReverbNation (reverbnation.com) will pull information from multiple sources and give you good demographic information based on everything that it can collect.

5. **Find out which listeners like your music.** Services like SoundOut (soundout.com), for a fee, will play your music for different listeners and demographic groups. Each will rate your song, and you can find out which ones take to the music better than the others.

6. **For touring, try Eventful (eventful.com).** Eventful (eventful.com) will let fans "demand" that you play in their area. This can give you location and other demographic information about your fans.

7. **For videos, use YouTube stats.** There's a little-known button to the right of the number of views of a video that looks like a little graph. You can get great demographic info out of this, find out the locations of your viewers, and find out what other views are referring viewers to see you.

7. **Ask them (surveys).** There are more ways than ever of asking your fans questions directly. Try using a Facebook fan page question or a form in Google Docs (docs.google.com). Other options include Free Online Surveys (freeonlinesurveys.com), Survey Methods (surveymethods .com), and Mister Poll (misterpoll.com). If you want to tailor the look and feel of the survey for your fans, then you may wish to use the pay sites SurveyMonkey (surveymonkey.com) or Zoomerang (zoomerang.com).

HOW TO CREATE A MARKETING PLAN

Most people like to write out a marketing plan so that they think through what they want to do. If you want a guide, visit IndieGuide.com/Marketing for a template that you can fill out. Here's what you want to do when you making your plan:

1. **Make a specific goal.** Make sure that you have specific goal, a date, and a target you can judge using numbers. (For example: Get $1,000 in sales by September. Get 3,000 Twitter followers by October 1.)

2. **List details about the competition.** Write down all of the bands that sound like yours, including well-known bands, and ones closer to your popularity. Determine where they have social presences, web presences, and publicity. Include at least one band in your city or region, so you can catch all of their local websites and publications.

3. **Make a profile of your fans.** Make a demographic profile of your fans. (Use the section "The Top Eight Questions You Should Be Able to Answer About Your Audience" for each audience, since you can have multiple audiences that have different marketing messages and needs.)

4. **List your products.** Write the mix of products, merch, and music that you are marketing. Make sure you have all of the conversion tools ready. If your message isn't sending people to at least one conversion tool, it's not a marketing message, it's just talking.

5. **List your communications.** Make a full list of every communication mechanism that's under your control (newsletter, blog, Twitter, Facebook, and others). Include advertising if you want to spend money for this. You'll be using these extensively to get the message out.

6. **List your collaborators.** Make a full list of everyone who can help you get your marketing messages to fans. Include a list of other bands you know that will help, including bloggers and Web sites. These can help broadcast your message to fans.

7. **Make a specific plan, and measure its success.** Pull together the details from the other steps and decide what you're going to do. Then, keep track of it using sales figures, Web site statistics, or other tools you have on hand so you can adjust as you get the message out.

TOP EIGHT EFFECTIVE MARKETING STRATEGIES

Below are eight effective marketing strategies that work no matter how much money you have to promote yourself. They are techniques that can get your marketing messages noticed by fans.

1. **Standing Out** There are more than three hundred thousand indie artists at CD Baby. The bestsellers all have stories to tell, but one of the most surprising ones is about an artist who wrote an entire album about sailing. While that topic alone isn't enough to get an album to the top-sellers list, the musician got her album reviewed in a popular sailing magazine, which got her tons of sales. A review of a sailing album in a *music* magazine would probably have gotten little notice. But because the review appeared in a *sailing* magazine, people read the article and bought the CD.

Dedicated music publications and sites review stacks of CDs and songs. Even if your band gets its album reviewed—and even if it's a good one—it just doesn't stand out. It's just one of many in a sea of other music reviews. Sailing magazines, on the other hand, don't get many albums to review; they get press packets for boats, sails, and gear. So when a packet arrives with an album, it gets noticed and written about. And if a review of an album is actually published, it stands out. This goes for *any* nonmusic specialty magazine, blog, or Web site. By targeting her niche, the woman's CD sales skyrocketed.

We call this the standing-out strategy. The great thing about it is, there's room for everyone. While your music probably occupies a musical niche depending on the type of music you play, this represents only one highly competitive channel for your music. By using any other channels where your music will be the only music to choose from, you'll get noticed.

This is a major shift in thinking that takes some getting used to. It's no longer necessary to stick to places where people listen to music. Forget radio—music can be played on any Web site. There are forums, podcasts, online zines, publications, and sites dedicated to activities where an existing audience might appreciate your music.

Our own experience of this started out accidentally, after we found inspiration in an usual place: an off-the-wall board game designed by Cheapass Games, called Deadwood. A card in the game led us to write a song called "Were All These Beer Cans Here Last Night?" Only a few weeks later, we hit on the idea to e-mail Cheapass Games and share the song that they had unwittingly inspired. We sent them the song, and, surprisingly, they wrote back the next day and asked if they could put it up on their Web site. Within a few months of its being posted, the demo was downloaded well over five thousand times. Soon, it took on a life of its own, winding up on blogs, message boards, and Internet radio stations, all without our help.

Their Web site was so popular that when we searched for "beer cans" on Google, our demo song was on the first page of links. This was great exposure, but it didn't end there. We applied the standing-out strategy and took this idea a step further. We teamed up with Cheapass Games to create an entire album of songs based on their games, *The Cheapass Album*. Best of all, they agreed to give it worldwide distribution along with their games.

Carla Ulbrich (carlau.com), who makes her living as a folksinger, summed it up best: "Go to where you're a novelty." Ulbrich did this by using her wit and off-center perspective to turn an unfortunate series of medical illnesses into inspiration for new music. After releasing albums on these topics, she found new audiences and not only gets traditional gigs but also plays lucrative gigs at medical conventions, where she's known as "the singing patient." At a convention like this, any music stands out.

2. **Piggybacking** Piggybacking can broaden your exposure by taking something people already know well and leveraging it for you. There are three different ways to apply this strategy.

o   *Ride Coattails* As we said in chapter 4, "Your Brand," one of the simplest ways to piggyback is to mention the bands that you actually sound like on your Web site. People who know those bands and search for them will find your site and are likely to give your music a chance. In fact, this is exactly how Web-presence services such as Last.fm work. The simplest way to piggyback is to cover a well-known song by a famous artist. These cover songs are usually an indie artist's best initial sellers. They act as a great gateway for people to discover the artist's original music. But music is not the only thing that you should piggyback on. Consider all the niches in the world and see if there's a place for your music inside one. And niches don't have to be small. We know of one band that wrote a song about the Indianapolis Colts before the team went to the Super Bowl. While Colts fans represent a niche, it's a large one. The band got a ton of airplay and articles, and a lot of fans bought its music because it successfully piggybacked on the Colts at a time when people were paying a lot of attention to them.

There is more than one way to ride on the coattails of another niche. For example, Pete Shukoff, of the group Nice Peter, wrote a song called "50 Cent Is a Pussy." The forums on his Web sites were buzzing after he released it, and he got a lot of angry comments but an equal number of supporters and new fans. He successfully piggybacked on the same guy he was dissing in his song. Even album art can provide you an opportunity for piggybacking. The art for Beatnik Turtle's *The Cheapass Album* was drawn by the renowned comic book and game illustrator Phil Foglio (studiofoglio.com). Foglio has millions of fans, and when we released the album, some people bought it just because they collect his artwork. Our album got listed on a Web site that tracks everything that Phil Foglio illustrates, and he even sold the album from his site.

Again, the place to start is not the traditional music mediums. Instead, brainstorm about concepts, ideas, or even events that can take you further than you would be able to go on your own. For example, when the *Star Wars* thirtieth anniversary came up, we leveraged a song that we had written for TheSongOfTheDay.com called "Star Wars (A Movie Like No Other)." We summarized the entire original *Star Wars* trilogy in a single song (and made fun of episodes I–III). Later we made a video using a mash-up feature at starwars.com. It ended up getting played over fifteen thousand times thanks to the active community at that site. That popularity also led to its being licensed by AtomFilms for use on its Web site and later to Viacom so it could be played on SpikeTV during a *Star Wars* movie marathon.

o *Ride a Tradition* Another way to piggyback is to make an album or a song about a holiday, festival, or other tradition that people know well. We did this twice over—once for St. Patrick's Day with our album *Sham Rock* (2008) and once for Christmas called *Santa Doesn't Like You* (2002). Like clockwork the albums get a slew of new sales every March and December. Christmas is especially potent in that we come up in searches for terms such as "Santa," "Christmas," and "holiday." The titles of songs, such as "Coed Naked Drunk Xmas Shopping" and "Smokin' the Mistletoe," get people to sample our music online out of sheer curiosity.

o   *Ride Trends*   Current events and popular culture provide opportunities for piggybacking as well. When a topic is hot, a large number of people are guaranteed to be searching for information about it. The Brobdingnagian Bards are always looking for trends to ride, so when the Monty Python musical *Spamalot* got popular, they posted a blog entry about *Spamalot* and also mentioned that they covered a Monty Python song previously. The post got a ton of hits, got them noticed by new fans, and resulted in sales.

3.   **The Agent**   Most bands start out promoting and representing themselves, because every band starts out small. But, when possible, it's a powerful advantage to have a person outside the band represent you. People tend to pay attention when someone who is not directly part of the band talks it up. There's an air of objectivity, even if it's promotional.

Agents are distant enough from the music that they can come up with promotional angles, strategies, and ideas that you might never have thought of. They can claim that you're the best band ever. And if they do something that's a little too outrageous, well, they're just an agent; it doesn't reflect directly on the band. It's also why agents are most useful during negotiations, because they can be mercenary. If you negotiate for yourself, and you give the other side a particularly hard time, they'll start to dislike *you*, rather than your agent.

Also, people tend to assume that you've reached a certain threshold of popularity simply because you can afford to have someone act on your behalf. Before she got an agent of her own, Carla Ulbrich would often pretend to be her own agent over the phone, employing a thick New York accent. When people asked to have lunch with the agent, she'd always be too busy, but they were always in luck because Ulbrich herself could make it.

4.   **Cross-Promotion**   Are you making a movie? Great! Promote your album in it. Do you make art? Plug your band Web site on your DeviantArt (deviantart.com) page. The best marketers put more than one product out there, and each of them promotes the others. For example, George Hrab (georgehrab.com) produces his *Geologic* podcast (geologicpodcast.com), which is a talk-show-style, fast-paced humor podcast. But he also plugs his music and has a built-in audience to reach when he puts out new music.

5.   **The Long Haul**   Most major-label bands are only profitable for a short time after they release, so for decades there was always an emphasis on the short-term, quick hit.

For some reason, musicians still think that it has to be true for them as well. But a sustainable career in music is not built overnight—especially when you don't have the money for billboard advertising and saturation of radio play. Instead, it requires "a long, slow burn," as Gavin Mikhail, a musician making a living from his music, says. In today's world, musicians need to allow development to occur naturally and gain an audience and momentum over time.

For instance, Brad Turcotte of Brad Sucks (bradsucks.net) created his own development cycle to maximize his exposure. In 2001, he released his album online in the form of MP3s, garnering some initial interest and some donations. This money allowed him to make a CD, and when he released this, he gained another surge of new fans. A little later, he released the source tracks to his music, this time making new fans among people who enjoy remixing songs. When he packaged the best remixes into another CD, another surge of new fans loved both the remixes and the original material. Finally, when he released his second album, it generated interest in his previous albums. This album cycle should continue as he releases additional albums and new material. As you can see, Turcotte's original material has generated exposure and income for him over the years.

Just as the album cycle takes time to gather momentum, getting noticed within a niche also takes time. Carla Ulbrich noticed that live festivals and conventions also have a cycle. Effectively breaking into each live festival and convention took about three years. Ulbrich needed that time to make the necessary connections and establish her reputation so that she could consistently get booked at events.

Most of the artists we've interviewed have agreed that it takes time to get noticed, develop a following, and acquire a steady income stream. Jonathan Coulton noticed, during his Thing a Week project, bursts of traffic for particular song releases: visitors to his site showed up in huge groups and quickly left. But with each surge, some stuck around, and his regular visitors steadily increased. This will happen for you as well. So whatever you do to get noticed, keep your mind on long-haul strategies.

6.   **Fans as Promoters** Each of your fans with a Twitter or Facebook account has ways of reaching hundreds of people. And these hundreds of people are actively listening to what your fans say because they are their friends and followers. While some musicians just focus on the press, fans now have audiences of their own. Your marketing campaigns should actively ask your fans to talk about what you're promoting. And if you do it right, they will look cool while doing it.

7.   **Make It Viral** Nice Peter (nicepeter.com) gets over one million views to his videos on Epic Rap Battles of History within days of being released. He told us that the secret to viral videos is to create things so "people look cool sharing it with their friends." We call this the "Nice Peter Principle." Knowing what you have—a song, video, image—that can make a person *look cool* when they share it with others will help increase your chances of making it go viral. It will also keep your own band members motivated and working toward the same goals. So always have a sound bite on the tip of your tongue about what you're doing next. Movies have trailers, and a band should have announcements of what's to come.

8.   **Stay Tuned** When radio DJs are about to play commercials, they never go directly into the ads. Instead, they announce what they're going to play after the break, to keep people tuned in. You should adopt this same technique. Always talk about your next project when you talk about your band, whether you're talking to the press, your fans, or other musicians. Here's why: your fans will be motivated to keep tabs on you until that next project is released. Also, it entices the press to ask questions about your upcoming projects and write future stories. It encourages people to get involved and help out. If you don't announce what you have planned, no one will know that he or she can help.

There are no rules to this new music business, so we suggest experimenting with many projects and ideas to see what works best for you. Just keep what sticks, and move on from what doesn't.

MARKETING TECHNIQUES

HOW TO PROMOTE YOURSELF ONLINE WITHOUT SPAMMING

"On their own, social networking sites appear to be either blunt promotional tools or much too intense interpersonal tools. But it doesn't have to be a one-on-one direct engagement with a stranger or 'here's our big rock video'—there's a middle ground," says John Flansburgh of the band They Might Be Giants. "The trick is about finding a friendly and appropriate level of interaction."

So how can you promote yourself without looking like you're spamming people and thus turning people off?

One of the easiest ways to do this is to add a signature to the bottom of your posts or e-mails that links to and talks about what you'd like to promote. This means your regular posts will end up promoting you in a more subtle way.

But on places like Facebook and Twitter, what kinds of topics should you post about? Ariel Hyatt, the founder of Ariel Publicity (arielpublicity.com) and an expert at social-network promotion, has a simple recipe that you can follow to help you appropriately engage your audience. She suggests a mixture of direct conversation, sharing of links, and cross-promotion. Here's a breakdown of how she suggests you should break up every ten posts you do:

- **Direct Engagement.** Approximately three posts out of every ten should be one-on-one conversations with your followers.

- **Shine a Light on Others.** Approximately two posts out of every ten should cross-promote and talk about others. "When you present a video of a song you love or recommend someone else's show you like, it's still about the aesthetic of what you're doing," notes Flansburgh. Why the link love? Because they'll talk about you in return. Retweeting is especially effective in cross-promotion.

- **Share Relevant Links.** Approximately two posts out of every ten should share links and ideas that your fans would like. Share a link to an article you read or a restaurant you visited.

- **Share Pictures.** Approximately two out of every ten posts should be photos. Visuals take very little time for people to look at and are easily enjoyed. Especially share pictures of things that you do as a musician that they don't normally see, like recording at the studio or waiting backstage.

- **Shine a Light on Yourself.** Finally, only one post out of every ten should be about you. By the time you've done the above, your self-promotion will make sense in light of everything else you talk about. In fact, it gives your fans something to repost (and if you've been shining a light on others, it's more likely to get picked up).

THE TOP SIX TIPS FOR WRITING GOOD COPY

Once you really start marketing yourself, you'll be surprised at how much writing—also called copy—you'll have to do. Here are some proven techniques to make your copy work.

1. **Draw them a map.** One of the most useful lessons we've learned about writing content for our Web site came from the book *The Tipping Point*, by Malcolm Gladwell, an examination of how and why trends are started. In *The Tipping Point*, Gladwell tells the story of an experiment performed at a college campus attempting to boost the rate of students getting tetanus shots. The researchers showed the first group photographs of the devastating effects of tetanus and gave the second group a written description. The expectation was that the grotesque visual images would better inspire students to get their shots. The result was counterintuitive: both groups came in at an almost identical (and low) rate. The researchers decided to run a second experiment, but this time gave one of the groups a map to the student health center, even though every student knew where the health center was because they had to visit there when they first showed up at campus. This time, more students in the group with the map got their tetanus shots.

What's the lesson here? We've drawn four from it, and we use them whenever we write for our Web sites:

o **Get to the point.** The content is less important than the message you want to convey. You can write paragraphs about why people should buy your album, but the only important sentence is "Click here to buy our album right now."

o **Call them to action.** Write "Call 555-2983 and book Beatnik Turtle today," not "If you are interested in booking Beatnik Turtle, you should call us at 555-2983." Direct readers to act how you want them to.

o **Keep it simple.** Anything you tell readers to do should be convenient. If you want them to buy an album, don't make them click ten times to do it.

o **Be explicit even when it's obvious.** The map in the experiment was unnecessary yet effective. On your Web site, it may seem unnecessary to write "Click on the button to buy the album" if the button says "Buy now," but it can eliminate any shred of confusion (and it acts as a call to action).

2. **AIDA.** An old marketing acronym reinforces these ideas: AIDA. It stands for four concepts that marketers use when drafting advertising or marketing materials:

o Attention

o Interest

o Decision

o Action

Take your readers through all four of these steps if you want them to respond to a call to action.

3. **Repetition and consistency.** Repetition is also important when influencing people to take action. If you want people to do something, keep repeating that message. Of course, this doesn't have to be done with words. For example, we have images of our albums throughout our site, each of which links to its respective ordering page. Featuring album artwork is one form of repetition. Try to think of as many different ways as you can to repeat your call to action.

4. **Salting.** Would you like to learn a technique that will make people take notice and pay attention to whatever you say? What if you could do it right now, in one easy step?

You would? Great. This technique is called salting, and we're using it on you now by asking a question that only we can answer. Effective salting piques readers' curiosity. Once you've salted their desire to know something, you're the only one who can quench their thirst. This technique is useful for sales, but it can also be handy for conveying information you want people to retain.

5. **Use images for every story.** Include an image wherever text appears. The Web is a visual medium. And less is more. Use graphics and photos to break up long blocks of text.

6. **Subject-Verb-Object (SVO).** Some musicians make the mistake of writing in passive tense. The best sentences use subject-verb-object form rather than forms of the verb "was": "The album was written by our band to show how complicated relationships can be," should be, "Our band wrote the album *Bizarre Love Pentagram* to show how complicated relationships really are in today's world."

HOW TO KEEP FANS ENGAGED AND COMING BACK TO YOU, YOUR WEB SITE, AND YOUR WEB PRESENCES

While it's often possible to get visitors to come to your Web site, the hard part is getting them involved—to come back repeatedly or to stay in touch via your mailing list or RSS feed. Think about the Web sites you check regularly. What do you like about these sites that keep you coming back? What made you subscribe to their feed, join their mailing list, or discuss things in their forums?

Usually, the secret ingredient is fresh, updated content that people *want*. News sites constantly post new stories. YouTube constantly features new videos. Blogs such as BoingBoing (boingboing.net) always have a new blog entry. Daily deal sites such as Woot (woot.com) and Tanga (tanga.com) always have a new product.

As a musician, here is what you can offer at your music Web site to keep people coming back:

1. **Updated Personal Content.** Most of the successful musicians we interviewed for this book communicated regularly with fans, using blogs, podcasts, video blogs, or newsletters. They personalized themselves to their fans, engaged in conversations with them, and had an easy way to promote their latest projects to their fans since they are always tuned in.

    If you do decide to do this, here are techniques that work:

    o   Make a consistent release schedule. Nice Peter has a Monday video blog, and George Hrab has a weekly podcast. As long as you are consistent, you can build an audience.

    o   Actually talk to the audience directly; say "Hey guys" rather than being formal.

    o   Ask questions and elicit comments. For example, the video show *Equals Three* (youtube.com/raywilliamjohnson) has a comment question of the day to get people to comment. If you include such a feature on your site, make sure to respond. Want to get fancy? Use Quora or Twitter to generate questions or suggestions.

o Have thick skin. Not all comments will be positive. And don't feed the trolls: ignore the haters, but be glad that they are there, because that means that people are listening.

2. **Episodic Project Releases.** Jonathan Coulton's episodic project Thing a Week promised fans one new song a week from September 2005 to September 2006. The lure of weekly updates kept people coming back for more, and his forums took off and became extremely active. Fans were always eagerly anticipating the next "thing" to come along.

We did something similar at TheSongOfTheDay.com by releasing a new song for every day of 2007. Visitors returned daily to hear each new song. Over the year, more people kept visiting, and interest in our band and its music grew.

One added benefit of an episodic project is that it tends to generate material for your blog and news feeds. Coulton would regularly blog about the new "thing a week" he was writing and has kept this level of involvement by blogging regularly since. Turcotte maintains an active blog as well, posting not only about his music and upcoming projects but also on topics related to his music, such as the software and equipment he uses, as well as commentary on the music industry—which leads us to a third method.

3. **Updated Nonmusic Content.** You can also use your Web site to cover topics beyond the scope of your band. These topics should be in some way related to what your band is all about, but by widening your focus a bit you can piggyback on the popularity of a larger topic. For instance, if your music speaks of social or political activism and your band feels passionately about an issue, then dedicating a section of your Web site to that issue would be a natural fit.

The Brobdingnagian Bards (thebards.net) did this years ago when they used their site to collect and catalog the lyrics and tabs of traditional Irish folk songs. Adding this section to their band's Web site was natural since the band was rooted in traditional Irish music. This section not only helped them catalog songs for their own repertoire but also became a destination among search engines—sending people directly to their site whenever they searched for information about an old Irish folk song. This piggybacking worked in their favor given that their own music aligned with the music people were searching for. Many new fans discovered the Brobdingnagian Bards simply by searching for their favorite Irish song and listening to free song samples of their music. An album purchase was just a few clicks and sample songs away.

We did this when we released the first edition of *The Indie Band Survival Guide* as a free downloadable PDF from our band's Web site. We wanted to share everything we had learned with other indie musicians. Because no books spoke directly to us as indies, and because we felt strongly enough about the subject to spend over two years researching and writing the initial guide, we felt it would be a natural complement to our band's Web site.

There are more ways to encourage people to return to your site beyond news of a new album for sale or a show next Saturday. The more regular, relevant content you can offer at your site, the more reasons people will have to stay tuned to your Web site and, ultimately, your music.

HOW TO MARKET YOUR MUSIC ON NONMUSIC WEB SITES

Any Web page can share music—it's not all about Internet radio, webcasting, streaming, podcasts, and video. There's an entire Web full of sites out there—blogs, zines, message boards, forums, social-networking sites—and any of them can share a link to an MP3 or embed a video.

Most sites are created by writers who are always hungry for new content, especially content aimed at the niche they're covering. So, rather than catalog Web sites by the kind of media they normally feature (music, video), categorize them by topic. Then find the most popular ones that relate to your music. A mention on the right Web site, blog, or message board can mean a lot of listens for your songs. Getting heard in this way allows people to easily share your music across social media ("going viral"). Plus, nothing on the Web really goes away. Your mention and song will remain on the Web and will be stumbled upon by future readers thanks to search engines and keywords.

For instance, when we wrote our album, *All in a Day's Work (2007)* (an album about the workplace), we prepared for the publicity campaign by listing each of the songs and figuring out which sites might be interested in the music. We came up with categories such as corporate culture, the workplace, the movie *Office Space*, cubicles, and so on. Then we searched to find sites that covered the topics and found workplace humor blogs that fit our list perfectly. As a result, we sent songs to a variety of workplace-humor blogs that poke fun at the corporate work world. Out of that list, a handful of sites wrote back saying they were happy to cover a song so on-target for their niche audience, and so they reviewed the album or featured the song, generating publicity.

To get played on a nonmusic Web site, follow these steps:

1. **Categorize your music by topic or genre.** For songs with lyrics, categorize them by topic. However, if you write instrumentals, categorize your music by genre and mood. For instance, a musician we met at a conference asked how he could get his ambient instrumental music heard on nonmusic Web sites, since it didn't have any obvious lyrical connections. We brainstormed a list of spiritual, meditation, and massage-therapy sites, message boards, and blogs he never thought to target. Additionally, this led him to a realization about the potential of getting his music used (and sold) at massage parlors.

2. **Brainstorm sites, blogs, Webzines, and message boards to target.** Once you've categorized your music, brainstorm what sites might enjoy each song.

3. **Find the sites that match your brainstormed list.** Once you have your list of general sites to target, use your favorite search engine to see what the most popular sites, blogs, and message boards are on the topics. You'll be surprised what you find.

4. **Contact the site and send them a link to your song or video.** Your submission itself should be informal, along the lines of, "You might like this song about snorkeling." Include the song or video (see chapter 2, "Your Music"; chapter 9, "Your Web, Social, and Mobile Presences"; and chapter 14, "Get Seen," for how to share your music in the best way and not as an MP3 file attached to an e-mail).

5. **Ask for links back to your site.** If they use the song, be sure to ask that they provide a link back to your own Web site and to where the song can be purchased in exchange for using the song.

6. **Send a thank-you note.** Once posted, send the contact a thank-you note since this will make it easier to contact them in the future should you have

more songs that tackle the topic they cover. Additionally, cross-promote their site on yours and through your Web, social, and mobile presences.

While this is one of the more informal ways of getting your music heard on the Web, because you're piggybacking on the popularity of each Web site and are using its interest in the topic to get your music in front of new audiences, this can be one of the most effective tools at your disposal.

HOW TO CREATE AND MANAGE A "STREET TEAM" OF FANS

If you have fans willing to help market and publicize your music, you should take them up on their offer, especially since they can put your name and music in places that you haven't even thought of. But without some direction from you, that enthusiasm can be wasted.

For instance, the Brobdingnagian Bards found their fans so enthusiastic about their brand of Irish Celtic music that the fans were posting links to their site and music all over the Web. The problem was, the fans were doing it in places that really wouldn't help get new fans of their type of music. They found that they needed to provide their fans a little guidance to make them more effective.

For you to get the most out of your street team and keep them motivated, you'll need to provide them with the following:

1. **Direction.** Without direction, your team is simply a mob. To get the most out of your team, you need to be clear on what you want them to do, and give them a time frame. Have a clear vision of what you want your fans to do and boil it down to a simple message such as, "Put up posters in a four-block radius around this venue" or "Share our new video using this link to all your Facebook followers." If you don't provide a clear direction, you could lose their interest or give them the impression that you don't care about their time or loyalty.

2. **Tools.** Providing your team with the right tools at the outset will make your team more effective. You'll need to give them posters to canvas the neighborhood or banners and music to post online so that it's easy for them to "just do it" and help you succeed.

3. **Rewards.** Most fans appreciate a reward as a thank-you for participating in your street team. Plus, laying out a reward at the outset of the mission

gives them something to shoot for. Rewards are up to you, so be creative. You can reward the top performer or the top few performers or anyone that meets your goals. Ideas as to what to reward are endless. Some suggestions include

- o   an unreleased song;

- o   an autographed CD;

- o   a T-shirt;

- o   other merchandise (buttons, stickers, posters, etc.);

- o   a live recording of your top street team member's favorite song;

- o   a house concert (see chapter 7, "Your Gigs," for more information);

- o   a spot on your next album; and/or

- o   a song in their honor.

4.   **A Clear Target.**   You won't know whom to reward if you're unable to measure everyone's effectiveness. You'll either have to do this manually yourself, designate someone you trust to manage the team, or have your team members report their progress to you via e-mail.

Although the above can be used off-line as well as online, there are tools available online, such as the one ReverbNation provides, which help you manage your fans and allow fans to report progress through trackable widgets and banners. Additionally, you can buy a street team that already exists. Services like Fancorps (fancorps.com) and FanManager (fanmanager .net) offer street-team management and personnel that can work social networks online. For more information on these and other fan-management services, head to IndieGuide.com/Marketing.

LEARNING MORE

Go to IndieGuide.com/Marketing for a clickable version of every link, Web site, and service mentioned in this chapter, as well as free extra materials to help you handle music marketing.

CHAPTER 12

THE STRATEGIC GOAL: to get the media to write and talk about you and your music to others

REFERENCE: IndieGuide.com/PR

What	Description
Band Bio	A one-page, one-paragraph, and one-sentence bio for your band's press kit
Band Photo	Formal band photo for press and marketing. Should be a 8"x10" 300 DPI JPEG
Press Clippings	Quotes and links to your best press coverage for your press kit and online presences
Info Sheet	A one-page sheet with the key facts about your band such as your name, hometown, band members, links, discography, bands you sound like, and other information to make it easy for journalists to write about your band
Song Samples	Samples of your music for the press
Press Releases	Press releases for each story that you want to put out
PR Newswires	A set of newswires you will use for your press releases (many are free and thus always available for releases)
Targeted Press Lists	A list of contacts for your press campaigns
Interview Talking Points and Sound Bites	When being interviewed, you should have talking points and sound bites ready to go to get your message across.
Publicist	Either get a publicist, or specify a publicity contact, even if it's you. Either way, the press needs a single contact if they want to interview you.

GET PUBLICIZED

"All is fair in love and PR."

—FELICE ECKER, FOUNDER OF THE MEDIA, MARKETING,
AND MANAGEMENT FIRM GIRLIE ACTION

THE WORLD appears completely different when you look at it through publicity-colored glasses. You start thinking about the press angle for everything you do as a band. You see potential press releases for every achievement. You start thinking about everything your band will do three to four months from now, because that's the lead time most media outlets need.

Every form of entertainment relies on the media to get people interested. While it would be great to just focus on playing music, musicians don't have that luxury if we want to get our music heard by as many people as possible. As Ariel Hyatt, the founder of Ariel Publicity (arielpublicity .com), said, "I don't care what business you're in, big or small, unless you spend forty percent of your time on promotion and marketing, you're dead in the water."

Although the Internet has made it much easier to communicate and get some attention, it's really only added another layer to your publicity campaigns, one you can worry about a little closer to the event itself. Publicity can be a large and mysterious world, so we're going to cover the parts of it that are important for musicians and break it into steps so you can conquer it.

UNDERSTANDING THE MEDIA AND PR

WHAT YOU SHOULD KNOW ABOUT THE MEDIA
AND PUBLIC RELATIONS

The Internet has changed everything that delivers content. In journalism, the Web has enabled more coverage of topics outside the mainstream, or ones that weren't as appealing to advertisers. Citizen journalists can cover subjects unhindered by political or financial influence or by a specific publication format or schedule. And Web-based reporters have short-circuited the process of journalism, forcing the older model to play catch-up.

Today, we have "new media" as well as the "traditional media." We will offer a definition here of each term, but the world is blending these topics, and that's why you need to research your media outlets carefully before submitting and never take their requirements for granted. To make things simple, in this chapter we will refer to press contacts as journalists whether they have a radio show, podcast, TV show, blog, or magazine or newspaper column.

While most people think that journalists find stories by pounding the streets and investigating, that's not the way it normally works. Although they occasionally do find stories the old-fashioned way, in reality most of the articles you read are based on press releases. You should also drop any illusions about journalists covering you just because you're playing good music. There's no shortage of good music.

What this means is that, if you want the traditional media to pay attention to you, you should get the stories directly into their hands. It also means that you will be competing with professional PR people who do this for a living. If this sounds tough, that's because it is. But you *can* do this yourself. You do have one thing going for you: journalists are always looking for a good story, and you can give it to them.

The two types of media are as follows:

- **Traditional Media:** The traditional media generally have formal submission guidelines, prefer press releases, and require three to four months of lead time. Examples include: newspapers and newswires, televised news and talk shows, radio programs, and magazines.

- **New Media:** The new media generally have informal submission guidelines, prefer personal messages to press releases, and don't require long leads. Examples include: blogs, podcasts, video blogs, and other Web sites.

WHAT EVERY MUSICIAN NEEDS TO KNOW ABOUT TODAY'S
MEDIA LANDSCAPE: PREFILTERS AND POSTFILTERS

In the past, there were two layers of filters that affected promotion: prefilters and postfilters. Prefilters were the gatekeepers who decided what music was made and publicized, such as music executives, agents, and A&R representatives. Postfilters were the publications and people that reviewed music such as newspapers, magazines, Web sites, and trusted friends.

Because prefilters are no longer a factor for indies—after all, any musician can now make and distribute music on their own—postfilters have grown more important. Now that music has been democratized, people are turning to others to help them find the gems "out there." Plus, today anyone can review and recommend music—whether on their blog, in a comment in a forum, through a post to their favorite social network, or even by writing a product review on Amazon. The traditional reviewers, who were at times influenced by the major players, suddenly have genuine competition from people who want nothing more than to share their opinions. This authenticity is the true currency of the Internet.

Postfilters are the primary way that people will find out about your band. As Jim DeRogatis, the former music editor for the *Chicago Sun-Times* and cohost of National Public Radio's *Sound Opinions*, says, it's the reviewers that help direct people to your music. "No matter how obscure a name I throw at you or you throw at me, the fact that we'll be able to, in no time at all, sample that band for ourselves is incredibly liberating. But you'd never know about [these groups] if I didn't mention it to you."

In today's Internet-enabled world, the types of postfilters have exploded:

- **The traditional music reviewers.** These are the music critics like NPR's *Sound Opinions* hosts, Greg Kot and Jim DeRogatis. Such critics get paid for giving their personal opinions about what is worthwhile. Nowadays they can be found not only in newspapers, magazines, and TV, but on blogs, Web sites, podcasts, and more.

- **Community-based filters.** Community-based filters are Web sites that let their own communities suggest and vote on what its members consider to be the best content. With a large enough community, this can be a powerful way to filter. Some examples of community-based filters include

StumbleUpon (stumbleupon.com), MetaFilter (metafilter.com), Digg (digg.com), and Reddit (reddit.com).

• **Editor-based submission filters.** These postfilters combine elements of traditional reviewers with community-based filters. A Web site that has editor-based submission filters will accept submissions from anyone, but an editor will sift through these and post what he or she thinks is worthwhile. An example of this type of postfilter is Slashdot (slashdot.org).

• **Aggregation filters.** Since so many opinions are now to be found, some sites aggregate reviews to give a more accurate picture. For instance, Rotten Tomatoes (rottentomatoes.com) takes reviews from known movie reviewers and quantifies their opinions into a combined approval percentage for each film.

• **Word of mouth.** The most important kind of filter there is. One that becomes even more powerful online thanks to social-networking sites like Facebook (facebook.com), Twitter (twitter.com), and Google+ (plus.google.com)

• **Advertising and marketing.** Although these are less effective than the other types of filters, advertising and marketing can have a powerful effect on what rises into people's consciousness.

As an indie musician, you'll need to target these postfilters. We'll talk about the techniques below.

THIRTEEN PR CONCEPTS YOU SHOULD USE TO PROMOTE YOUR MUSIC

Use these PR techniques to promote your music:

1. **Think publicity, always.** Everything your band does should be considered material for press coverage. When you're planning anything, from a performance to an album launch, ask yourself, Is this sufficiently newsworthy? If necessary, alter your plans to make your new project even more press-friendly. While some musicians just focus on music, remember that music is entertainment. And entertainment and publicity go together like peanut butter and chocolate.

2. **PR is an ice pick.** Bob Baker (bob-baker.com), author, teacher, and music-marketing guru, said it best when he said that if you want to punch through a wall, you should use something sharp like an awl. The more narrowly you define your audience, the more effective your PR campaign will be, since you can focus your energies on the outlets that reach your audience. Plus, because you understand your audience more deeply, you can also write a more targeted message that will likely cut through the noise, get picked up by the media, and resonate with your audience.

3. **PR is a Crock-Pot, not a microwave.** The Internet has made us impatient. We expect information, and gratification, immediately. Unfortunately, PR takes place in people time rather than Internet time. Even successful PR campaigns take months, even years. The goal of your campaign is twofold: getting coverage for your upcoming event and spreading the word about your band in the long term. The first press write-ups in a PR campaign are hard to get because you have nothing to build on. But once you have some press clippings, it gets easier to get more stories. This means you need to start small. For your first campaigns, target local newspapers, blogs, and anything else that seems to be within your arm's reach. Use those initial press clippings to get mentions in more widely read or prestigious outlets.

4. **It's still about who you know.** You get two things out of press coverage. One is the clipping itself, and the other is a new press contact who now knows you, liked your story, and is likely to cover you in the future. Always send thank-you notes to journalists who mention you, and do your best to get to know them personally. Professional publicists personalize press releases to some journalists because, by establishing a personal connection, they can get more of their stories covered.

5. **If the media didn't cover it, it never happened.** The media is like a public memory. If you had an event and the press never covered it, it's as if it never happened. Because of this, you should try to get at least some kind of clipping about every major event that you do, even if it's only a mention on a blog. It's the best way to establish the history of your band.

6. **Journalists' secret pleasure: getting a scoop.** If there's one thing that journalists love, it's being the first to break a story. Giving a journalist the scoop on what your band is up to, before sending the press release to others,

works especially well if you know a journalist personally. Keep in mind that this can also work against you, because sometimes other outlets will lose interest if the news was already released. If you do this, keep track of which stories are under wraps and which have been released. This is a technique for more established bands since what they do tends to be newsworthy.

7. **Two ways to get coverage: make coverage happen, then make it so that they spontaneously cover you—be easy to contact.** A PR campaign boils down to a two-pronged strategy: sending out press releases to try to convince journalists to write a particular story and making it as easy as possible for the press to cover you if they decide to do so.

You can do a few things to increase the likelihood that journalists *spontaneously* write stories about you:

o Write clear press-contact information on your Web site, so it's obvious whom reporters should ask about interviews. Also, provide all the tools they would need to write a story, such as bios, fact sheets, and images.

o Get blogs to write about you. Both traditional-media and new-media journalists watch blogs for story ideas.

o Piggyback on events that are already being covered by the press. For instance, you might offer to perform at a noteworthy charity event. (Note: many charities have publicists. You should ask if they do and work with them.)

o Add, "If you are a member of the press and want a free CD, write to us at . . ." to all of your Web presences, to welcome journalists to get your music.

o Brainstorm and execute projects that are unusual, interesting, or newsworthy.

When we began our Song of the Day project to release a song every single day for a year, we only announced it to our fans. But word about it spread as people blogged about it, generating a lot of interest and sending more people to the site. In another instance, Todd Martens at *Billboard* magazine wrote about our band because he read about us on Lawrence Lessig's blog (lessig .org), and Caryn Rousseau of the Associated Press wrote about us after reading a short blurb about us in a Chicago-happenings blog called Gapers Block (gapersblock.com). None of these stories began as a press release, but they weren't entirely spontaneous because the seeds were planted in other media.

8. **Use polite persistence.** The most important qualities of a media campaign are consistency and persistence. Both of these qualities will establish you as a serious source of news for journalists. So you need to send quality press releases regularly. Once you develop relationships with the press, you can send more direct and informal messages.

o **No means no, but . . .** If you get a no, accept it, but remember that it just means they won't print *this* article at *this* particular time. They might still pick up a future release, so don't take them off your list.

o **It's the second e-mail that counts.** Some journalists won't even talk to you until you've followed up after sending the first one, even if you are a professional publicist. We've heard stories that some outlets don't even contact you back until you've written *five* times. So when you e-mail press releases, wait a week, then send a follow-up if you don't hear back. You always have an excuse: spam filters sometimes eat e-mails, so it's acceptable to confirm whether they received your earlier e-mails.

o **Never send an old story.** Persistence does not mean sending reworded versions of old stories to the same outlets. Make sure that every new release covers new news. It's okay to refer to older events in a new release, as long as there's new content or a new angle.

9. **Two steps forward, one step back.** When you get major press coverage, your site will immediately get a huge number of visitors over a short time, perhaps a day or so. And after that initial burst of traffic, your site will go back to normal, but with a slightly higher number of regular visitors. People will often read a news story or find a link on a bulletin board and click through for a closer look. After checking that one page and satisfying their curiosity, most will leave. Only a few will be hooked enough to stick around.

Jonathan Coulton had this experience throughout his Thing a Week project as certain songs got coverage. For instance, he recorded a unique cover of the song "Baby Got Back," which, after some good blog coverage, had him deluged with listeners. The majority just downloaded the song and went on their way. But after the visits cooled off, his Web statistics indicated he'd gained a few more regular visitors. We noticed the same trend with our Song of the Day project.

10. **The two magic words: "solicited materials."** When it comes to any physical mail you might send, there are two magic words: "solicited materials." Use them when you can. If you get in touch with a journalist and he or she tells you to send your materials, that's an invitation to use those magic words on your envelope. These words will move your press release to the top of the stack since it's expected. If you do send a press release that was solicited, be sure to write this on the envelope and in the cover letter. And you should still follow up with a phone call to make sure that it arrived.

11. **Never make them wait.** If a journalist reaches out to you, never make them wait if they get in touch with you for a story. They have deadlines. If you make them wait, you might miss out on a chance for publicity.

12. **The best place to start: find bands similar to yours, and see who covered them.** One of the simplest ways to figure out where to get coverage is to study bands with similar music to yours who are a step or two ahead of you in terms of popularity and success. Simply perform a Web search on those bands to find out where they've gotten press and contact the journalists that covered them.

13. **Research the journalists.** Use your favorite search engine to research anyone who is interviewing you, reviewing you, or you want to get in touch with. This can give you the information you need to get covered, as well as an idea of what kinds of articles they write. Especially read any blogs that they write, since you can get a sense of their personality and what they've been up to lately.

PREPARING FOR PUBLICITY
WHAT MUSICIANS SHOULD KNOW ABOUT
THE TRADITIONAL MEDIA

Traditional media are still formal, which makes them harder to approach. Because of this, many musicians don't even bother trying for coverage. It's true that the new media is becoming more and more effective at getting the word out, but a good media campaign should embrace both kinds.

Traditional media need large lead times—they often have three to four months of stories queued up, so you will need to contact them early. They will also need an official press release and your press kit. But you can now start with informal e-mails that tickle their interest. The only time you will need their physical address is when you send them a CD.

The key factor of a traditional-media outlet is its target demographic. Traditional outlets are acutely aware of who makes up their audience and what they are interested in. This isn't surprising, considering most of these media companies make their money from advertising and their success rests on their advertisers knowing what demographics are being targeted. This means that traditional-media outlets are looking for perfect-fit stories for their demographic.

Focus on solving problems for each journalist you target. Journalists are interested in the following:

- **Finding Relevant Stories.** Journalists are always on the lookout for interesting stories that will be appropriate for their demographic. People buy kickboxing magazines to read about kickboxing. People check the local newspaper when they want to do something fun, such as see a band over the weekend.

- **Hitting Deadlines.** Journalists are tasked with filling a certain amount of space before their deadline. To be safe, they usually build up a three- to four-month buffer of stories.

- **Getting the Facts.** Journalists need all the information to flesh out the story, including facts and photos. Research takes time, and if it takes too much time, they may cut their losses and skip the story altogether.

- **Capturing the Zeitgeist.** Journalists want to write stories of the moment, identifying and covering the latest trends.

The more you can meet journalists' needs, the more coverage you will get. This might mean that you write targeted press releases to particular media outlets based on their focus and demographics. If you send a general press release, keep the above goals in mind when you write it and give outlets enough hooks to take your story in different directions for their own needs. And always consider piggybacking on a story that is big at the moment.

WHAT MUSICIANS SHOULD KNOW ABOUT THE NEW MEDIA

The new media are informal, fast, and usually inconsistent in quality. These online outlets are mostly run by people who are simply covering what they personally love. Generally, they won't write their stories or record their podcasts ahead of time the way traditional media do. In fact, they often don't have a regular release schedule. New-media journalists are usually skeptical of the traditional media and love to cover topics that the traditional media won't.

And of course, one of the topics that traditional media ignore is indie music. Many new-media proponents argue that traditional media are keeping good indie music from the people who want to hear it. (And who are we to argue?) In short, being an indie band is an advantage, not a disadvantage, when it comes to new media.

Ironically, new-media journalists dislike anything that looks like promotion. For example, when we worked on getting a blog review of our fifth CD, *All in a Day's Work,* we sent an e-mail to the Office Humor Blog (officehumorblog.com) because the album seemed to be a perfect fit. Indeed, the writer liked it and decided to cover it. But take a look at how the writer started the review: "Last week I received an e-mail from a person representing a band called Beatnik Turtle—a band that apparently has an office-themed album coming out August 7. Normally I'd write off such an email as some sort of spam, but I decided to check out the Beatnik Turtle Website to see what they have to offer and I'm glad I did."

A member of the traditional media would *never* start an article admitting that an e-mail from a representative of the band caught their attention. (And if they did, most of their articles would start that way!) But in this case the writer was not only telling the story of how he found out about it, he was also disclosing, in the interest of transparency, that he found out about it from the band itself.

So the traditional media expects you to send them unabashedly self-promoting materials, but usually ignores them. The new media, on the other hand, would love to write articles about you but *doesn't want to get anything that seems like promotion!*

That's not the only irony. Traditional media write supposedly neutral or unbiased articles based on these press releases. Those writing for the new media, in spite of rejecting outright promotion, usually take a personal or biased point of view of news, events, and entertainment (most are even written in the first person just like the above blog).

Unlike the traditional media, the new media don't feel the need to please their audiences because they aren't usually trying to sell anything to them. They cover topics because it's their passion, not because they are trying to hit a particular demographic or drive sales for their advertising department. This gives the new media an authenticity that is lacking in the traditional media.

The new media don't usually have a backlog of news and don't feel pressured to meet deadlines. They often cover stories immediately. But because they print news whenever they want, they often have a bigger appetite for news than the traditional media. The exceptions, of course, are the largest and most popular examples of blogs and new media. They tend to act more like the traditional media, lining up stories ahead of time and sometimes reporting on press releases.

Just as you have to fit in to the needs of the traditional media, you will also have to fit in with the new media to get covered. But the process is entirely different. New-media journalists want stories that are personally interesting to them. Their interests are easy enough to figure out by looking at the topics covered by their site. Most bloggers and podcasters find stories on their own. The best way to convince them to cover you is to encourage them to make the story their own and find a unique spin.

In general, the new media love covering niche stories, ones outside the mainstream. They love poking fun at the traditional media and also glom on to stories about bucking the system. As an indie, you will often have these stories. For instance, one of our fans blogged about how he was frustrated by the digital-rights-management (DRM) restrictions that Napster imposed on his music and used our album as an example. This was a number of years ago, when the music industry did not release any of its digital downloads in DRM-free formats. We disliked DRM as well and only made our music available on Napster through CD Baby, which put us in every digital music store. So, we sent the blogger DRM-free versions of all of the songs he'd bought. The blogger was so happy about it, he wrote a new entry in his blog about it.

We wrote a blog entry about it ourselves, and sent a link to the Stanford Law professor Lawrence Lessig. Since he was talking about DRM in his blog, it was highly relevant to him, and he picked up the story. And because Lessig was so influential, other blogs then picked it up.

While pitches to traditional media need to be formal, the opposite is true for those to new media. Some do accept press kits, but sending one is usually a mistake. If you're *lucky*, they'll ignore it. If you're not, they will publicly criticize you for your shameless self-promotion. Here are a few ideas for getting new-media coverage:

- Send a short e-mail consisting of nothing more than "Hey, I thought you might like this," with a link to a blog entry or song, using a nonband account.

- Get someone else, preferably a fan of the site who has suggested material in the past, to send an e-mail on your behalf.

- If the site accepts comments or features a message board, find a way to relate your song or story to the discussion at hand. Since site owners usually read their own Web site's comments, this is an authentic way to give them the idea for a story.

- Find sites that you like, and tell the site owners that you're with a band, and that you love their blog or podcast or video show. Then tell them they may like your song, album, or story, and send it to them. While this is self-promotion, it's also a meeting of equals that new-media types sometimes appreciate. This also opens the possibility of cross-promotion. For example, we did this when we found a podcast doing a story about people who talk on their cell phones, annoying everyone around them. We submitted our song "Do You Mind" (bit.ly/doyoumindsong), which is about that very topic, and got it played on the podcast.

- Read a site's most recent blog entries and articles or watch their most recent videos. These can all give you hooks and ways to tie your music to what they are working on.

Remember that the new media will cover stories soon after they learn about them. Some will post stories within a week, some the same day. And, of course, some are unreliable and won't cover a story even if they say they will. And most will get at least one thing wrong when they write about you, so check it over—they are also usually receptive to fixing it.

HOW TO MAKE A PRESS KIT—ONLINE AND PHYSICAL

When a journalist receives a press packet from you, he or she will ask two questions: Who are these guys? And, What do they want from me? The press kit answers the first question. Your press release answers the second. The good news about your press kit is that you can use it over and over with any release that you send out.

A press kit consists of the following:

1. **Band bio.** You can create two kinds of bios: one for the press, the other for bookers. The band bio for the press should always fit on one page and feature a picture of the band. This bio should tell a story that tickles the readers' interest, giving them just a flavor for the rest of your press materials. Don't make this a history of the band. The band bio for bookers should provide a history of the band, as well as each musician, so that a potential booker can see how much experience the band collectively has.

If you'd like examples, go to IndieGuide.com/PR for a place to start.

2. **Band photo.** Visuals can decide whether a kit is read or tossed. Avoid the standard pictures of the band in front of a brick wall; try to stage photos that are distinctive and memorable. Journalists will often look at the band photo before listening to the music, and it can color their perceptions of what they hear.

3. **Press clippings.** Nothing in your press kit is more effective than press clippings. They provide real-world, objective validation of your band's success. Also, journalists hate missing a story, and the right clippings can make them feel as if they've been missing out on something great. Use these guidelines to make your clippings sheet:

- Choose the best of the best.

- Your clippings page should be no more than two pages, front and back.

- Take the best quotes or snippets from the clips, and put them in a list on the sheet.

- Feature articles should be included whole (which could make the clippings longer than two pages, but a feature article warrants it).

- Reviews and fan quotes are both fair game.

4.   **Info sheet.** Since your bio is a story about your band, you will need a separate info sheet that lists details such as when your band was founded, your discography, what your music sounds like, and other details journalists might need for their story. This should be no longer than two pages. You'll want this online as well so that they can easily cut and paste the information. Here's a list of everything that you should consider adding:

o   **Your Name.** So that they can spell it right!

o   **Sounds Like.** A one- or two-sentence blurb about your band and its music. Include bands you sound like.

o   **Basic Information.** Web site address, genre, date founded, and hometown

o   **Discography.** List each album, the date released, and a descriptive blurb. For our info sheet, we include thumbnail images of our album covers to add some color.

o   **Band Members.** Instrumentation and list of band members

o   **Radio Plays.** If you have any radio play, indicate where and when.

o   **Live-show Info.** List venues where your band has played live and any tours you've done.

o   **Press.** You may wish to list in one place all the media outlets that have covered you. Unlike the clippings page, this is just a list of the outlets, articles, and dates.

o   **Upcoming Projects.** You should list the projects you are currently working on.

This info sheet takes longer than you'd think because it calls for brief, targeted writing. The trickiest part is keeping the information up to date.

Review your info sheet monthly and add to it as you get more press, plays, and exposure.

5.   **Song samples (online press kit only).** Pick three of your strongest songs and add them to the online press kit. Use an embedded Flash Player so people can just hit play if they want to hear what you sound like. If you have

multiple pages in your online press kit, keep the player on the left or right side of every page.

Your goal is to give the press samples of every type of media you create: text, photos, music, and video. Find the best of what you have of each, and put it on your pages to give them a taste. Do not set music or video to play automatically on these pages, because you don't want to annoy people who just want your bio or photo.

6. **Press releases (online press kit only).** You should include your prior press releases in your online press kit so the press can refer to what you've done before.

7. **Video (online press kit only).** If there's a video on the online press kit, it's nearly always going to be the first thing that they try out.

8. **Make sure it's consistent, accurate, and arresting.** Once you're done, check it over to make sure that your press kit meets these key points:

- Keeps the format consistent for all pages of the kit.

- Studies have shown that you only have about six seconds to grab attention with your press kit. It should be visually arresting and should give journalists the information they want quickly.

- Uses pictures: they are often the first thing that people will look at and can really improve journalists' reaction to the press kit.

- Your contact information is on every page of the kit. Include name, e-mail address, phone number, and Web site address. Remember: they may lose the front page.

HOW TO WRITE A PRESS RELEASE

Press releases are mostly aimed at traditional media, but while you are unlikely to send the new media your releases, they may end up going to your site to research you and read them. Press releases work best when they incorporate current trends in pop culture. It's easier for journalists to sell their audience on a story it is already familiar with rather than a completely new one.

Press-release writing can be difficult. You might find yourself laboring over each word. We find it to be the most demanding kind of writing that we do. See IndieGuide.com/PR for ideas and samples to work with.

Although we provide the steps to write it yourself below, another option is to pay services to write them for you. If you are looking for help, see Beat Wire (beatwire.com) or Music Industry News Network (mi2n.com). And go to IndieGuide.com/PR for links to more services.

To write a press release, here are the basics:

1. **Follow these guidelines:**

    o **Length.** It should be one page long.

    o **Contact Information.** Add your publicity contact information at the top of each page. Include a name, phone, and e-mail and Web site addresses.

    o **Release Date.** If there's a date that the story should be released (such as the release date of an album), put it at the top. Otherwise, add "For immediate release."

    o **Headline.** The headline, often written in all caps, should be designed to catch the journalist's attention. It's a good idea to use salting here.

    o **The Lead.** This is the first sentence or two of the press release. There are two types. A news release should answer the questions who, what, when, where, why, and how. A feature story should have a hook that is attention-grabbing or amusing.

    o **The Press Release Text.** Tell your story briefly, succinctly, and make it as compelling as possible. Aim it at your audience members' interests as you write it, and read it out loud several times to make sure that it's punchy. Use small words and subject-verb-object sentence construction for more impact.

    o **Call to Action.** Your story should have a call to action.

    o **Mention Recent and Future Projects.** Near the end of a press release, it's a good idea to mention recently finished projects as well as future ones. You never know what the press will pick up on.

    o **Envelope Teasers.** When you mail the press your materials, write further information on the envelope itself. For instance, Carla Ulbrich, a folk musician, always writes a special note if she'll be in town, such as "Playing in your area at the Riviera on March 12!"

If you'd like model press releases to start from, we have a template for you to use, and have posted some examples at IndieGuide.com/PR.

2. **Have an editor (or someone else) look at it.** If you are serious about getting coverage, have someone else look it over. Spelling errors, grammatical errors, or obvious mistakes can waste all of your hard work.

PLANNING AND EXECUTING YOUR PUBLICITY CAMPAIGNS

HOW TO RUN A PUBLICITY CAMPAIGN

Press campaigns can be as simple as sending out a press release, and as complicated as a highly orchestrated mailing campaign simultaneously promoting a tour and a new album. No matter what you are trying to do, stick to these steps:

1. **Determine your goal.** Your most effective press campaigns will have well-defined goals. Goals help determine which media outlets to target and how to best schedule your campaign.

    Some example goals include:

    o   Get articles written about a CD-release party.

    o   Get a review of your album.

    o   Get coverage of a big charity show.

    o   Get attention for a music video.

    o   Increase your draw for an upcoming tour.

    These are, of course, just examples, but the point is that they don't always have to be big goals. Any goal will help determine the later steps.

2. **Prepare a targeted press list.** Your press list is simply a list of the submission contacts at each outlet. If you haven't worked with that outlet before, you will have to research to find the right person. The easiest way to start is to find bands similar to yours, and find out where they've been covered. Then just reach out to the same journalists.

    This is where publicists have an advantage, because they have already gathered a large database of contacts and can put together press lists for new campaigns quickly. Many publicists will send an e-mail with personalized notes to each contact to raise their response rate. If you don't know who they are, spend a bit of time and research them yourself. This will help you target your releases.

Also note that each media outlet will respond to different aspects of your stories. Music journalists will be concerned with your music and your influences, the local paper will want to know about your latest shows, and so on. You may need different press releases for each of these targets, and they will each have different deadlines, so plan carefully. And keep in mind that you shouldn't send every press release to every outlet. Some of your press releases will go to just a handful of outlets.

3. **Plan the timing.** Traditional-media journalists need lead times of around three months. They want to know about the news before it happens, so that they have the necessary lead time to break the news the moment it does. New-media journalists tend to want info closer to the date that it happens. No more than a week or so ahead of time. For tours, send the press release as soon as details are available.

4. **Update your press kit.** Before you send out your press materials, it's a good idea to look over your fact sheets, bios, clippings, and other materials. Details change quickly with bands, and it's worth your time to make sure everything is up to date. Often, we'll find that our fact sheet mentions future events that have already taken place. We also often find new information to add, such as new places where our music has been played.

5. **Write press releases.** Use the section above for the steps to writing a good press release. They should be targeted for each type of outlet to be most effective.

6. **E-mail press releases.** Most outlets prefer e-mail press releases. Make sure you have a compelling subject line and a punchy lead, because the subject line might be the only thing a journalist reads before deleting your e-mail. Provide links to your online press kit in the press release. Links to songs, and especially videos, are also recommended.

7. **Snail mail CDs.** You should only spend the money to send a paper press release when you have a CD to promote. And you generally should only send a CD if it's requested, or if the outlet definitely requests CDs. If you do send a package, you'll need paper versions of your press kit, your

press release, and a pitch letter. The pitch letter should summarize the press release and should tease the journalist into reading more.

8. **Use polite persistence: send follow-up e-mails and use track-back.** Remember that some journalists won't even read your release until you've followed up—sometimes several times. After your campaign begins, track your progress by searching for your band name in search engines and watching the referrers page of your Web-site stats. You'd be surprised how often reporters write about you without informing you of it.

9. **Send thank-you messages.** If you get a story covered, send a thank-you, but don't expect a reply. You want to use each successful article to build a relationship with the press. The more you know them personally, the more articles they are likely to write about you.

HOW TO BE INTERVIEWED

If your press release hits home, you might be called for an interview. How well your interview goes will depend partly on your personality and partly on preparation. Interviews are much like stage performances: you need to practice for them just as you'd practice for a show. The difference is, you will never be sure what questions you'll be asked. Here are some techniques that will help you prepare.

1. **Research the journalist.** A few minutes of searching the Web on the person interviewing you can reveal a lot of information that can help you do a good interview. You can learn their point of view and the kinds of stories that they write. If you can find their blog, you can see what they have been up to lately, and you can bring this up when you first meet with them. This can give you an instant connection that can make the interview go well.

2. **Know what to expect.** By the time you're contacted to do an interview, the journalists usually have an idea of the story that they want to tell. Most of the time, they are interviewing you to fish for original quotes that will match their story (which they often have partially composed—sometimes just in their heads) and so you can perhaps fill in some details that weren't covered in your press release or press kit. It's rarer to get a feature story, where a journalist will interview you to learn what you're really about. Your goal during the interview is to give journalists what they're looking for while subtly blending in the points you want to get across. It's a delicate balance.

Unless it's a Q&A-style story, you'll be lucky to see more than two actual quotes from a one-hour interview. You don't have much control over these stories, except for how you answer questions and the points that you manage to squeeze in. After your first interview or two, you will probably be frustrated by the errors—most journalists get at least one thing wrong in every article. They will misspell your name, get your Web-site address wrong, get the story out of order, or take something you said out of context. This is why you will normally just take one or two quotes out of the article for your press list.

Combat these problems with talking points, sound bites, and other techniques we talk about below.

3. **Prepare talking points.** Talking points are just a list of the points you want to cover, with short statements ready to go for each point. You will usually have two types of talking points handy for interviews. One consists of answers to basic questions such as, "Who are your influences?" and, "Where do you get your ideas?" The other includes points that you want to introduce to the interviewer, such as your latest projects and anything that your band will be doing over the next few months. If the interview seems to be getting offtrack, you should try to pull it back to the talking points, because that will be the strongest material.

4. **Make sound bites.** Sound bites are short packaged statements you can prepare ahead of time that are easily quotable. They are useful for print journalists, who are looking for easy quotes to drop into their piece, but they're especially useful for radio and TV interviews. If you give journalists a good sound bite, they are more likely to use that than something you said off-the-cuff that might not reflect positively on you.

5. **Prepare stories.** Have stories ready to go for interviews. Be specific and engaging, since it gives journalists hooks to write about. For radio and television, stories can make an interview truly memorable.

6. **Give them fact sheets and follow-ups.** When the interview is done, send journalists an e-mail with the key facts that they can use for the article. Also, thank them and offer to clarify anything that you think was unclear. These two steps may save you a lot of grief in the future. It will also help cement your relationship with them, which is an even more important objective.

HOW TO USE PR NEWSWIRES AND PRESS SERVICES
TO BLAST OUT PRESS RELEASES

Newswires accept press releases and blast them out to all of their subscribers, who are journalists of every type. Many publications rely on these wires as sources of fresh stories, rather than doing their own. When we were covered by the Associated Press, for example, the story went to many publications, and newspapers in different parts of the country picked it up. Newswires are a particularly good place to get coverage because of this.

The good news is that there are some newswires that you can submit your own press releases to. Use the following steps:

1. **Put together your press release.** Use the steps from earlier in the chapter. And definitely pass it in front of multiple people, to make sure it has no spelling errors or problems.

2. **Choose press wires.** There are free and paid versions of press wires.

   o Free newswires: try Music Industry News Network (mi2n.com), Rock and Metal (rockandmetal.com), and Free Press Release (free-press-release.com).

   o For-pay newswires: try Beatwire (beatwire.com) or Music Submit (musicsubmit.com).

See IndieGuide.com/PR for links to dozens more press wires, both free and otherwise.

HOW TO GET INTO SITES THAT AGGREGATE NEWS STORIES

Sites such as Slashdot (slashdot.org), Fark (fark.com), MetaFilter (metafilter .com), Reddit (reddit.com), StumbleUpon (stumbleupon.com), and Digg (digg.com) have large audiences and are key targets for Internet campaigns. The best part about these sites is that they don't only post news stories. They can, and often do, post links to songs, videos, or whatever is related to one of their interests. They are always happy to send their users to something entertaining. This can provide you with a lot of traffic in a short amount of time. Each has a different method for getting posted, whether that be passing a community vote or impressing a small group of editors.

Here's how to get posted on news aggregators like these:

1. **Participate in the site, make a profile, and learn how it ticks.** Each of these sites has a particular character and different ways that they take submissions. Your story has to fit perfectly, and it should come from a profile on the site that has an established history. Participate in the sites yourself before submitting anything for your band.

2. **Make the story title controversial, titillating, sexy, arresting, or suggestive, or target news or events that the readers are interested in.** On these sites, remember that they are based on user-submitted links chosen by editors or by votes. The title or subject line of what you submit is everything. If the subject line doesn't make you want to immediately click on the link, keep working on it.

Take a look at the stories that get picked up at each of the sites to see how to grab a site's interest. Stories at Slashdot should have a geek element. MetaFilter's front page looks like a series of comments about headlines, so sensational stories tend to work. And Fark tends to pick up news of the weird, strange, stupid, or amazing.

HOW TO GET YOUR MUSIC REVIEWED

Today, there are more new-media reviewers of music than ever. Unfortunately, there's also more music submitted to those reviewers than ever. Getting reviews is still an important part of any PR campaign, since you will want to add quotes from reviews to album pages in digital music stores and press kits.

Getting music reviews is similar to running a press campaign, including making a press list and following up. Fortunately, there are also new options such as services that will get you your first review, as well as MP3 blogs.

1. **Make sure your online presences, including your online press kit, are up-to-date.** Music reviewers might go to your Web sites and online press kit for information about your music. You want to make sure that they find the latest and best information about your music. Some of them will ignore music from musicians that don't have a solid presence or, even worse, comment on any problems they see in the review.

2. **Make a list of music-review outlets.** Use the following methods to generate a list of music-review outlets besides just listing ones that you personally like to read:

o   Find media outlets that review your genre of music.

o   Search for reviews of independent artists similar to your style of music and add each reviewer to the list. You will be able to research them more when you choose actual reviewers rather than just media outlets.

o   If you are touring, add local media outlets in cities that you are playing in, since they are much more likely to write a review.

o   Include MP3 blogs in this list. You can find an excellent list of MP3 blogs at the Hype Machine (hypem.com).

o   Consider kickstarting your first review by using services like Review You (reviewyou.com), where you can pay to get your first guaranteed objective music review. Once you have quotes from a real review to work with, it makes it more likely for you to get more reviews in the rest of your campaign.

The list of review sites changes often, so head to IndieGuide.com/PR for the latest links to music review sites.

3.   **Follow submission guidelines carefully and track everything that you send.**   Most music-review sites get so many submissions that they automatically rule out anyone who can't follow the basic instructions. Once you send it, follow up, and keep track of your submissions.

4.   **Link to any reviews that you get, add them to press kits, and send a thank-you.**   Keep track of all reviews that you get, and if they're good, post links to your social media and update your press kits and Web presences. And always send a thank-you to the reviewer. Then, keep their name handy for the future. That reviewer is very likely going to want to review your next album. Keep track of the bad reviewers as well, so you know whom to avoid.

HOW TO HIRE A PUBLICIST

If you're feeling overwhelmed by this, publicity is one area where finding or hiring someone to help makes a lot of sense. Publicists can provide some key services such as:

•   help you assemble a press kit and bio;

•   brainstorm, plan, and implement press campaigns;

- find angles to your stories that fit with what the media are looking for;

- write press releases;

- give you ready-made press lists appropriate to each press release, based on journalists that they already know and have worked with before;

- send your press releases under their letterhead, which gives it a better chance of getting noticed;

- put together your press clippings for your press kit;

- follow up with media after your campaigns;

- set up and coordinate interviews.

To hire a publicist, do the following:

1. **Figure out your budget.** You can spend anything between under a hundred dollars for a single press release to spending six to ten thousand dollars a month to run a PR campaign. Your budget will determine what kind of services you can get.

2. **Choose a publicist.** Find a publicist in your area if you can so that you can work directly with him or her. Also, services like Ariel Publicity (arielpublicity.com) do an excellent job of handling new media. You can also see IndieGuide.com/PR for links to more publicist resources if you need to find one.

3. **Use them effectively.** If you hire a publicist, this will help you be more effective:

    o   Tell them of all the events that you have planned for the next year at least. This includes album releases, major concerts, and anything else that the traditional press will require a lead time for.

    o   Inform them of any newsworthy event. Remember that these can be small things.

    o   Give them all the press contacts you've developed on your own. They will be better able to make use of connections that you have already made.

o   Make sure that they have copies of all of your press materials.

o   Give them high-quality MP3s of your best songs. The media outlets that accept music will sometimes ask for an MP3 before the entire album.

o   Make sure to give them enough lead time for any story that has to go to the traditional press. If a story misses the deadline window, there might be nothing a publicist can do for you.

TRACKING YOUR CAMPAIGNS AND BUILDING ON SUCCESSES

HOW TO DETERMINE THE EFFECTIVENESS OF YOUR PUBLICITY CAMPAIGNS

One problem with the press is that they rarely tell you they've written a story about your band, even if you sent them a press release. The only way you'll know is if you discover the story yourself. Fortunately, there are tools to help you do this. To track mentions of your band, do the following:

1.   **Make sure you are using Google Alerts on your band name, your band members, and possibly your album names.** Most of the coverage that people decide to write about our band we learn of from Google Alerts, which is constantly looking for our name whenever it appears in blogs and anywhere else on the Web.

2.   **Regularly check the referrer list on your Web site.** If you have a Web site, you can check to see what links people clicked on to get to the site. These are usually called referrers. You can use this to find stories or blog entries about your band that you didn't know about. Even better, you will be able to see how many people have come to your site from each link, so you can learn which articles are the most effective at sending you new fans.

3.   **Consider using advanced tools.** If you want more advanced tools, sites like ReverbNation's BuzzTracker can provide tracking in more sites and blogs than you can otherwise reach.

THE FOUR THINGS YOU SHOULD DO ONCE YOU'RE COVERED

Many musicians think that they are done once they have some coverage, but there are some important steps to do afterward.

Consider undertaking these actions every time you get some significant coverage:

1. **Write a thank-you.** The ones most likely to cover you in the future are the ones that have already covered you once before. And the best way to help ensure that is to keep the relationship after the story comes out. Acknowledge the story, thank them, and then add them to a list of journalists for the future. This is your future press list.

2. **Save a copy and keep an archive.** If you have a story that's online, it might be gone next week. You have no guarantee that it will hang around on the Web. Since we've been around for over fifteen years, many of the review links of our music no longer exist (heck, even some of the publications don't exist anymore). Save the story when it comes out. We prefer using tools like Scrapbook for Firefox (addons.mozilla.org/en-US/firefox/addon/scrapbook), which captures not only the text but also the Web page and all its images. We also use tools like Evernote (evernote.com) to save the text.

3. **Update your press kits, quote pages, and public presences.** Now that you have coverage, update all of your press materials online and off-line. Also, consider talking about the coverage you receive in your blog, Twitter, Facebook, or any of your Web presences.

4. **Keep an eye on Web sites that cover you for the comments.** The comments on stories can often give you very interesting feedback, or even more quotes. Sometimes, you can even get in touch with commenters and forge a relationship with them by reaching out.

LEARNING MORE

If you want to read about publicity, we recommend *Public Relations for Dummies*, by Eric Yaverbaum and Ilise Benun, and *Guerrilla Music Marketing Handbook* and *Guerrilla Music Marketing, Encore Edition*, by Bob Baker. Also, head to IndieGuide.com/PR for a clickable version of every link, Web site, and service mentioned in this chapter, as well as free extra materials to help you put together your press campaigns.

CHAPTER 13

THE STRATEGIC GOAL: to get more people to hear your music and to grow your fan base

REFERENCE PAGE: IndieGuide.com/Heard

What	Description
College Radio	Running a college radio campaign is in the reach of indies and can result in some regular airplay.
Commercial Radio	Expensive and exclusive, this is available to indies with a bankroll.
Public Radio	Shows like *All Songs Considered* and local public radio are all opportunities to get heard.
Webcasts/Internet Radio	Webcasting is the radio of the Internet, and there are a lot of stations and shows, which provide opportunities to get played.
Podcasts	Podcasts are like Internet radio shows that people can subscribe to. There's a multitude of music-related shows, as well as talk shows that feature music, many with huge audiences.
Internet Video/Video Blogs	Internet video sites have allowed people to put on their own TV shows, for their own following. Many feature music.
MP3 Blogs	MP3 blogs review and feature music for fans who are looking for new things to listen to.
Streaming and Social Music Discovery Sites	There are tons of sites that allow people to discover music and share what they like, such as Pandora (pandora.com), Last.fm (last.fm), and Spotify (spotify.com). All are accessible for independent musicians and have large user bases interested in new music.
Music Archive Sites	Sites like Archive (archive.org) and Etree (etree.org) feature recorded and live-performance music and can expose your band to new audiences.

GET HEARD

"Radio has no future."
—LORD KELVIN, BRITISH MATHEMATICIAN AND PHYSICIST,
PRESIDENT OF THE BRITISH ROYAL SOCIETY, 1897

OF COURSE, for people to discover music, they have to hear it. But we hope that when you think about getting your music heard, the first thing that comes to mind is not radio. Radio is no longer the best method for indies to get heard and gain exposure—especially in today's post-Internet world. With the Internet there are more places to get your music "out there" and to get discovered by fans than ever before—from digital streaming and social music services to MP3 blogs, podcasts, video blogs, and more. Plus, thanks to the convergence of computers and media, people can listen to your music in more places than was ever possible in the past: whether on their computer, their phone, their iPads, or on their TV through set-top boxes pulling content via the Internet or through their gaming-console platforms. We're going to cover all these methods below.

PREPARING TO GET HEARD
TOP THREE THINGS TO DO TO PREPARE YOUR MUSIC
FOR GETTING HEARD
To maximize exposure, you will need to do the following to get your ready music for broadcast or on the Web:

1. **Prepare your music files correctly.** Name and ID3 tag your music files so they advertise you when people hear them on the Web. See chapter 2, "Your Music," for how to do this properly.

2. **Make sure your music is registered appropriately.** Any plays on radio, TV, or elsewhere may generate income for you (though only big players generate significant earnings from the amount of plays they get). Make sure you're appropriately registered so you get the royalties owed to you. See chapter 5, "Your Rights," for more information.

3. **Prepare your Web presences.** As people discover and listen to your music, they'll want to learn more about you. Make sure your Web strategy funnels them to your Web site so you can capitalize on any listens you get.

WHAT "NO" REALLY MEANS TO MUSICIANS TRYING TO GET THEIR MUSIC HEARD

Getting heard is all about submitting your music to those places that will play your music. This means you'll run up against people who get to decide whether your music is chosen or not. This may leave you feeling a bit vulnerable. After all, what if they say no?

First, don't take silence as a no. Venues or mediums might not respond to your song for many reasons—many of which have nothing to do with you or your music, such as that it got lost, it didn't fit their format, they ran out of time, they've been on vacation, or they forgot. This means it's up to you to follow up. Most places that accept music submissions don't even tell you if they've decided against using your stuff. Also, a series of well-managed follow-ups can sometimes make the difference in getting your song played. Some of the methods we discuss in chapter 12, "Get Publicized," will come in handy here. Many of our follow-ups have gotten us plays, so don't skip this essential step.

Second, if you submit a song somewhere and they don't accept it, simply move on. Don't use rejections as critiques. If you want feedback about your music, go to other musicians or producers. The good news is that there are so many places to get heard today that it's simply a numbers game. You will get played. Make the best music, craft the best publicity materials that you can, and send them as far and as wide as you can. What you can control is your submissions and follow-ups.

THE NUMBER ONE THING YOU CAN DO TO HELP YOU GET HEARD

Throughout this chapter we'll talk about all the places where you can get your music heard and the steps you need to take to make it happen. The number-one tip, however, won't appear in any of the steps: ask your network if they have any connections or opportunities for you to get heard.

What gets lost is that people, not technology, are what really make things happen. And someone you already know likely has a connection who can help you get heard—whether it's getting your music placed in rotation at a radio station or webcast or getting you connected to a video producer making a YouTube Web series or to a podcaster. Always build on what's within your reach and grow from there.

HOW TO MAKE SURE YOU DON'T LOSE THE
RIGHTS TO YOUR MUSIC

Anytime you submit your music to a site or service so it can get heard, there will be a user agreement to check out. We discussed user agreements in chapter 8, "Your Web Strategy," but it's worth repeating, especially for music-related sites.

1. **Read every agreement carefully before signing up.** Some sites will have agreements that may require you to concede more rights than you're willing to give up. We've seen sites that, if we'd agreed to submitting our music, would have had us give up some of our licensing rights! For instance, one site stated that if we used their service and later quit, they'd still have first right to license our music to others for up to a year after terminating.

2. **Keep a list and check back.** You'll want to check back every once in a while on the services you have your music on since many of these agreements reserve the right to change their terms—sometimes without notice. If they do send a notice to you, be sure to review the new agreement.

GETTING PLAYED OFF-LINE

FOUR WAYS TO GET YOUR MUSIC HEARD ON THE RADIO

There are four ways for indie musicians to get on the radio:

1. **College Radio.** College radio is well within your arm's reach and we'll go over the steps of launching a campaign later on.

2. **Commercial Radio.** Commercial radio is difficult and pretty much reserved for major labels and acts. However, there are some ways to get on.

3. **Public Radio.** Similar to commercial radio, there are opportunities here where you can get heard.

4. **Satellite/Cable Radio.** There are some areas where indies can get heard.

WHAT EVERY MUSICIAN NEEDS TO KNOW
ABOUT COLLEGE RADIO

College radio works the way that most people think commercial radio should work: you send them your music, and if they like it, they'll play it. It's uncomplicated and far less expensive than dealing with commercial radio. But this doesn't mean it won't take hard work to get your music played. It requires time, effort, and follow-up. The good news is that college radio is within your reach.

Not all college radio stations work the same, but there are some things they have in common.

- **The College Radio Staff.** College radio is run by students: they are the people whom you need to convince. They're the DJs. They run the station, pick the music, and read the news. And the best news is that college radio is inclusive, playing every style and genre out there. No matter what kind of music you create, there's a college radio show that will play it.

  Naturally, most college stations only allow current students to staff the station, to make sure that as many as possible have the opportunity to work in radio. This includes the DJs as well as the music directors who decide what goes into the station's rotations.

  Typically, students who take part in radio are genuinely excited about new music. Most of the ones we've met have unconventional tastes and prefer music outside of the mainstream—beyond commercial radio. Most love discovering something new—a new band, a new sound, a unique song—and sharing it with their listeners. Many are musicians themselves and love discussing music endlessly.

- **The College Radio Music Director.** Many stations stick to a particular genre or style of music during daytime hours: alternative, rock, hip-hop, and so on. They play a rotation of preselected music. Typically, the music director determines what music to include in this daytime rotation, although some stations may let a committee of staff members decide. Like the music they play, music directors' personalities run the gamut. Some share music decisions with the DJs and staff, while others can be dictators. In true tail-wagging-dog fashion, some decide based on what charts in the *College Media Journal*. DJs, however, also have a say in what music is played, although it's typically limited. College DJs can technically play whatever music they want as long as they meet a certain number of plays of the preselected music. For instance, at KRUI in Iowa City, Iowa, where one of this guide's authors worked, the station divided music into heavy, medium, and light rotation slots. CDs (well, records at the time) were physically labeled with red, blue, and yellow stickers corresponding to how often a particular song should be played during the hour. DJs were supposed to play a certain number of songs every hour, favoring the heavy-rotation songs and going down from there.

Because the music directors are students, you need to keep their motivations and schedules in mind if you want to convince them to play your music. Getting in touch with them will be at their convenience. Generally, student music directors keep irregular office hours and, because they're students, might be at class or in bed with a hangover when you call.

- **The College Radio DJ.** In the end, though, it's the college radio DJ who actually controls which songs air and when. Contrast this with commercial radio, where DJs are simply on-air personalities with no control over the music (despite frequent talk of a certain song being "requested"). Music on commercial radio is decided by music directors and is typically programmed into computers beforehand. After the daytime college-radio rotation, evenings and weekends are usually dedicated to shows that focus on a particular niche. These generally focus on music radically different from the kind featured in the daytime format, such as a thrash metal show on a station that normally plays country. Latin, punk, folk, jazz, alt-country, bluegrass, ambient, or even children's music might be spotlighted.

Some of these are long-established shows that have been inherited and handed down through the years from student to student. Others are the original invention of a particular student who received approval from the staff for the format. The songs played on a particular show are decided by the student or students who control the show at that time. These shows tend to appeal to a limited but targeted college and college-community audience.

THE TOP FOUR REASONS TO DO A COLLEGE RADIO CAMPAIGN

If one of your goals is to get played on radio, a college radio campaign is your best bet. But a full-blown college radio campaign might actually be a distraction from better opportunities that could spread your music further for the same or less effort. There are four reasons why you may want to do a college radio campaign:

1. **Exposure.** If your music is added to a station's rotation, you likely will reach potential fans. Most of the benefits of this airplay are somewhat indirect, however. Your song will get played, but will the DJ announce the title correctly? the band name? Will he remember to announce anything at all? If he doesn't, the radio play won't necessarily help you make new fans. Unlike with online mediums, you can't click on the band name to go to the Web site or instantly buy a track.

When listeners decide to buy your music, they'll have to do a Web search, which could lead them astray. And there's no good way to determine how many times you've been played even if you do get added to the rotation. It could be thousands. It could be once. Although there are some stations that actually tweet or list what they played online, generally stations have no obligation to tell you. In comparison to the Web, which tracks plays and downloads, you have to listen to the radio station yourself to confirm if and when you get played.

2. **Charting in *College Media Journal*.** The *College Media Journal*, or *CMJ*, is to college radio what *Billboard* is to top-forty commercial radio. It's an expensive industry magazine that tracks what's "hot" on college radio. If your music is played often enough across multiple college stations, you have a shot at getting charted in *CMJ*. This can provide recognition by a trusted, objective authority that your music has momentum in the college market. This can generate interest in your band from the press and record labels. For many bands and labels, charting in *CMJ* is a major goal.

But charting for the sake of charting can be a distraction from what's really important: building your fan base. Many alternative outlets for your time, energy, and money can be more effective. Most campaigns that succeed at *CMJ* charting do so by paying radio promoters to perform the intensive promotional work and follow-up necessary to get airplay in multiple college markets.

3. **Boosting concert-tour draws.** College radio listeners like attending concerts. Timing your radio campaign to your tour schedule can be a great way to boost your draw. If coordinated with a publicity campaign, listeners in the area will become familiar with you and your music and will be more likely to check out your show. For instance, posters on campus advertising your upcoming show are more likely to resonate with the college community when timed to coincide with radio airplay. Offering complimentary tickets to the station to give away to listeners will increase their incentive to play your band's music on the air, announce and advertise your show, and have you come to the station to be interviewed and perform.

4. **Performance royalties.** As discussed in chapter 5, "Your Rights," one additional benefit of college radio airplay is that each play counts as a performance for the author/publisher. If you've registered with a PRO, you are eligible to earn performance royalties, although it's likely the handful of radio plays you may get won't get caught in their surveys.

HOW TO RUN A COLLEGE RADIO CAMPAIGN

Follow these steps to get your music played on college radio:

1. **Coordinate with your publicity campaign.** If the purpose of your college-radio campaign is to boost draw for a tour, coordinate carefully to maximize the effectiveness of the campaign. This means planning ahead and building in enough time to get your music to each station, to convince the station to add your song, and, if possible, to schedule an interview or performance in-studio well before you pull up on campus in your van. Because this will seriously affect your planning, determine if this is one of your goals early on. See chapter 12 , "Get Publicized," for more information.

2. **Compile a list of targeted college radio stations and shows.** You'll need to identify stations and any shows that specialize in your style of music. You also need to identify people at the station or show to contact.

   o To identify stations and contacts, use your favorite search engine to identify stations. See also IndieGuide.com or the radio directory at Yahoo! (dir.yahoo.com/news_and_media/radio/stations/college _and_university). You can also buy resources such as *The Indie Bible* and *The Musician's Atlas,* both of which list college radio stations as well as other resources.

o   To identify shows, you can use the books listed previously, although it's hard to find a complete, up-to-date list, since those books can become outdated compared with the pace at which college shows pop up and disappear. You typically have to search each station's Web site for information on its shows, unless you live in the area and already know what those shows are.

You should submit your music directly to the person most likely to play it. To get in the general rotation, send it to the music director or the submission address they provide. If you want to get into a specialty show, find that DJ's address and send it directly.

3.   **Set up a tracking system.** You'll need to keep track of to whom, where, and when you sent your music and press material. If you don't have your own system or database software, a simple spreadsheet is fine, or you could use the downloadable one we created at IndieGuide.com/Heard.

4.   **Call in advance and establish a relationship with the music director or show host.** When your list is finalized, call all the stations to double-check the contact information and find out exactly what materials they expect to receive.

Also, you will want to talk up your band and music. This is what professional independent radio promoters do for labels—and you're up against them. The key to getting your music played and in rotation is to build a personal relationship with the music director of the radio station or host of the show you're targeting. If you're going to be on tour in their area, tell them the date and venue to spark additional interest.

You may want to skip this step, but don't make that mistake. The key to any successful college-radio campaign is making direct contacts and creating a personal connection. This will give you a leg up against bands that simply "submit and forget."

5.   **Prepare your press kit.** See the chapter 12, "Get Publicized," for how to create a press kit. Keep in mind radio stations are not the press—they only need the most basic information. Also, pay attention to their submission guidelines and tweak your press kit accordingly.

6. **Mail your stuff in.** Some stations are happy to get MP3s or digital files. Others want a CD mailed in. If they want the CD, follow these tips:

o If your CD is not already in a standard jewel case, put it in one. In general, CD libraries at college radio stations are based on the size of the standard jewel case, so thin cases or paper folders are inconvenient for them.

o If your CD is shrink-wrapped, remove it. Save them time and hassle.

o Label the case with the top two or three "radio-ready" songs you want them to hear. You don't want them losing interest in your CD by track three when track six is the best song on the album.

o If you contacted the station and they told you to send in a CD, write "SOLICITED MATERIAL" on the outside of the envelope so they know it was requested by them.

o If you are touring in the station's area, write the date of your show on the envelope because this gives them another reason to consider your CD sooner rather than later. It also tells them when you will be in their area so they can announce your show, schedule an interview, or get you to play live on-air.

7. **Call and verify delivery.** After a few days, call your contact at the station to verify that they received your material. This is another opportunity to talk more about your music and upcoming shows. Ask when they'll listen to it and consider it for rotation. Note this date in your tracking system. If they didn't receive your music, resend it.

8. **Follow up to verify it was added to the rotation.** Call your contact again a few days after they said they'd listen to it and find out if your music was added to the rotation. They are used to these calls from radio promoters. Note that being added to the rotation does not necessarily mean you will get played—it's usually up to the DJs to decide when to play the songs. It's likely you won't know if your music was played unless you listen to each station or they keep a log on their Web site.

Does getting played on the radio seem like a lot of work? It should come as no surprise that an entire industry sprang up around orchestrating these campaigns.

HOW TO HIRE A RADIO PROMOTER OR PLUGGER

Eighty percent or more of the music you hear on daytime rotation at college radio stations is chosen thanks to the work of radio promoters. They offer three advantages over doing a college radio campaign yourself:

- **Existing contacts.** Promoters know the stations and shows and have the necessary relationships in place.

- **Comprehensive service.** Promoters do all the work promoting, following up, and verifying that your music has been added to the rotation.

- **Hype.** Promoters are good at schmoozing college DJs and music directors and convincing them that your music is "hot." Radio promoters typically only accept clients whose music they feel is worthy of promotion. After all, their reputations are on the line when they try to get bands played. Promoters tend to be tenacious, with the capacity for barefaced selling that the job calls for. And because they act as your agent, it's easier for them to hype your music as "the best ever." One music director told us that, each week without fail, he'd get a call from a promoter describing the "hottest group ever" with "the best song," insisting it be immediately added. Every week the promoter would have a new "best song ever." And although the tactic didn't work on this director, it always seemed to work with his junior music directors, who would approve the new song for rotation. They loved the attention this promoter gave them, how important it made them feel. If you have the money, a radio promoter may be an option for you. Fees can range anywhere from $2,500 to $40,000 or more depending on the scope of your campaign (there are a lot of college radio stations out there), the services you want (they'll charge you less if you do all the grunt work and mailing), and the duration of the campaign.

Radio promoters range from those that specialize in radio to broader PR firms. Some promoters specialize in particular music genres such as urban or country since they know that part of the industry. Promoters are not cheap. One word of warning: promoters get paid to try to get your music into rotation, *not to actually get it played*. Once your campaign is over, all they'll owe you is an invoice and a report on which stations they contacted: "talked to so-and-so," "left message," "will review CD."

To find a radio promoter, follow these steps:

1. **Identify promoters and publicity firms.** Use your favorite search engine to identify radio promoters or go to IndieGuide.com. Keep in mind that PR firms may do radio promotion as well.

2. **Research the promoter.** Since promoters get paid whether your music is played on the radio or not, you need to be wary of any scams or poor performance. Do an Internet search to see if there are any negative stories. Get references.

3. **Hire the promoter.** If you hire the promoter, make sure you get timely reports about their progress so you can check up on their work.

ONE ALTERNATIVE TO HIRING A RADIO PROMOTER

If you've decided to spend money to promote your music, you might consider as an alternative to a traditional radio promoter, whose campaign will be limited in time and scope, paying someone who's not a professional in the field. Find someone in your network with the right personality and skills to handle the steps. One individual calculated that, for the amount of money he spent on a radio promoter for six weeks, he could have financed his own promotions person for six months. And unlike a radio promoter, who has to allocate limited resources among many clients, a part-time promotions person works for you alone. Of course, your promotions person won't have the established relationships in place that a radio promoter already has, but with a little research even a newbie can be effective in this role. Just remember that your new hire will be competing against people who do this for a living.

HOW TO GET HEARD ON LIVE-MUSIC SHOWS
AND PLAY IN-STUDIO PERFORMANCES

If you're touring or have a gig within a college station's broadcast area, find out if the station has a live-music show. Live-music shows typically run during the day and feature in-studio performances and interviews with bands and musicians performing in the area that night or weekend. Getting on the air in this way works out well if you plan it out in advance so you can arrange appearances when you're in town.

1. **Search for live-music shows on college stations in the area you're touring.** Use the resources in the "How to Run a College Radio Campaign" section listed previously to find shows in the area you're touring. Even if the

station doesn't have a live-music show, they may still want you to come in to do an interview, play some songs off your album, and give away some tickets.

2. **Contact the station and see if you can come in.** Call the station, mention when you'll be in town and available, and ask if there is a slot where you could perform. Most college stations are more than happy to have bands from out of town come in during the afternoon before a show and play a few songs, give away a few tickets, and get interviewed by the DJs.

3. **Show up early.** Show up early, since you'll need time to set up for the performance. While you set up, use the time with the staff to get to know them and cement your relationship so it's easier to submit music to them in the future.

4. **Record the show.** When our band does these in-studio performances we record them since this material can be used for our Web site, reserved for our street team as a reward, or even sold (as a special performance or as part of a live compilation). Often we get this recording from the station itself, so be sure to ask if they'll do this for you.

5. **Send a thank-you.** Most people forget to do this step, but sending a thank-you note makes it easier to get invited back next time you're in town or reminds them to add you or keep you on rotation.

WHAT EVERY MUSICIAN NEEDS TO KNOW ABOUT COMMERCIAL RADIO

Commercial radio does not work in the idyllic way still portrayed in some movies and TV shows. Unlike college radio, it doesn't accept unsolicited submissions. A commercial radio campaign can cost anywhere from tens to hundreds of thousands of dollars. Part of that money goes to independent promoters, who control access to the stations and block other music from getting added to the playlist. A radio promoter is different from an independent promoter. While a radio promoter tries to get music added to the rotation, an independent promoter acts as the gatekeeper and tollbooth for each station.

Given this, even major labels will often try to chart their artists on *CMJ* before launching a commercial radio campaign. As we explained above, it's better to start with a college campaign, even if your goal is to eventually get played on commercial radio, since a *CMJ*-charted band has an advantage in getting added to rotation on commercial radio.

Your best bet for getting into a commercial radio station's rotation would be to hire a radio promoter who specializes in commercial radio. But this is rarely economically feasible for independent musicians. In fact, the amount of effort you would need to invest to get your music on commercial radio would probably be sufficient for you to become a professional radio promoter yourself. This is why most indie bands avoid commercial radio altogether.

HOW TO GET PLAYED ON COMMERCIAL RADIO
(THROUGH THE BACK DOOR)

Although getting played on commercial radio isn't likely, there are a few backdoor ways you can use:

- **Local Music Shows.** Some commercial radio stations have shows that feature local artists, such as WXRT's *Local Anesthetic* (wxrt.radio.com /shows/local-anesthetic), hosted by Richard Milne out of Chicago. These shows will accept submissions from any local band. Unlike what's played throughout the day, the host of the show chooses the music that will be featured. Sometimes, as is the case with Milne's show, the host will ask a band or artist to come in for a live interview or in-studio performance. Such shows can be a good way to get heard because they usually have larger audiences than college radio shows and they love promoting quality local talent.

- **Syndicated Specialty Shows.** Some commercial stations air syndicated shows that specialize in a certain type of genre and that accept submissions. These syndicated shows are similar to local music shows in that the show host typically decides what to play. Unlike the local music show, syndicated shows span multiple markets and have larger listenerships. Examples include *Little Steven's Underground Garage* (undergroundgarage.com) and the long-running *Dr. Demento Show* (drdemento.com).

- **Talk Shows.** Talk shows are another way to get played on commercial radio. If one of your songs is on a topic being discussed, they might just play it if it's brought to their attention. A play on a talk show helps make your music stand out more than one on a standard music rotation. This happened to us when we sent our version of the Irish song "Tell Me Ma" (bit.ly/tellmemasong) in anticipation of St. Patrick's Day to Jonathon Brandmeier, who has a morning show in Chicago.

To get played on these shows:

1. **Identify the shows.** For local music and talk shows, if you're like us, you already know the show or shows in your area you'd like to be heard on. But if you don't know if such shows exist locally, check the Web sites of the stations in your hometown that play your type of music. For syndicated specialty shows, use the resources in the "How to Run a College Radio Campaign" section on page 323.

2. **Follow their submission guidelines.** For local music and talk shows, follow the submission guidelines on the station's Web site. Local music shows are usually flooded, so make sure you obey the guidelines carefully, and as we outline on page 325 with college radio campaigns, follow up on your submission.

Of course, no formal submission guidelines exist for talk shows. Instead, you'll want to contact the show's producer. Other times, getting your music directly to the hosts works best. It helps if you're personally familiar with the show so you can tailor the message. When Jonathon played our song, all we had done was e-mail the show and send an MP3.

3. **If you're played, send a thank-you.** If you're played, be sure to send a thank-you note to the host or director of the show since it helps build your relationship with the person and makes it easier to get played on the show in the future.

HOW TO GET PLAYED ON PUBLIC RADIO

Public radio is a great way to get your music played because the audience is much larger than that of college radio and it isn't as gated off as commercial radio. In fact, Felice Ecker, one of the founders of the media, marketing, and management firm, Girlie Action (girlieaction.com), says National Public Radio (NPR) is one of the most important online outlets for breaking new music.

Public radio stations play the general NPR news feed and then add their local news at the end. Then, throughout the day, they will alternate shows between locally produced ones and nationally produced ones. Each show has a producer of its own who makes decisions about the stories and music that are included.

The steps to get your music heard on public radio are similar to those you follow to get your music played on college radio, so see the "How to Run a College Radio Campaign" section on page 323. It was in following this method that we targeted the producer of *Eight-Forty-Eight*, Chicago's local public news show on WBEZ, and got a song from our debut album played.

After e-mailing the producer, we sent a CD. Keep in mind that it may take awhile for the song to make an appearance, and, even if it is played, the producer will likely not get back to you. In fact, it was a friend of ours that managed to alert us to the fact we were played on the show. Skeptical, we searched the radio station's site and discovered that our song had actually been aired—despite the fact no one from the show informed us.

HOW TO GET PLAYED ON SATELLITE/CABLE RADIO

Satellite radio works like satellite television, the signal being beamed from orbit rather than from local towers. Satellite radio services like Sirius/Xm (siriusxm.com) require a subscription but have been chipping away at terrestrial radio's listenership. While the services started off by being built into cars, they are also available through the Web and mobile devices.

Although they haven't adopted the independent-promoter system of terrestrial commercial radio, it's still often difficult to get your unsolicited music in rotation. While satellite radio is organized into channels of music genre, nearly half of the channels are talk shows or other programs. The steps to get your music heard on such a talk show are similar to those outlined in "How to Get Played on Commercial Radio (Through the Back Door)," so follow them if you're targeting a specific show.

Additionally, Sirius/XM will take submissions of music through its music programming department. To submit your music for consideration at Sirius/XM, head to siriusxm.com/contactus for the most up-to-date information on where to send your recordings.

THREE NONRADIO OPTIONS TO GET
YOUR MUSIC HEARD "OFF-LINE"

There's more to getting your music heard "off-line" than radio. Here are six other options for getting your music in front of audiences:

1. **Theater and Comedy Groups.** Working with live theater is an opportunity often neglected by bands. These shows can be a great way to stand out and get your music in front of a new type of fan. Theater and

comedy groups are always looking for ways to improve their shows and there's nothing like having live music to add to the energy. These groups are trying to get gigs themselves, and so saying they have live music can make their show stand out.

We used this to good effect when we hooked up with a sketch-comedy group, the Dolphins of Damnation, and got a run of shows at Second City in Chicago, partly because they were able to promise a band with the sketch comedy (which made for a bigger show as well boosting the draw). We were heavily promoted, appeared in the program, and were able to sell our albums. Plus, the comedians ended up getting us new opportunities we couldn't have gotten on our own. For instance, years later, they used our recorded music as part of yet another Second City show. And years after that, one of the actors in the second show created his own production company, and, when he created his own TV show, he commissioned us to write all the music. The show went on to be aired on television nationwide and showed in over twenty-eight million homes. All these opportunities helped build our band résumé. Music at a theatrical performance of any kind stands out, just as actors would at a concert. We've found that these shows often have an easier time getting critical attention and mentions in the paper. It's also a good way to get publicized, and a good excuse for a press release.

If you're interested in getting your music in a theatrical performance, hook up with the local theater, improvisation, or sketch-comedy community in your area. (These are three distinct communities, if you can believe it, although there is always some crossover.) Many local artists are putting on their own shows, and you never know who might be looking for music unless you get involved.

2. **Film, Television, and Web Video.** There are a variety of ways to get your music into film, TV, and Web video. This is more true now than in the past since production companies have found indie musicians to be less expensive than major labels, easier to work with, and, thanks to the Internet, easier to find. Opportunities for you include the following:

o **Community Television.** Some community television stations have shows that need music. Given the copyright obstacles involved in using major-label music, they are always on the lookout for precleared alternatives.

o **Video Production Schools for Film, TV, and Web.** With the Internet, you can make your music available to any schools in the world that specialize in video production. If there are any in your area, you can hook up with them more directly and provide your music for their use (usually just for exposure rather than money). And if the film takes off, it could create a lot of interest in your work.

o **Music Aggregators.** Film, TV, Web video, and commercial producers often rely on music aggregation services that act as middlemen between musicians and producers. See chapter 5, "Your Rights," for more information about getting your music into these services.

o **Creative Commons.** Sites based on a Creative Commons license make music available to many types of creators, including producers of film, television, and Web series. See chapter 5, "Your Rights," for information about using Creative Commons to promote your music.

To better your chances of making producers aware of your music, mention that your music is available for film, TV, and video use on your Web site (which helps get your site showing up in searches for "film music") and ask your social networks if they know of any opportunities. Although it should be obvious that music can be used for anything at all, sometimes you have to draw producers a map. You might just give them an idea.

3. **Battle of the Bands** Battle-of-the-bands contests are live events that pit one band against one or more other bands. By the end of the night, someone (the audience, a panel of judges) decides who was "the best." Some of these contests require a fee to participate, but others are free.

While we have never seen music as a competitive activity, competition can motivate some musicians. If you win one, you can publicize it. But even if you don't, you can at least expose your music to new listeners. They can be worthwhile, whether you win or lose.

GETTING PLAYED ONLINE

THE TOP FIVE THINGS EVERY MUSICIAN NEEDS TO KNOW ABOUT GETTING HEARD ONLINE

As cool as getting heard on the radio is, getting heard online is where the action is. Plus, online opportunities are the most effective because they link directly to your Web site and music stores and they tie to your Web strategy. The exciting thing about getting heard online is since music is just data, *any* Web site can feature your music on its pages—not just Web sites dedicated to hosting your music.

Here are five things you need to know about getting heard online:

1. **Find out "where the party's at."** The difficult part about deciding where to spend your time and energy on the Web is determining whether a given Web site is popular. Most don't display their statistics, so you'll need to rely on public traffic aggregation sites like AttentionMeter (attentionmeter .com) and SiteTrail (sitetrail.com), which include social analytics to get an idea of their traffic and social reach. But don't judge a site on traffic alone since it could be targeting a dedicated, but niche, audience. If you write songs about beer, for example, you'll want to target the most active Web sites and message boards about beer to promote your music. Even a modestly popular Web site can have a dramatic effect if its audience is mostly people who would probably enjoy your music for one reason or another.

2. **Ask, Who is the target audience?** The first thing to do with any Web site is to figure out what audience it is targeting. For instance, lots of sites out there say they're a great place for indie music to get heard, declaring all these benefits right on the front page. The problem is, as a listener, you wouldn't stay on a page that speaks directly to bands. A site like Amazon, on the other hand, devotes its front page to selling to customers, although links are on there as well for setting up your own store. YouTube also does a good job of balancing its front page between featuring the latest videos for viewers and explaining how to submit your own on the side. So, think twice about signing up on any site that doesn't strike this balance. Most likely, the sign-up agreements aren't fair to the musicians, because if these sites aren't making their money off listeners, it's coming from somewhere.

3. **Evaluate the Web site's design and look and feel.** Often, it's possible to tell how good a site is simply by how well it's designed. If it has a lot of bad links or looks like it's out of the 90s, it probably won't be worth your time. People have to spend money to make sites look good and work well, and this investment is a good indicator of how seriously they take their endeavor.

4. **Check the site's Google PageRank.** One of the quickest ways to judge a Web site's popularity and trustworthiness is to check its Google page rank. To do this, install Google Toolbar (toolbar.google.com) in your browser or use a free site like PRChecker (prchecker.info). Google ranks Web sites from one to ten and is based on the number of sites that link to it along with a host of other constantly shifting criteria. A four or five or higher is quite good, although these numbers change whenever Google tweaks its methodology. Keeping up with the latest changes to Google's page rank on blogs about search engine optimization (SEO) will help you interpret the numbers more effectively.

5. **Check your favorite search engine.** You can use search engines to find out who is linking to a particular site. For instance, in Google, enter "link: www.beatnikturtle.com" to see every site that links to ours. It won't take long to learn if a site is a scam, since posts complaining about it will be in the first few pages of results.

HOW TO GET PLAYED ON INTERNET RADIO, WEBCASTS, AND WEBCAST SHOWS

Webcasting streams music, talk, and news to people through the Internet using multimedia players or dedicated mobile apps. While terrestrial radio took the "Internet waves" initially by simulcasting radio feeds through the Web, there are now a variety of Internet-first radio stations such as Radio Paradise (radioparadise.com), Slacker (slacker.com), and SkyFM (sky.fm). In addition, sites such as Live365 (live365.com) and SHOUTcast (shout cast.com) have become platforms for anyone to create their own radio station. The explosion of personal mobile devices has only led to the growth in these stations since their Webcasts are no longer tied to a bulky desktop computer.

As a result of this growth, there are more "radio" stations and shows that you can get your music on than ever before. Plus, most stations are covered by PROs to ensure musicians get their performance royalties. Targeting these stations and the shows they air is within your arm's reach. To get played on Internet radio, do the following:

1. **Find Internet radio stations.** There are aggregate sites that help you find stations that play your type of music. Check out FilterMusic

(filtermusic.net) and StreamFinder (streamfinder.com) for listings. There are dozens of aggregators, so for a complete listing, see IndieGuide.com/Heard.

2. **Target stations.** Each webcasting station has a format that it plays in rotation. Follow the steps in the "How to Run a College Radio Campaign" section to target these stations.

One note: while many of the stations you find may focus on "indie music," we suggest avoiding those. People often forget that indie music is not a style, just an indicator that a band is not on a label. There are indie bands in classical music as well as power punk, but the two don't necessarily mesh well on a radio broadcast. Focus instead on those stations that play your style of music so your music can piggyback on other popular songs in your genre. That way you get it in front of people who may already be predisposed to your music.

3. **Target specific shows.** Many webcasting stations have genre-specific shows, talk shows, and more. Each show may have its own Web site and submission policy. If you want to get played on these stations, you can target and reach out to them directly using the same steps as outlined above in the "How to Run a College Radio Campaign" section.

4. **Submit your music to the webcasting platform, if possible.** Places like Live365 accept music submissions by allowing artists to upload their tracks to their music library, which makes your music available to the webcasters to pull into their playlists. In other words, submitting your music doesn't guarantee plays, but doing so does make them more likely.

HOW TO GET PLAYED ON PODCASTS

Podcasting is "Internet radio on demand" and one of the best ways for indies to get heard. Podcasts are shows about a particular topic that anyone can put together, uploaded to the Internet as an MP3 and made available for people to download either at their Web site or through a podcast host.

Almost every human interest is addressed by a podcast. There are literally thousands of podcasts—some just starting, others disappearing (called "podfading"). It's hard to imagine a radio show about, say, crocheting, but a search on Podcast Alley returns over twenty podcasts, with titles such as *Crochet Unraveled*, *CrochetCast*, and *Crochet for Men*. The same holds true for music podcasts. Name a genre and there's a podcast that covers it— and ones that cover its subcategories. Best of all, they're all looking for music to play. The podcasting world is a universe of niches, and no niche is too small.

But podcasts aren't only talk shows. Sometimes podcasters produce a short-run series of podcasts on a particular social, political, charitable, or other cause. Another trend is for authors to podcast their books in serial form. Notable authors who have done this include Scott Sigler (scottsigler .com), J. C. Hutchins (jchutchins.net), Tee Morris (teemorris.com), and Mur Lafferty (murlafferty.com). Once these podcasts run their course, the podcast ends. And yet all of these need music.

Podcast audiences tend to be small but very dedicated to the topic of the podcast or the personality doing the show. Tapping a podcast in the right niche can build a strong connection with a lot of potential fans. That said, some podcasts, such as *Keith and the Girl* (keithandthegirl.com) and Adam Curry's *Daily Source Code* (curry.com), have consistently large audiences. The same is true of music podcasts such as Brian Ibbott's *Coverville* (cover ville.com).

Production values vary greatly as well. Some podcasters use state-of-the-art recording and production techniques, with results that wouldn't sound out of place on the radio, while others sound as if they recorded their show with a cassette recorder while cooking dinner. Some maintain rigorous schedules, updating their shows at the same time each week, while others upload new podcasts "when they get around to it" or disappear altogether ("podfade") because of lack of interest or more pressing commitments.

Thanks to copyright laws, most podcasters are often in desperate need of "legal" music to play. Since any music they use needs to be licensed, and since major labels charge a lot for this or don't allow it, many podcasters turn to indie artists for music.

To get played on podcasts, do the following:

1. **Choose a license that allows podcasters to use your music.** There are multiple podsafe licenses, but our favorites are issued by Creative Commons (creativecommons.org) and are free to use and easy to understand, even though they are written by lawyers. They are flexible with regard to what rights you want to allow. See chapter 5, "Your Rights," for more information.

Additionally, you can add yourself to a podsafe collective. These are associations such as Mevio's MusicAlley (musicalley.com), created by podcasters to help them find music that's precleared for podcasting. This means you can upload your songs to these sites and podcasters will know that they are podsafe to use in their shows for free since you agreed to their user agreement. Doing so is a simple way to make your music available to podcasters worldwide, but note that each collective uses different licenses. Some are based on licenses that are subject to change at the collective's discretion.

2. **Browse podcast directories for podcasts that play your genre of music.** Instead of waiting for podcasts to come to you, you can search for some on your own. You can find podcasts that specialize in your style of music by searching Podcast Alley (podcastalley.com), Podcast Pickle (podcastpickle.com), and iTunes. Make sure to look for podcasts that are still active and posting regularly.

3. **Browse podcast directories for podcasts that cover topics that relate to your music.** *Saturday Night Live* is a popular, long-standing sketch-comedy show, and yet on each episode they have a guest band perform twice. It breaks up the monotony of the sketches and gives the audience and talent a break from the format. Similarly, many "talk" podcasts will feature a song or two, either because it's related to the subject or simply to break up the dialogue. For example, we reached out to a podcast for coffee drinkers with our song "Coffee," and the podcaster played it. Follow the steps outlined in "How to Market Your Music on Nonmusic Web Sites" in chapter 11, "Your Marketing Strategy," to brainstorm and target podcasts in this way.

4. **Follow the submission guidelines and contact the podcaster.** This rule is simple: read each podcast's submission guidelines and follow them carefully. Most music podcasts have a preferred method of delivery, file format, and information they need about the band (such as Web site address, bio, etc.). If they don't have a preferred method for receiving songs, see chapter 2, "Your Music," and chapter 9, "Your Web, Social, and Mobile Presences," for the best ways to share your music, rather than attaching the MP3 file to an e-mail. Sharing your music the proper way will not only let you see the listening stats but may make it easier for the person you write to post and share the song at the site. When you contact podcasters be sure to offer them something in return for playing your song. Tell them you will blog and tweet about them to send your fans in their direction.

5. **Follow up to see if the podcaster has received your song and e-mail.** If the podcaster doesn't write back, send a follow up e-mail a few days later to check in. Offer to send some extra songs or more information. You might feel like you are being annoying, but just remain polite and persistent until you receive an answer.

6. **If you get played on a podcast, promote it by linking to it on your Web, social, and mobile presences.** Be sure to cross-promote. Show your appreciation by linking to the episode on your site and mentioning it in all of your presences.

7. **After getting played, send a thank-you e-mail.** Send an e-mail to the podcasters letting them know how much you appreciate the play. Send them a link to your online posts so they can see how you publicized them. Then offer them some more music you think that they will like. Let them know that you will be in touch when you have new music out that they can use. Doing this will make it easier to get played in the future.

HOW TO GET PLAYED ON INTERNET VIDEO, VIDEO BLOGS, AND WEB SERIES

Like podcasts, Internet video, video blogs, and Web series on sites like You-Tube or Vimeo can feature music as well. Unlike podcasts, where the music may be spotlighted, a video typically uses music in the background as part of the soundtrack (if not used as the theme or end credits).

Although this medium is still growing and evolving, many of the steps to get played on videos are identical to the steps for getting on podcasts, with one key difference: instead of podcast directories, browse YouTube to find shows that could match your genre of music (YouTube.com/shows).

TWO CREATIVE WAYS TO GET PLAYED ON INTERNET VIDEO, VIDEO BLOGS, WEB SERIES, AND PODCASTS

1. **Theme Songs.** Podcasts, video blogs, Web series, and videos often need a theme song. Some podcasters and video bloggers turn to indie musicians they know for a song that's already been recorded. Others request that a new song be created especially for them. If you have a knack for this type of songwriting or have a song that naturally fits, reach out and ask. If they use your theme, you're likely to get mentioned each show (or multiple mentions over time—our band has been mentioned for years on

long-running shows). You'll also get cross-promoted and linked from the Web site for the show as thanks. (Although it never hurts to ask for this, just to make sure.)

2. **Incidental Music, Beds, and Bumpers.** Listen to any commercial or public radio format and you'll notice that music—typically instrumental music—is used in a variety of ways to grab the attention of the listener and keep the show moving along. It's also used to introduce particular segments. Incidental music works well in radio and TV, but is often ignored in podcasts and video blogs. And yet this kind of music can really help these shows sound more professional. If your existing music lends itself naturally to incidental music such as beds (music played underneath talk) and bumpers (music played before or after talk), or you enjoy writing instrumental music, it's worth reaching out and exploring this option.

HOW TO GET PLAYED ON MP3 BLOGS

MP3 bloggers are essentially freelance music reviewers. The main differences between MP3 bloggers and traditional music journalists is that they provide an actual copy of the song they're reviewing (as an MP3) and they tend to only write about the music they like and are deeply passionate about. These are the buzzmakers you want talking about your music that we discussed in chapter 11, "Your Marketing Strategy."

Like podcasts, the audience sizes for MP3 bloggers vary from a handful up to tens of thousands of listeners. Not all MP3 bloggers post their contact information. As more and more publicists zero in on tastemakers to get the buzz out about their client's music, MP3 bloggers become further inundated with submission requests. With the popularity of mobile devices, there are sites with apps like Shuffler (shuffler.fm) that aggregate MP3 blogs into one "music magazine."

To get played on MP3 blogs, follow these steps:

1. **Search Hype Machine for MP3 blogs that may play similar artists to you.** Hype Machine (hypem.com) is an MP3 blog aggregator that posts the latest MP3 blog entries. Search the site for artists that are similar to you, and the engine will come back with a list of MP3 blogs that are playing that music. These are the blogs that most likely will play your music if you contact them. You can also search by genre.

2. **Contact the MP3 blogger.** If the blog provides a way to submit music, follow the instructions or e-mail the blogger if an address is provided.

3. **Monitor the MP3 blog for your play and send a thank-you.** If you have your alerts set up correctly (see chapter 9, "Your Web, Social, and Mobile Presences"), the alerts will tell you when your music's covered. Send a thank-you to the blogger to show your appreciation and help build the relationship.

HOW TO GET PLAYED ON SOCIAL MUSIC DISCOVERY SITES LIKE LAST.FM AND GROOVESHARK

With social music discovery sites, not only can people discover your music, but you can learn more about who's listening to your band. Two examples of these services include Last.fm and Grooveshark. Both services provide artist dashboards and insight into how your music is being listened to. You can access this information once you sign up as a label or artist while also controlling your Web presence and "claiming your music."

We discuss Last.fm in detail, including how to claim your music that's already on the service, how to upload more of your music, and how to manage your presence in "Your Web, Social, and Mobile Presences" (ch. 9). Since Grooveshark follows a similar process as Last.fm, we recommend following the same steps outlined in that chapter.

HOW TO GET PLAYED ON DIGITAL STREAMING SERVICES SUCH AS SPOTIFY, RHAPSODY, RDIO, AND MORE

With digital streaming services, people can discover your music and share it with others in social playlists or through their social networks. For instance, Spotify is integrated with Facebook, so it's easy for listeners and fans to share your music within the network.

Most streaming services don't accept music sent in or uploaded by artists. Instead, a majority of them get their music from digital aggregators such as CD Baby, TuneCore, Nimbit, and others (see IndieGuide.com/Sales for a full listing). To get your music heard on these streaming services, follow these steps:

1. **Get your music on a digital aggregator service.** We discuss digital aggregators in detail in chapter 6, "Your Albums, Merchandise, and Sales."

If you don't have a digital aggregator for your music, you may want to look at which streaming services you would like to get played on and find an aggregator that will serve it.

2. **Check to see if you're already on the streaming service.** If you already use a digital aggregator for your music, you may be on them already. For instance, a list of services CD Baby automatically submits to can be found on its Web site (members.cdbaby.com/digitaldistributionpartners. aspx). Note that some digital aggregators charge money to submit your music to streaming services, so if you're not up at a service, you may need to contact them and pay to be included.

Keep in mind these services are constantly changing, evolving, and, yes, disappearing, so we recommend staying on the lookout for new sites as they appear. We're going to cover eight below, but there are many, many more— Zune, Verizon, iHeartRadio, Nokia, and so on. For a more comprehensive list of the places to get your music heard, head to IndieGuide.com/Heard.

HOW TO GET PLAYED ON PANDORA

Pandora (pandora.com) is a "personalized" music station delivered over the Web and through mobile devices. By entering your favorite artist or song into a search box, it creates a "station" that plays similar music based on the Music Genome Project. The Music Genome Project created a way to group music into hundreds of musical attributes so similar songs and artists could be paired. Getting your music on this service can help people discover your music when listening to established artists in your space.

To get your music played on Pandora, you'll need to send it to them directly. To do so, follow these steps:

1. **Register for a Pandora account.** Pandora has tied its submission service to listener accounts, so you'll need to register first if you haven't already.

2. **Make sure your CD has a UPC bar code.** Pandora will only accept submissions of CDs that have bar codes.

3. **Follow Pandora's submission policy.** Go to Pandora's policy page (submitmusic.pandora.com) and follow the instructions. You'll need to upload MP3s of your music so they can first listen and determine if your

music is acceptable for their service before you send anything in. If accepted, they will send you a mailing label so you can send in the CD.

HOW TO GET PLAYED ON TURNTABLE.FM

Turntable.fm is part music streaming, part chat room, and part game. It allows people to be DJs in an animated nightclub where they compete and play music in real time to a crowd of listeners. The listeners vote on whether the song the DJ is playing is "awesome" or "lame." Positive votes give the DJs points, but too many negative points will stop the music and give the next DJ control of the turntable. Getting on this service can help people discover your music and introduce it to others.

Turntable.fm gets the music it plays from music aggregators, so follow the same steps as in "How to Get Played on Digital Streaming Services such as Spotify, Rhapsody, Rdio, and More."

HOW TO GET HEARD ON MUSIC ARCHIVE SITES

You can post your music at music archive sites so others can hear it. The most famous music archive is the Internet Archive (archive.org/details/audio). The site hosts a vast collection of music from 78-record collections to live recordings to "community music" that includes Nine Inch Nails's *Ghosts I–IV.* To add your music to the archives, follow these steps:

1. **Choose a license that will allow the Internet Archive to host your music.** To use these sites, you'll need to license your songs under a Creative Commons license (creativecommons.org) so your songs can be shared and uploaded. See the "Your Rights" (ch. 5) for more information.

2. **Create an account at the Internet Archive.** Creating an account will allow you to upload your music.

3. **Upload your MP3s.** Make sure they are properly tagged (see chapter 2, "Your Music," for more information).

HOW TO GET HEARD ON LIVE-MUSIC ARCHIVES

Fans have a long tradition of trading live music performances. Naturally, with the Internet, the practice has gone online. Live-music archives allow people to freely trade recordings of performances that fans attend. These live-music archives have some unique characteristics. First, they tend to be

THE INDIE BAND SURVIVAL GUIDE

picky about sound quality and prefer music files that use lossless encoding (such as WAV files). Second, they often insist that any files traded in their networks be made freely available to all, and for nonprofit purposes only. And finally, they are usually careful to only trade music from bands that allow it.

Perhaps the most well-known live music site is Etree (etree.org), which has teamed up with the Internet Archive (archive.org/details/etree). Etree has software, resources, and information about uploading to and browsing their live-music archives. To upload or "seed" your music to the archives and to announce the taping of your live shows by fans, follow these steps:

1. **Register at Etree and follow the instructions.** Head to Etree's wiki (wiki.etree.org) to get the latest information and learn how to encode your band's performance so that you can add it to this archive.

2. **Register your band at Bands That Allow Taping.** Etree provides a list of bands that allow the recording and trading of their music at (wiki.etree .org/index.php?page=tradefriendly). To get on this list and to encourage the recording and taping of your live shows by fans, create an account and register yourself at Bands That Allow Taping (btat.wagnerone.com).

THREE ADDITIONAL WAYS TO GET HEARD ONLINE:
MUSIC CONTESTS

From online battles of the bands to songwriting contests, countless places exist to "compete" against other musicians to get your music judged and heard. Below are a few opportunities:

1. **Online Battles of the Bands.** Battle-of-the-bands contests are usually live, although many are appearing online by pitting a band's recorded music against that of other bands. If held online, the "performance" is usually a Web page with the band's posted songs.

2. **Songwriting Contests.** Some contests focus simply on your ability to write songs. Songwriting contests have been around for quite a while and often require an entry fee to participate. That's the way a lot of these contests make their money—from the musicians. There are innumerable songwriting contests you can enter, with perhaps one of the most famous being the John Lennon Songwriting Contest (jlsc.com). Some lists of songwriting contests

can be found at the Muse's Muse (musesmuse.com/contests.html) and IndieGuide.com/Music. Many of these songwriting contests offer prizes for first place, including recording gear, instruments, and even record-label contracts.

One notable and free songwriting contest that occurs weekly online is Songfight! (songfight.org). Songfight! typically posts a song title or titles on their Web site. Musicians have one week in which to write and record a song based on that title and e-mail it in. Songs are made public for visitors to stream and download so they can vote on their favorite. The prize for winning is bragging rights for the week.

3. **Album Challenges.** The goal of an album-challenge participant is to write, record, and produce an entire album in one month. Most album challenges were inspired by National Novel Writing Month (nanowrimo.org), which challenges authors to write a 175-page (fifty-thousand-word) novel within the month of November. Three of the major album challenges that you can participate in are the Record Production Month Challenge (rpmchallenge.com), February Album Writing Month (fawm.org), and National Solo Album Month (nasoalmo.org). The RPM Challenge and February Album Writing Month (fawm.org) occur in February, while the National Solo Album Month (nasoalmo.org) occurs in November alongside National Novel Writing Month. Each of these contests is free.

A surprising number of musicians take part in these challenges. According to Christopher Grenier and David Karlotski, two of RPM's organizers, they've had musicians from all seven continents participate (yes, even Antarctica!). Karlotski states that one of the purposes of the RPM Challenge is to "get musicians back to why they do music in the first place: to create music for the sake of music and not focus on whether it's commercial or not." In fact, that's what we found when we participated in the RPM Challenge ourselves. We had a blast writing the music and got an album out of it to boot. We also connected with other musicians on the RPM Web site and discussion boards and even met a bunch of them in person at the Chicago celebration party, which was held simultaneously with parties in many other cities all over the world.

One notable participant in RPM was Bob Boilen of the band Tiny Desk Unit. Boilen is a host and director of National Public Radio's *All Songs Considered*. As a participant he highlighted RPM and some of the bands that participated (including ours) on his NPR show. Best of all, sites such as RPM make their participants' music available free to the public year-round on an online jukebox. So it's yet another place to be heard.

4. **Nonmusic Web Sites.** Sometimes people forget that any Web site can share an MP3 file. Each has their own audiences that can be tapped to expose your music to new fans. These are excellent ways to get played. In fact, in our case, we've gotten tens of thousands of plays of some of our songs from posts on nonmusic Web sites. See chapter 11, "Your Marketing Strategy," for how to get played on Web sites that don't specialize in music.

HOW TO PAY TO GET PLAYED

If you've got the money, there are many ways to pay to get played, and we'll share a few here. However, you should always be skeptical about services that ask for money to get you played, so you'll want to do your research since some services may be questionable.

Naturally, if your music isn't available for sale yet, you should hold off spending any money to get your music played (unless you just want exposure and are not worried about sales). To pay to get played, follow these steps:

1. **Use pluggers or promoters.** Pluggers and promoters do not lead to guaranteed plays. You pay instead for someone to submit your music to radio stations, podcasts, webcasts, or other outlets. Whether it gets aired is up to those outlets, not the plugger.

One of the better services for this is Ariel Hyatt's cyber-PR service (arielpublicity.com), since Hyatt has good relationships with many new media outlets with large audiences. See IndieGuide.com/Heard for more links to radio promoters.

2. **Use automatic submission services.** Some services will blast out your music to many different outlets, in hopes that they will play the music or use it in a radio show or webcast. Since these are less personal than promoters, the success rate is lower. Examples include Live365 (live365.com) and Music Submit (musicsubmit.com). For more options, see to IndieGuide.com/Heard.

3. **Pay for play on streaming services.** Music-discovery sites like Last.fm (last.fm), Grooveshark (grooveshark.com), and Jango Airplay (jango.com) all have platforms that let listeners stream music, and each have

pay-for-play options to get your music featured. Before paying any of these services for airplay, get to know the site like a user so that you can experience what you will be getting out of it. These services are free to join for listeners and artists, so it's worth it to check them out. For a list of other streaming services, see IndieGuide.com/Heard.

LEARNING MORE

Go to IndieGuide.com/Heard for a clickable version of every link, Web site, and service mentioned in this chapter, as well as free extra materials to keep up with all the new places and techniques to get your music heard.

CHAPTER 14

THE STRATEGIC GOAL: to create, record, and use video to grow your fan base

REFERENCE PAGE: IndieGuide.com/Seen

CHECKLIST

What	Description
Video Host	A site that hosts your videos. See chapter 9 for the steps to get on such sites.
Video Streaming Hosts	If you want to handle live streaming concerts or appearances, you should have a video-streaming host such as Ustream (ustream.tv) or Livestream (livestream.com) or a virtual presence in a place like Second Life (secondlife.com). For even more intimate appearances, use Google Hangouts (www.google.com/tools/dlpage/res/talkvideo/hangouts) or Skype (skype.com).
Video Editing Software	Software or tools to edit your videos
Video Camera	A camera to capture your video. This could be a dedicated video camera, a Digital SLR, or just the camera on your laptop or mobile device.
Sources for Video Clips, Audio Clips, and Still Shots	If you make videos, you will likely need sources for video clips, still pictures, and audioclips in order to help you with production. You should have sites such as Creative Commons, public domain sites, and photo sites ready to go for your production.
Video Crews and Actors	Either bring friends together or recruit video crews and actors from video schools, theater communities, the general public, or sites like Craigslist.
Finished Videos	Note that you can create many different types of videos, even for the same song, including animated videos, machinima, music videos of live performances, or behind-the-scenes videos.
A Content-ID Account on YouTube	YouTube uses a service called ContentID (www.youtube.com/t/contentid) to identify when copyrighted audio or video are played on their site. The owner can decide to disallow the content, collect revenues via ad sharing, or just collect statistics on it. Since you, as a musician, likely own the copyright for audio and possibly video of your own, you will want to use this yourself.
Video Statistics Sources	Use tools like YouTube or VidStatsX (vidstatsx.com) to give you statistics for your videos so you can track the demographics of who is watching and where they are located.

GET SEEN

"The way to get people to share your videos is to make one that makes the person watching it look cool to their friends for sharing it."

—PETER SHUKOFF OF THE BAND NICE PETER AND COCREATOR OF EPIC RAP BATTLES OF HISTORY ON YOUTUBE

THERE IS no question that video has taken over the Internet. It's become one of the best and most powerful ways to get content and discover new music. And the trend is just starting. Here are some surprising statistics about one video service—YouTube—as reported at the end of 2011 by Mashable (mashable.com), an independent news source that covers digital culture, social media, and technology ("YouTube in 2011: How Its Busy Year Affects You," at mashable.com/2011/12/31/youtube-in-2011/):

- 48 hours of video are uploaded every minute, resulting in nearly 8 years of content uploaded every day.

- More than 3 billion videos are viewed per day.

- 70% of YouTube traffic comes from outside the U.S.

- YouTube's demographic is broad: mostly consisting of 18- to 54-year-olds.

- YouTube has 800 million unique visitors each month.

- 100 million people take a "social action" on YouTube (likes, shares, comments, etc.) every week.

THE INDIE BAND SURVIVAL GUIDE

- Every minute more than 500 tweets contain YouTube links.

- An auto-shared tweet results in six new YouTube sessions on average.

- Nearly 17 million people have connected a YouTube account to at least one social service such as Facebook and Twitter.

- More than 20,000 partners from 22 countries are now involved in the YouTube Partner Program. YouTube says hundreds of its partners make more than $100,000 a year.

Besides the large viewership, video has become important for musicians for another, nearly hidden reason: sharing is built into video services. It's easy and frictionless. Embedding, linking, or sharing video on your social networks are all just one click away. There's a reason why the term "viral video" is so common but "viral audio" is not. There's no audio service that's equivalent to YouTube for sharing audio.

Because of this, video is the best way to harness your audience, social networks, and the Internet to get your music heard. Everything you need is built in to video hosts, and the best part is that you don't need to explain to your viewers how to share it; they already know how, and if they like it, they'll do it. In this chapter, we'll talk about how to harness this incredibly powerful marketing tool, how to make videos, share them, and become part of the second video revolution in music since MTV—but this time, one that every musician can participate in.

CREATING YOUR OWN VIDEOS

HOW TO PREPARE FOR VIDEO PRODUCTION

When you sit down to make a video, you quickly realize that nearly everything that you've done to prepare your music business so far comes into play. Your music and audio, brand, Web presences, and everything else you've done are all part of it. Here's a checklist to go through before you do your video.

1. **Prepare your audio.** One of the biggest mistakes you can make is to make a video before the audio is complete. The audio should be fully mastered, and the audio source for your video program should NOT be an MP3 file, as some musicians mistakenly use. YouTube will reencode the audio, which will end up with a poor-quality result. Use the final mastered

WAV files in your production. See chapter 2, "Your Music," for a complete rundown of everything that you need to do for recording, mixing, and mastering your music.

2.   **Prepare your Web and social presences.**   Use the checklist in chapter 8, "Your Web Strategy," and follow the instructions in "Your Web, Social, and Mobile Presences" (ch. 9) on how to sign up with YouTube and other video-hosting services. If you do this right, it should be tied in with the rest of your Web presences so that when you share a new video, it automatically posts to your social networks.

3.   **Prepare your brand.**   Nearly every aspect covered in chapter 4, "Your Brand," will be used in videos, especially the imagery, logos, and avatars.

4.   **Prepare your stores.**   If sales are your target, your channels better be ready when you post the video. The link to purchase your song should be the first thing beneath the video, to capture an impulse buy. Chapter 6, "Your Albums, Merchandise, and Sales," covers this, including how to include stores within YouTube.

THE TYPES OF VIDEOS YOU CAN MAKE

When you sit down to make a music video, you will find that there are actually many different options that musicians use successfully. In chapter 2, "Your Music," we provided a list of different versions of songs that you can offer your fans for sales or promotion. The same is true for video. Here's a list to get your own ideas flowing:

1.   **Music Videos.**   MTV made traditional music videos popular (that is, until they stopped actually broadcasting music videos). Online video has given music videos new life.

2.   **Animation Videos.**   With the amount of computer animation as well as real-world animation available, there is no end to the different types of animation video you can make. We'll cover some of these later in the chapter.

3.   **Video Mash-up.**   You can take your music and set it to video using video clips, images, or anything from popular culture. This is known as a mash-up—combining different elements into a new work.

4. **Still-Photo Videos.** Want to make a shareable video quickly? You can just put up a static picture or a little GIF animation and show it while playing your music. One incredibly popular video on YouTube is Nyan Cat (www.youtube.com/watch?v=QH2-TGUlwu4), a looped GIF animation of a cat flying on a crazy background with a strange song that almost seems to be sung by a lolcat. Not only did this video not take much time to make, the person who made the video didn't even create the GIF or the song. She just threw them together and put it up on YouTube.

5. **Video Songs.** Jack Conte and Nataly Dawn of the popular indie band Pomplamoose (pomplamoose.com) helped popularize a form of music video on YouTube called the "video song." This type of video revolves around making the music: you see the musicians recording the exact audio that you're hearing in the video—no lip-syncing or fake playing. In fact, if you hear a sound, you'll eventually see it appear in the video—as one of the "rules" is there're no hidden sounds. For many examples of this type of video, see Pomplamoose's YouTube channel (youtube.com/PomplamooseMusic).

6. **Machinima Videos.** Programs like Poser (poser.smithmicro.com) have made it possible to make computer-animated people that already move like real people, which you can use to make videos. But even that can be far more complicated than just taking your favorite video game and using the game engine to make a video. This is called Machinima (machinima.org/machinima-faq.html), and it has become its own video genre. One example is the machinima Web series *Red vs. Blue*, which uses the Halo game engine (roosterteeth.com/archive/?id=88&v=more&s=1).

6. **Anime Music Videos (AMV).** Fans that love Japanese animation (anime) sometimes go out of their way to use their extensive knowledge of anime shows and movies to match the music to animation clips. There are award shows for AMVs at anime conventions and entire Web sites devoted to this. See AnimeMusicVideos (animemusicvideos.org) for information on this subculture.

7. **Live-Music Video.** Any video and sound you capture from your live performances are fair game for music videos and can provide great alternate versions of songs. Keep in mind that you don't have to just put up recordings of your live performances as they are. You can splice them together and mix them with your music to feature highlights.

8. **Remix Videos.** Another type of video is created by making music from the actual sound contained in video footage. For example, Nick Bertke, an indie musician better known as Pogo (pogomix.net), has created new music from snippets and bits of audio from popular movies such as *Alice In Wonderland, Terminator,* and *Wizard of Oz.* His remixes have led to various commission deals, including Disney Pixar, which had him create a video remix to promote the movie *Up* (bit.ly/upular-pogo). Another group, The Gregory Brothers, use video footage from news or viral videos to create songs with "unintentional singers." Through the judicial use of Auto-Tune, the band splices up the footage and creates songs. For an example, see their *Auto-Tune the News* series (youtube.com/schmoyoho) or the wildly popular "Bed Intruder Song" (bit.ly/bedintruder-gregorybros).

9. **Creating regular video content.** Like a blog or podcast, you can create regular, behind-the-scenes content about your life as a musician. You can let your fans in as you write new music, tour, do a charity event, or prepare for an album release. You can also share your views or let people into your life. To do this is to vidcast, or video blog. For a good example of this, see what Nice Peter, creator of the incredibly popular Epic Rap Battles of History (youtube.com/erb) does on his second channel Nice Peter Too (youtube.com/NicePeterToo).

TOP FIVE CLASSES OF TOOLS FOR EDITING
AND POSTPRODUCTION

Once you decide to make a video, you will need to decide what tools to use. Because there are so many different kinds of video, we will provide a list of some options for each type, but this is another area that changes quickly, so go to IndieGuide.com/Seen for more links.

1. **Free Tools that Come with Your Operating System.** If you have a Mac, you have iMovie, and Windows comes with Movie Maker. Linux has many options due to the open source nature of the operating system, although OpenShot video editor (openshotvideo.com) is one of the most popular. These are all simple and easy-to-use tools and an excellent place to start until you get the hang of them and decide to get more fancy.

2. **Free Downloadable Video-Editing Software.** Note that the free options for video editing depend on the operating system that you use,

although you can consider tools such as Wax (debugmode.com/wax), Avidemux (fixounet.free.fr/avidemux), or VirtualDub (virtualdub.en.softonic .com). See IndieGuide.com/Seen for a full set of links to video-editing resources, since there are numerous options. In most video production, you will often need to work with photo and image editing, so free tools like Gimp (gimp.org) come in handy.

3. **Non-free Video Editors.** Perhaps the best-known video editors are Final Cut Pro for Mac (apple.com/finalcutpro) and Adobe Premiere for Mac or Windows (adobe.com/products/premiere.html). But there are a ton of options, which we provide links to at IndieGuide.com/Seen.

4. **Animation Editors.** If you want to make an animated movie, using tools like the free and open-source Blender (blender.org) can help (and can also be used for regular video). Also see Adobe's Flash (www.adobe.com/ flashplatform) or Poser (poser.smithmicro.com) for making computer -animated people. For stop-motion or drawn animation, try MonkeyJam (monkeyjam.org), or Clayanimator (clayanimator.com). And for animating titles, try the free Pinnacle Videospin (videospin.com). You can go to IndieGuide.com/Seen for more in this space.

5. **Online Video Editors.** There's no need to install anything on your computer if you want to just edit online. YouTube has its own editor now (youtube.com/editor), or you can go to its resources page (youtube.com/create) for a set of links to both video-editing as well as online-animation-editing tools that have images and options ready to go.

TOP FOUR CLASSES OF CAMERAS YOU CAN USE
FOR VIDEO PRODUCTION

Video cameras are now extremely prevalent, since they are present on nearly every type of phone, mobile device, or computer out there. They have also gotten very good at handling low-light situations, which has increased video quality tremendously.

You can certainly use any type of camera you want for your production, but consider these classes of options:

1. **Dedicated Video Camera.** If you decide to get a professional, prosumer, or home video camera, simply make sure that it exports the output into computer files that you can easily work within your editing software.

Go to IndieGuide.com/Seen for links to the latest cameras that work well for music-video shooting.

2. **Digital SLR.** SLR cameras are not only good at taking still shots, they turn out to do a great job of video, even in low light. And they are particularly portable. On top of this, they can be mounted on a tripod or steadicam, making them one of the most versatile devices you can get. They also export the final video easily into computer programs. Many videographers have decided to start using digital SLRs instead of dedicated video cameras because of this. If you'd like some links to cameras you can buy, go to IndieGuide.com/Seen for links to the latest cameras that work well for music-video shooting.

3. **Mobile Devices and Phones.** The latest cameras built in to phones are now of such high quality that they are a viable way to capture video. They also easily export to a computer. You can even edit them using apps directly on the device if you want to make videos quickly. Or use mobile apps like MadPad (itunes.apple.com/us/app/madpad-hd-remix-your-life/id460309682?mt=80), which allow you to mix video and audio in novel ways.

4. **Laptop Computers or Mounted Digital Cameras.** Your laptop computer or a mounted digital camera on your computer can act as a video source. Indeed, many YouTube videos are just shot with laptops by using the cameras and microphones built in to the video makers' computers. This isn't a very good option for many music videos, but it may work well if you want to make a quick personal video.

THREE KEY FACTORS FOR SOLID VIDEOS

Just as details matter in audio production, so, too, do they in video production: the difference between a good video and a great one has to do with things that you might not think are important at first. For example, just as you learn to tune your drums when you record them, you will learn that if you clap loudly once at the beginning of a video take, you'll be able to sync the audio between multiple sources. Here's what you want to be aware of when making video:

1. **Video quality is primarily about audio quality.** Low lighting can work out fine using today's cameras, but poor sound quality is noticed immediately. You know that microphone on the video camera you have? It's

probably terrible. As a musician, you have no excuse for low sound quality. Here's how to do it right:

o Use fully mastered music from WAV files in the video editing, not MP3 or other compressed formats. Video sites will compress the sound again at aggressive bit rates, and you will not get a good final result.

o For live music, get an audiofeed off the soundboard.

o Invest in mics. If you must capture live audio yourself, buy, rent, or borrow good-quality external microphones. Most on-camera mics record poorly, so use a separate recorder, slate it (just clap your hands), and blend in your video editor. See vimeo.com/10568081 for a great example and go to IndieGuide.com/Seen for more info.

o Once your video is edited and ready to go, extract the audio as a WAV file and export it to an audio-editing program to apply compression, EQ, and volume normalization on the final audiotrack. Do not alter the length, or it will be difficult or impossible to reimport and sync with the video. It's critical to do this post-processing in WAV format rather than in MP3 or another compressed format.

2. **Good lighting is important, and it is cheap and easy to do right.** Poor lighting is the second most common way to make a video look amateurish. Here are some simple tips: first, for an incredibly cheap and simple lighting solution, go to the hardware store and buy three clip-on work lights. They work surprisingly well for video. Then go to the grocery store and get some wood clothespins and some wax paper. Clip the wax paper over the lights with the pins to diffuse them if they're too bright. A second idea is to use the standard three-light setup by having a crew member adjust the lighting while the director looks *through the camera* at the room. All cameras pick up lighting differently. The standard setup includes the following:

o **Key light:** a light pointed at the subject and placed just behind the camera, to the left or right.

o **Fill light:** a light on the opposite side of the key light, aimed at a shallower angle to the subject. Adjust it until you fill in the shadows caused by the key.

o **Backlight:** a light set behind the subject and pointed at it to illuminate its edges. Backlit subjects look more three-dimensional. If you only have two lights, skip this one.

3. **Stick with jump cuts.** Don't overdo the transition effects. Although there are a multitude of options for transitions between clips, such as wipes, fades, and designer cuts, nearly every cut in movies is just a jump cut without transition effects. You know you're looking at amateur work when there are too many distracting effects between shots. It's the content that matters, not the edits. You'd be fine using a fade-in at the beginning, jump cuts between, and a fade-out at the end.

HOW TO MAKE A MUSIC VIDEO

There's a lot to getting filming right, and of course filming is a subject that fills entire books. Here are the basic steps that will let you pull off a music video if you want to dive into it on your own.

1. **Make a storyboard.** Make a storyboard by using Post-it notes laid out on a large piece of paper to plan out your shots. Stick figures and other simple drawings will do. Post-its allow you to move or remove shots as necessary.

2. **Hold a preproduction meeting.** Get your crew and performers together to discuss the shoot at least once beforehand to go over the plan. You'll avoid a lot of problems this way. Also keep a lot of duct tape on hand.

3. **Set aside a full day for shooting.** A three-to-five-minute video can get done in one day if it's not too complicated.

4. **Use a video clapper board to name your shot and provide an audio clap to help you sync your sound in post-production.** When you record music, you probably label your takes so that you can remember what they were when you go to mixdown. Do the same thing when recording video. You'll appreciate it later when you edit your shots together. You can use a classic Hollywood video clapper board, a whiteboard, or even a notepad. Keep the shot number in the frame at the beginning of each shot so that you know what take it is. And don't forget to film a clap at the beginning of each shot to help sync the sound between audiosources. You can use a video clapper, but any loud sound will do—including just clapping your hands. This simple procedure will

allow you to line up and sync your various audio sources with the video for the shot by making it easy to find the audiospike caused by the clap.

5. **Consider shooting indoors.** Filming outdoors can be difficult in that the weather and light can change quickly and unpredictably. If you do shoot outdoors, you may need to use your lights to help maintain consistent lighting.

WHAT MUSICIANS SHOULD KNOW ABOUT
YOUTUBES CONTENTID SERVICE

The reason video-sharing has succeeded while audio-sharing has failed is not because people prefer video as a format. People like audio just fine, but all attempts in the past to make audio simple to share with others was hampered by current copyright law and the fact it was one of the first mediums to get disrupted by the Internet. It took the music industry by surprise and as a result they took many of the early audio-sharing services like Napster to court where they were subsequently shut down. With video, copyright law is even more complicated considering that three rights are at stake: the sync right, the performance right, and the mechanical right. But the key difference is that YouTube, with its video-sharing capabilities, came years after Napster and it had Google as a financial backer to try and negotiate deals.

Once YouTube came into prominence, the major labels negotiated with Google and worked out agreements to share in the revenue that YouTube was making from the traffic. At the time, YouTube was just following what every other Web site host was required to follow, a congressional bill called the Digital Millennium Copyright Act (DMCA). This requires anyone who runs a Web site to take down copyrighted material if the owner requests it. But YouTube went beyond this. It also initiated a new service called ContentID that recognizes audio and video content. This allows the creator of that content to request a takedown, share the revenue of the ads on the page, and track metrics.

Keep in mind that if you end up using copyrighted video or audio (such as a cover song or a video clip you don't own), your video could end up being flagged with ContentID—even if you clear the video or audio use with a legal contract.

Finally, if you have original songs and videos, you can use ContentID to protect your own work. Go to ContentID (youtube.com/t/contentid) for AudioID or VideoID and use it with your own content.

HOW TO FIND PRECLEARED AND ROYALTY-FREE VIDEO CLIPS AND PHOTOS FOR YOUR VIDEOS

As you make video, you may find that you want to get royalty-free images and video clips to enhance the final product. There are sources, found all over the Internet, that can add new dimensions to your video.

1. **Check out free sources.** It turns out that there are many free sources of video and images. Public domain recordings are always free, and there is also a great deal of material licensed under Creative Commons (CC), some of which allow commercial use, while others require you to go back to the creator to get the right, so read the license carefully. The Creative Commons site (creativecommons.org) allows you to search multiple sites for precleared material. Also see the Internet Archive (archive.org/details /movies), PD Drama (pddrama.com), PD Comedy (pdcomedy.com), and Funny Videos and Funny Video Clips (video-clips.co.uk). Or go to IndieGuide.com/Seen for even more resources.

2. **Use YouTube's built-in Creative Commons tools.** You can access more than ten thousand videos from C-SPAN, Voice of America, Al Jazeera, and others via the CC tab on YouTube Video Editor (youtube .com/editor).

3. **Research loop and sample services.** There are sites that produce royalty-free video clips that can be used within your music videos such as iStockphoto (istockphoto.com/video), Getty Images (gettyimages.com/ footage), and BBC Motion Gallery (bbcmotiongallery.com).

4. **Make sure that you understand the terms, and verify that clips are royalty-free.** Be sure to read the agreements carefully before down-loading, buying, or using them. The important point about these tools is that they must come with a license that allows you to mix them with your own video royalty-free.

HOW TO GET HELP IN MAKING VIDEOS

The best solution for video is to get someone else to do it for you. While you might enjoy making videos—we certainly do!—the process is time-consuming and has a steep learning curve, even though the equipment and software are accessible. There's a wealth of resources available for you if you would like to take advantage of it.

1. **Video Communities.** Communities like Creative Cow (creativecow .net) and Videomaker (videomaker.com/community) are great places to visit. If you have Final Cut Pro, you can see the Final Cut Pro resources page (apple.com/finalcutpro/resources/communities.html).

2. **Theaters and Film Schools.** Students who go to theater or film school study every aspect of video and are looking for experience for their portfolios. These can provide you with actors, crew, camerapeople, and anything else you need—sometimes just in exchange for giving students the credits.

3. **Community-Access Television Stations.** Community-access television stations are incredible resources for video. If you join one, you can get training, crews, and equipment, and they will often let you broadcast the final product on the TV station. These stations often feature soundstages with professional lighting rigs and even green screens for more elaborate effects.

4. **Online Training and Resources.** YouTube has a page for creators, Creator Hub (youtube.com/creators) and Vimeo has a Video School (vimeo .com/videoschool). Both are worth checking out. For more tutorials and links to useful articles, head to IndieGuide.com/Seen.

THREE WAYS TO STREAM VIDEO CONCERTS ON THE INTERNET

Here are just three ways you can use video to stream concerts to your fans. We've covered the details elsewhere in the book, but since we're talking about video here, this is a reminder.

1. **Use video streaming services to broadcast your live shows.** See chapter 7, "Your Gigs," for the steps to simulcast and record your live performances at venues. Note that most of the streaming services will also record the video, and thus will give you more video to post when you're done.

2. **Use voice/video tools to throw an intimate concert.** Using tools like Skype and Google Hangouts, you can grab a laptop or mobile device and perform intimate concerts for your fans. Check out Gavin Mikhail (youtube.com/gavinmikhail), who uses Google Hangouts to stream live, intimate performances; record the result; and then post it to YouTube afterward.

3. **Use virtual-world sites like Second Life.** See chapter 9, "Your Web, Social, and Mobile Presences," for information on Second Life. And check out wiki.secondlife.com/wiki/live_performances if you'd like more information on how to perform there.

PROMOTING YOUR VIDEOS

THE TOP SIX TIPS TO INCREASE THE NUMBER OF VIEWS
FOR YOUR VIDEOS

1. **Make the title into a "click me."** You will get more clicks if you make the video title suggestive, sexy, bizarre, funny, or controversial. Also, fill in the keywords and tags to get more views.

2. **Ask for thumbs-up and subscriptions.** Just asking for a thumbs-up and subscriptions will boost both. Drop them into the video any way you can. These will help increase the number of views.

3. **Organize your channel by content.** If you make multiple video projects, such as a video blog, music videos, live content, or "making of" content, you can create playlists or more than one channel to organize them. You want to make it easy for your fans to find just what they want.

4. **Cross-promotion works.** Leave comments for similar bands, musicians, and video bloggers. You can appear in each other's videos and cross-promote one another. Contact them and offer up ways to creatively work together—play on each other's videos, co-write, and more. See youtube .com/watch?v=M0bAm_YxmPw for ideas.

5. **Pay for promotion (if you want to).** If you have money, and want to promote your videos, Google makes it easy to run ad campaigns. Try www .youtube.com/advertise/en/adwords.html.

6. **Make sure that your videos autopost to Twitter, Facebook, and any of your other presences.**
   If you aren't telling your fans to check out your new videos, who are you telling? If you use the autoposting techniques from chapter 8, "Your Web Strategy," every time you post a video, your autoposting tools will automatically post a tweet every time you put up a new video.

SEVEN WAYS TO USE VIDEO TO PROMOTE YOUR MUSIC

New marketing techniques for video promotion exist. Try these ideas to boost your views and your sales:

1. **Put a Buy link in the first line of the description.** For music videos, you want to capture the impulse purchase by providing a link *right beneath* the video. Make it simple, and fit it on one line: "Buy the song: <Link>." If you can, provide an affiliate link so that you get an extra cut.

2. **Add a video coda.** Video codas are extra video clips that appear after the music video (for example, check out Pomplamoose's "September"—youtube.com/watch?v=xycnv87N_BU—and keep watching to the very end of the video). There are two reasons why you might want to add a video coda. First of all, it's simple for your fans to rip the audio into an MP3 (see youtube-mp3.org as an example). If there's extra audio material there, unrelated to the song, it makes it more likely that they will just buy the track rather than try to do some MP3 editing. Second, it allows you to plug other videos, merch, products, or music.

3. **Brand everything.** Your logo, colors, avatar, and bio all help you connect the rest of your musical presence to the videos. Also, consider adding a "bug" in the video (the little picture or logo in the corner of the screen—see youtube.com/watch?v=4l8Zkr5T1wQ).

4. **Use annotations.** Annotations can be either little word bubbles or areas of the video that can be turned into links (see youtube.com/t/annotations _about). Used correctly, these can promote your other videos, projects, merch, or music sales. And if you haven't asked for thumbs-up or subscriptions in the video itself, you can do it using annotations. Want to get even fancier? Show your other videos at the end and make them linkable: youtube .com/watch?v=VERgMOcHz6c.

5. **Use YouTube's message feature.** You can send messages to your channel subscribers using their messaging feature. John Flansburgh of the band They Might Be Giants often uses this feature to write the band's subscribers about upcoming tours, new albums, and where to purchase their music. Messages appear in your subscribers' recent activity feeds (on their homepages) and on your channel page in your recent activity feed.

6.   **Post regularly to your channel feed.** Any content you share—uploaded videos, comments on other videos you make, favorites, likes, playlists, and more—are posted on your channel's feed. Any of your activity can be seen by any of your subscribers on their homepage. By posting items to your feed regularly, you can keep your channel active and increase the likelihood of your subscribers visiting and watching your posted videos.

7.   **Embed stores.** If you become a YouTube partner, you can embed a store within your channel, allowing you to get sales directly out of YouTube. See chapter 6, "Your Albums, Merchandise, and Sales," for information on how to sell through YouTube.

HOW TO GET FEATURED ON YOUTUBE

Ever wonder how videos are featured on YouTube? Besides just choosing videos they like, YouTube does accept submissions. Simply send an e-mail to editor@youtube.com. The video, of course, has to be original. To see how, check out this video about it from YouTube itself: youtu.be/3eZTh94Fapg.

HOW TO USE STATISTICS ON YOUTUBE TO UNDERSTAND YOUR VIEWERS, MAXIMIZE YOUR VIEWS, AND PLAN YOUR VIDEOS

There are a surprising number of statistics that you can get out of your videos, beyond just views. Note that your goal is to get the number of views of your videos to be higher than the subscriber count since this shows you're reaching more people than just your subscriber base. And note that one person can count for multiple views—especially if you're linking to your other videos at the end.

Here's how to get useful statistics out of videos.

1.   **On YouTube, use the analytics tool.** Log in to your account to see extended statistics using the Analytics button next to each video. This gives you more than information about the number of views, including demographic and location information for your viewers. Google provides information about this here: psupport.google.com/youtube/bin/static.py?hl=en&guide=1714169&page=guide.cs.

Also note that tagging can be effective: using stats and YouTube's Insight tool (youtube.com/t/advertising_insight), you can find what keywords are driving your traffic. If you choose your tags appropriately, then you can piggyback on related videos. You can use the "hotspots" data to find out if people are skipping over any parts of your video so that you can fine-tune your videos.

2. **Try third-party tools.** Google has opened up its system to allow other parties to get stats for you. They can go beyond even what Google provides. Try VidStatsX (vidstatsx.com) for more data on your videos.

HOW TO BECOME A YOUTUBE PARTNER AND GET A CUSTOMIZED YOUTUBE CHANNEL

YouTube makes its money off of ads on the videos they show. Because of this, they would like the owners of video channels to promote more views. To encourage this, YouTube will let some owners of YouTube channels be "partners," which is well worth doing if you are a musician.

If you sign up as a partner, you can do the following:

- Share in the income from the ads, giving you a new source of income.

- Customize the look of the channel, allowing you to put up custom links and a custom heading and color scheme for the channel.

- Post longer videos.

- Put a store into the channel, allowing you to sell music and merchandise directly from your YouTube page.

Becoming a YouTube partner isn't automatic: you need to apply and become accepted. (Or, they may reach out to you.)

Here's how to maximize your chances of a partnership:

1. **Meet the minimum requirements.** According to the YouTube Partnership FAQ (http://www.youtube.com/t/partnerships_faq), the following are minimum requirements:

   o You create original videos suitable for online streaming.

   o You own or have express permission to use and monetize all audio and video content that you upload—no exceptions.

   o You regularly upload videos that are viewed by thousands of YouTube users, or you publish popular or commercially successful videos in other ways (such as DVDs sold online).

Note that the second point is key with a music-based channel: if you perform cover songs, you may need to prove that you have the rights to make videos. See chapter 5, "Your Rights," for information on sync rights, which are required for cover songs in videos.

2. **Try to get as many views as possible first.** The more views you get, the more likely it is that they will accept your partner application.

3. **Make a partner request.** Make your request at www.youtube.com/partners. Here is a tutorial video that may help clarify the process: youtube.com/watch?v=_2Jn8uu27jU.

LEARNING MORE

Go to IndieGuide.com/Seen for a clickable version of every link, Web site, and service mentioned in this chapter, as well as free extra materials to help you put together video for your music.

PART FIVE

CONCLUSION AND LEARNING MORE

CONCLUSION

THE STRATEGIC GOAL: to learn more about additional resources, information, and material that's within your arm's reach

REFERENCE PAGE: IndieGuide.com/Seen

NO ONE knows where the music industry is headed. As Jim DeRogatis said, "If anyone says they know what it will look like in five years, they're lying." And he's right. But no matter what happens to the industry, we do know one thing: musicians will always be able to do it themselves. New opportunities to connect with fans and get your music out there are appearing daily. The amazing thing is that they are within your arm's reach.

We hope that this guide helps you recognize when these new opportunities appear and how to take advantage of them for your music. But know that you're never alone. We'll be keeping up with these opportunities as well as all the latest tools, sites, and resources at IndieGuide.com, where you can join us and a community of motivated musicians.

LEARNING MORE

We are glad that we've been able to share so much information in this book, but there's always more to learn. We're constantly researching and have a waist-high stack of books that we read—and not all of them are music books. A lot of them are business books, psychology books, or other topics that we found relevant in putting together our own music business. Because you're holding this book (and reading to the conclusion), you are probably the kind of person who, like us, is always trying to learn more.

BOOKS, BLOGS, AND NEWSLETTERS
We recommend the following to get more information about the music business:

1. **Recommended books** If you're hungry for even more info, like we are, we boil down the books that we liked the very best at IndieGuide.com /Conclusion. We cover every book that we mentioned in this guide on this page, but we'll also share others that we found thought provoking and useful for our own music career.

2. **Blogs and newsletters** Today's music business moves fast, and every week new ideas appear for taking advantage of the latest social networks and services . We particularly like Bob Baker's newsletter (bob-baker.com). We also like blogs from Derek Sivers (sivers.org), Hypebot (hypebot.com), Musformation (musformation.com), Know the Music Biz (knowthemusicbiz .com), and Digital Music News (digitalmusicnews.com). But go to IndieGuide.com/Conclusion for clickable links, and even more Web sites and information worth reading.

MUSIC-BUSINESS SCHOOLS

You have a choice: you can take a few years learning on your own or you can spend a bit of money, attend a music-business school or class, and get taught what to do from people who are actually in the business. The added benefit of getting taught, beyond speeding up the process, is that they teach you all the good habits and things to do right off the bat.

1. **Full Degree Programs** You can always enroll in a music-business school and earn a degree. Nearly every major university has a music-business program. There are also colleges that specialize in the music business such as Berklee College of Music (berklee.edu), Belmont University (belmont.edu), and Columbia College (colum.edu). As Don Gorder, chair of the Music Business/Management Department at Berklee College of Music, says, with today's Internet-powered music industry, the emphasis on a curriculum needs to be on "thinking-outside-the-box classes like Emerging Music Business Models, where we give students an overview of the new business models that are developing, and give them latitude to develop their own. This promotes the mindset of what you need to start your own business." For a complete list of music business schools, see IndieGuide.com/Conclusion.

2. **Online Courses and Certificates** With the Internet, you don't need to leave your house to go to class. There are a lot of online classes that you can

attend no matter where in the world you live. BerkleeMusic (a separate organization from Berklee College of Music) (BerkleeMusic.com) and Full Sail (fullsail.edu) are two such online music schools. Online schools tend to cover a wide range of courses, with many allowing you to earn college credit should you choose to pursue a full degree. As Dave Kusek, the CEO of BerkleeMusic, says, "We survey our audience constantly so we find topics that people are interested in and then deliver it. Asking questions like where are the jobs? And if you're going the DIY route, what is it that you need to know?" For a complete list of online schools, see IndieGuide.com/Conclusion.

Of course, if you are in the Chicago area, join us at Music Industry Workshop (miworkshop.com), where we teach music business based on the guide. Come out for one of the free weekly open houses so you can check out the school and see what it's all about. Depending on the night, you may catch us hanging out there.

CONNECTING WITH MUSICIANS

Beyond options to connect online, keep in mind that there are conferences, workshops, and organizations that will allow you to network with other musicians and people in the business. Organizations like ASCAP (ascap.com), BMI (bmi.com), and the Grammy organization (grammy.com) all allow musicians to connect with each other.

INDIEGUIDE.COM

You're holding more than just a book—it's a portal to an extensive and free Web site we created called IndieGuide.com (IndieGuide.com). Think of it as the musician's back office. While this book can explain how, why, and what you should do, IndieGuide.com can show you *where* to go and *whom* to talk to. Not only does it contain all the links mentioned in this book, but it's also a guide to all the useful musician resources, services, and tools that can help you get your music out there and win fans. Knowing how fast the Internet changes, the site is the place to stay up to date. To get all this information, as well as additional how-tos, exclusive materials, downloadable forms, and a way to connect to other motivated musicians like yourself, head to IndieGuide.com.

CONTACT US

We'd love to hear your suggestions, ideas, and comments. You can get in touch with us by mailing ContactUs@IndieGuide.com or going to the Web site and using the contact form. Also, follow us on Twitter at @IndieGuide and, if you like our music, at @BeatnikTurtle.

But enough reading about music—it's time to get out there. After all, there's no better time than now to be a musician.

ACKNOWLEDGMENTS

THEY SAY no book is created by just the authors. That was true for the first edition of the guide and it's true for this one as well. First, we'd like to thank our agent, Rick Broadhead, for realizing our potential. We wouldn't be writing this second edition, let alone have written the first, if it weren't for him. Thanks for the continual guidance and encouragement!

Thanks to all at St. Martin's Press for their help, knowledge, and support in bringing this second edition of the guide to life. Special thanks to our editor, Yaniv Soha, for bringing this completely remixed and remastered version to life. We think his jaw hit the floor when we showed him how we took the first edition, turned it completely inside out, and reinvented it into this even more practical and expanded edition.

Thanks also to the editor of our first edition, David Moldawer, for believing in us and the work in the first place. And to Mike Levine, our editor at *Electronic Musician* magazine.

We'd like to thank everyone involved in Beatnik Turtle. Without the band, there'd be no book. In no particular order, we'd like to thank everyone involved in the band and with TheSongOfTheDay.com: Tom Roper, John Owens, David Hallock, Chip Hinshaw, Tom Susala, Mike Hernandez, Mike Combopiano, Chris Joyce, Ryan Lockhart, Drew Swinger, John Lisiecki, Matt Scholtka, Caroline Bruno, Cheyenne Pinson, Dana Huyler, Ted ("Hi, my name's Ted and this is still my song about ants") Blegen, Alison Logan, Steve Owens, Dugan O'Keene, Eric Elmer, Jerry Waggoner, Danielle Wetle, Tom Hordewel (and his alter ego Tom Beeyachski), Mike Holmes, and everyone else who has been a part, past and present.

Many who helped make this guide a reality don't know it, and although we'd like to keep it that way so they don't get a swollen head, we really should thank them. These have been our advisers and mentors—people who have helped pioneer the areas that made it possible for musicians to do it themselves and inspired us. These include, in no particular order, Lawrence Lessig, Derek Sivers, Janis Ian, Eben Moglen, Bruce Schneier, Richard Stallman, Steve Albini, and Eric Boehlert.

We also want to thank everyone we interviewed for the guide. In no particular order, we'd like to thank Chris Anderson (thelongtail.com), Derek Sivers (sivers.org), Jim DeRogatis (jimdero.com), Jeff Price (tunecore.com), Norman Hajjar (guitarcenter.com), Mark Wordsworth, Peggy Manning (fistralpr.co.uk), Holly Anderson (eventful.com), Sharon Howell (lewispr .com), Richard Jones (last.fm), Christian Ward (last.fm), Sarah Jones, Todd Martens, Mur Lafferty (murlafferty.com), Fletcher Lee (leeproductionsinc .com), Patrick Faucher (nimbit.com), Matt Scholtka (scholtkadesign.com), Michael Freeman, Ariel Hyatt (arielpublicity.com), Bob Baker (bob-baker .com), Mike Dolinar (getmadbaby.com), James Ernest (cheapass.com), Scott Alden and Derk Solko (boardgamegeek.com), J. C. Hutchins (jchutchins.net), Brian Austin Whitney (jpfolks.com), Don Gorder (www.berklee.edu), Dave Kusek (www.berkleemusic.com), Dan Hetzel, Brett Ratner, Tim O'Reilly (oreilly.com), Jed Carlson (reverbnation.com), Andre Calilhanna, Jordan Glazier (eventful.com), George Sanger aka "The Fat Man" (fatman.com), Norman Hajjar (guitarcenter.com), Panos Panay (sonicbids.com), and Felice Ecker (girlieaction.com).

We'd also like to thank all the great indie musicians we interviewed and talked to: Gavin Mikhail (gavinmikhail.com), Grant Baciocco (throwing-toasters.com), Simon Wainwright (hopeandsocial.com), Roo Pigott (www .hopeandsocial.com), David Taylor II aka DT (davidtaylor2.com), Andrew McKee and Marc Gunn (thebards.net), George Hrab (georgehrab.com), Carla Ulbrich (carlaulbrich.com), Peter Shukoff of Nice Peter (nicepeter .com), Jonathan Coulton (jonathancoulton.com), Brad Turcott (bradsucks .net), Brett Ratner, the Gregory Brothers (gregorybrothers.com), and Yvonne Doll of the Locals (localsrock.com), Nataly Dawn and Jack Conte (pomplamoose.com), and John Flansburgh (theymightbegiants.com).

Additionally, we'd like to thank the editor of the first online *Survival Guide* that started this all, Brad Weier, for his excellent work, as well as Erik Balisi for his initial help. We'd also like to thank all the musicians who e-mailed us after reading the online *Survival Guide,* the first edition, and IndieGuide.com. Their continued advice, insight, suggestions, and questions helped make this second edition all the better.

We'd like to thank Katelyn Cohen (katelyncohen.com) for all her assistance with IndieGuide.com and Beatnik Turtle. Her tireless research, thoughts, and insights on the new music industry have been a big help not only to us but to indie musicians everywhere.

And especially to Matt Scholtka for the hours of phone conversations, the excellent graphic arts work, and the hordes of crazy ideas that we will get to one day. Oh yes. We'll get to them eventually.

And lastly, we'd like to thank everyone who has been part of Beatnik Turtle and TheSongOfTheDay.com past and present, as well as the friends, family, and fans of Beatnik Turtle.

RANDY WOULD LIKE TO THANK . . .

I want to give my heartfelt thanks to my parents, Glenn and Susan Chertkow, for their support. Thanks to my sister Heather and brother-in-law John Cumings, and of course my adorable nieces Chloe and Eva. Thanks also to Grandma Alaine Klein and Grandpa Eddie Klein for the encouragement. Thanks to my good friends Tony Downing, Heidi Downing, Dana Huyler, Steve Levy, Jay Kline, and Bradley Trenton Malloy Quinn for the personal support. Also, thank you to the Pegasus crew (pegasusmuck.com) for the research, banter, distractions, abuse, and senseless violence, including Shannon Prickett, Andrew Crawford, Tom Shekleton, James Tripp, and Jessica Firsow. And also my thanks to Vylar Kaftan (vylarkaftan.net).

I want to thank everyone who has worked with me in music, David Bloom (bloomschoolofjazz.com), the perfect set group, and Berklee College of Music. And especially my departed and much-missed sax teacher, Frank Schalk. And Paul Maslin at PMWoodwind (pmwoodwind.com) for his excellent saxophone advice. Also, thanks to New Trier's music department, especially James Warrick and John Thompson. Also the great team at MIW, especially Reggi Hopkins for all of the support and great projects that we're doing together. And the excellent instructors including Coleen Spapperi, David Taylor aka DT (davidtaylor2.com), Dan Hetzel, and Ricco Lumpkins.

I need to say a special thank-you to my co-wokers at my day gig, especially Dave Matuszewski for his understanding while I wrote the book.

Also thanks to Zin Fooks, Jimi McCafferty, Dan Noah, Quinn Obermeyer, David Roth, Andy Franklin, Tommie Carter, Kim Freeark, Mike Pones, Tom Wiers, Vino Nachiar, Tommie Carter, Jeremy Bragg, and Mark Daavettila. And also to folks that have had to listen to me blather on about the manuscript, such as my personal trainer, David Bush (abodyofknowledge fitness.com), and my incredible MT, Debra Ann Christiansen (inneradvan tagemassage.com).

And more than any other, my thanks to Jason for the friendship as well as the hard work. As you've often said, you set sail on a course, and never know where it'll take you. We certainly never expected to be where we are now, and I can't wait to find out where we wind up next.

And, finally, to Peggy Mahoney: I guess this is the second time I have to apologize, and return him back to you. Hope you still want him back.

JASON WOULD LIKE TO THANK . . .

First and foremost, a big thanks is owed once again to my wife, Peggy Mahoney, for all her love, support, encouragement, and understanding as I put another set of long hours into the guide, Beatnik Turtle, and work. I'm thankful to have a wife like you. Thanks also to Liam (and his alter ego, Super Liam), who always wonders what I'm doing typing words on a computer screen when there are games to be played, princesses to save, and bad guys to fight. Love you both!

Everything in this guide stems from Beatnik Turtle. And everything about Beatnik Turtle stems from my parents, Jim and Jean Feehan, who, for some reason, allowed me to build a home studio years ago in their basement. Little did they know their decision, made on a whim, would result in countless musicians traipsing through their home at all hours of the night, instrument cases banging up their walls, and a never-ending stream of Beatnik Turtle music sound-tracking their lives as they struggled to complete the crossword, do the dishes, or watch TV. Despite their inconveniences, they've constantly worried more about us than themselves ("Did you guys eat?"). Although they may still have no idea what the hell we're doing with Beatnik Turtle or how I got into writing books, they certainly are proud nonetheless. And I'm proud to call them my parents. Thanks, Mom and Dad for all the support! Love you both!

I'd like to thank the rest of my family, including my brother, Jared Feehan, my cousins John and Jeff Franzen, and my grandparents William and

Ester ("Sick of Sandwiches") Grommes. I'd also like to thank my fun and supportive in-laws, Joe and Collette Mahoney, as well as Chris and Moria Waldron, for all their support, advice, and encouragement throughout the writing and work with the books and IndieGuide.com.

I'd like to thank everyone at work once again for their understanding and encouragement throughout this project. That includes Jim Citrin for unknowingly inspiring me to get into this book-writing thing, everyone in my legal department—Dave Rasmuessen, Tricia Spence, Terry Thornley, Heath Brewer, and all the law clerks I worked with, including Doug Reisinger and Marcella Hein, who agree with me that "What We Need Is Some Interns in Here." It also includes everyone in the IT department—Rick Abel, Tom Roper, Mark Czazasty, Mark Andrus, and those in the Irish office I set up—Paul Coyle, Frank Ryan, Richard Brady, Nick Ryan, Gabriel Tanase, Ivor McCormack, Sally Ann O'Connor, Eibhlin Ni Oison, John ("Hang in there!") Grisolano, and all the others of whom there are too many to name unfortunately. They've made working and living in Ireland the past few years fun and rewarding. And while I'm at it, I hereby rescind the acknowledgment for Tim Schmidt that I put in the first edition, and instead apply it to this edition.

I'd like to also say there's something amazing about this Internet thing and all the great IT professionals creating awesome collaborative tools like Google Docs, Skype, and the like that can really bridge a 3,500 mile gap between Randy in Chicago and me in Dublin, Ireland. If these tools didn't exist, I'm not sure how we would have managed to complete this on time. And the cool thing, it's all just getting better and better.

Lastly, I'd like to thank Randy for co-writing this. As always, we not only poured our all into it, we accomplished it and came up with a hundred more ideas we now have to do!

INDEX

ABOUT THE AUTHORS

AND BEATNIK TURTLE

RANDY CHERTKOW

Professionally, Randy Chertkow is an information-technology specialist with over eighteen years of experience in enterprise-class IT departments in Fortune 100 companies. He has a bachelor's in business administration in information systems from the University of Iowa and a master of science in computer science: data communications, with a secondary concentration in artificial intelligence, from DePaul University, where he graduated with distinction. Randy has played music all his life, including jazz, rock, and classical music. His instruments include baritone, tenor, alto, and soprano saxophones, flute, Bb and bass clarinet, guitar, bass, and anything else he can get his hands on. He started at the challenging New Trier High School jazz program and went on to study jazz at Berklee College of Music, then completed a Perfect Set course at the Bloom School of Jazz. He writes, records, and performs with Beatnik Turtle as well as performing with theater companies around Chicago. Randy also writes sci-fi and fantasy (story quake.com) and about computer topics (effectivemonitoring.com).

JASON FEEHAN

Professionally, Jason Feehan is both a practicing corporate attorney and an IT director working for a multinational executive-search firm. Recently, they sent him overseas to start a new office in Ireland and reinvent its software development department. He plays guitar and keyboards, sings, records, engineers, and produces. He founded Beatnik Turtle in 1997, growing it from a four-piece band into an eight-piece rock machine with a full horn section and a recording studio all its own. Unfettered by a formal music education, he often learned to play instruments as he wrote the music, using nearly anyone in arm's reach who could play or claimed to be able to play a musical instrument. He is a prolific songwriter and has written close to a thousand songs, three of which are actually not too bad.

BEATNIK TURTLE

The authors' band, Beatnik Turtle (beatnikturtle.com), is a horn-powered pop-rock band based in Chicago. They have recorded twenty albums, released over four hundred songs, and successfully completed a song-of-the-day project, where they released one song for every day of 2007 at the Web site TheSongOfTheDay.com. They've written music for TV, commercials, films, podcasts, theater (including Chicago's Second City), and have licensed music to Disney/ABC Family and Viacom.